The Future of the Nation State in Europe

THE FUTURE OF THE NATION STATE IN EUROPE

Edited by
Jyrki Iivonen
The Finnish Institute of International Affairs, Helsinki

Edward Elgar

Published by
Edward Elgar Publishing Limited
Gower House
Croft Road
Aldershot
Hants GU11 3HR
England

Edward Elgar Publishing Company
Old Post Road
Brookfield
Vermont 05036
USA

British Library Cataloguing in Publication Data
Future of the Nation State in Europe
I. Iivonen, Jyrki
320.1094

Library of Congress Cataloguing in Publication Data
The Future of the nation state in Europe / edited by Jyrki Iivonen.
p. cm.
Papers from a conference held in Helsinki on April 10–11, 1992, under the auspices of the Finnish Institute of International Affairs and the UNESCO Commission of the Finnish Ministry of Education.
Includes index.
1. National state—Congresses. 2. Nationalism—Europe—Congresses. 3. Europe—Politics and government—Congresses. I. Iivonen, Jyrki, 1950– . II. Ulkopoliittinen Instituutti (Finland) III. Finland. Suomen Unesco-toimikunta.
JC311.F95 1993 93–28599
321'.05'094—dc20 CIP

ISBN 1 85278 740 6

Printed in Great Britain at the University Press, Cambridge

CONTENTS

PREFACE

Jyrki Iivonen

The future of the nation state has been one of the major issues in recent European development. European integration, originally believed to lead to the formation of a more coherent union of European states, has been under way for several years now. Simultaneously with that process, in Eastern Europe the collapse of the Soviet Union and the socialist system has been followed by the formation of new nation states. As late as in autumn 1989, it was widely believed that Europe was finally on a threshold of a new and more peaceful era, during which prosperity would expand over the whole continent. It was further believed that after the disappearance of the two-bloc Cold War international system it would become easier to solve inter-state disputes by peaceful means.

By 1992 it had become clear that the future of Europe was not that sunny. On one hand, the formation of the European Union by the most developed European democracies had run into difficulties, when disbelief in new arrangements started to grow. In the East, on the other hand, the formation of new nation states on the ruins of multinational socialist states had already led to a number of violent conflicts and even wars. The myth of the disppearance of the nation state was also questioned: if Western European integration was about to fail and if multinational socialist empires were gradually divided into separate nation states, the basic unit of the European system of states would, after all, remain the same as before.

This was the general political situation in Europe, when the Finnish Institute of International Affairs and the UNESCO Commission of the Finnish Ministry of Education organized an international research conference in Helsinki on 10-11 April 1992. The articles of this book are based on the presentations given at that conference and completed by the authors during the summer of 1992.

The contributions have been divided into four sections. The articles by Finland's former foreign minister, Doctor Paavo Väyrynen (Helsinki), Professor Ernest Gellner (Cambridge) and Professor Aira Kemiläinen (Vantaa, Finland) deal with the concept of 'nation state' and its definition. The second section consists of two historical articles by Professor Giovanni Arrighi (Binghamton) and Professor Erik Allardt (Helsinki). The former discusses the development of historical capitalism, while the latter connects the question of the nation state to different forms of technology.

In the third section, we deal with various contexts of the nation state. There we have four articles, written by author Jaan Kaplinski (Tartu, Estonia) on the future of national cultures in Europe, by director Ali Kazancigil (UNESCO, Paris) on the effects of European unification on the nation state, Professor Allan Rosas (Turku) on the decline of sovereignty in the international law and Professor Raimo Väyrynen (Helsinki) on the relationship between territory and nation state. Finally, in the fourth section, certain regional processes with an impact on the ethnic development of the area will be analysed, German unification by Doctor Thomas Henschel (Mainz), prospects of Russian civil society by Professor Risto Alapuro (Helsinki) and East European political development by Professor Maté Szabo (Budapest).

The financial arrangements for the conference were taken care of by the Finnish Ministry of Education, while the Finnish Institute of International Affairs has prepared the publication. It is the firm belief of the organizers of the conference that the question of the nation state in Europe will remain one of the most important and interesting issues to be studied by social scientists in the future as well.

CONTRIBUTORS

Risto Alapuro, Professor of Sociology, University of Helsinki, Finland.
Erik Allardt, Professor of Sociology, University of Helsinki; Chancellor, Åbo Akademi University, Turku, Finland.
Giovanni Arrighi, Professor of Sociology, State University of New York at Binghamton, USA.
Ernest Gellner, Professor of Social Anthropology, University of Cambridge, Great Britain.
Thomas R. Henschel, Researcher, Department of Political Science, University of Mainz, Germany.
Jyrki Iivonen, Senior Research Fellow and Editor-in-Chief, Finnish Institute of International Affairs, Helsinki, Finland.
Jaan Kaplinski, author, Tartu, Estonia.
Ali Kazancigil, UNESCO, Director of the Division for the International Development of Social and Human Sciences, Paris, France.
Aira Kemiläinen, Professor of History (emerita), University of Jyväskylä, Vantaa, Finland.
Allan Rosas, Professor of State Law and International Law; Director, Institute for Human Rights, Åbo Akademi University, Turku, Finland.
Maté Szabo, Professor of Political Science, University of Budapest, Hungary.
Paavo Väyrynen, Dr. Pol. Sc., former Minister for Foreign Affairs, Helsinki, Finland.
Raimo Väyrynen, Professor of Political Science, University of Helsinki, Finland.

Part I

CONCEPTS AND DEFINITIONS

1. INTRODUCTION: NATION STATES IN EUROPE

Jyrki Iivonen

1. DIFFERENT EUROPES

The European state system, as it has emerged during the last centuries, has based on the idea of the nation state, that borders between states should be analogous to those between nations. After the First World War, in particular, efforts were made to construct the European system in such a way that different states would be ethnically as homogeneous as possible. Even then it was understood, of course, that nation states were an ideal type only that could not exist in a pure form. Even states described as 'pure' nation states actually had their own national minorities that, however, had already been acculturated by the dominant ethnic culture. In France, for example, the formation of the nation state was an enforced process during which various local identities were crushed.[1] A similar process took place in certain parts of Great Britain, officially called the United Kingdom of Great Britain and Northern Ireland.

It is a curious fact that in 1919, partly as a result of the Versailles Peace Conference, two new multi-ethnic states entered the political map of Europe, namely Soviet Russia (since 1922 the Union of Soviet Socialist Republics) and Yugoslavia. In both countries, efforts were made to create an ethnic-free identity, where the loyalty of the population would be directed to the state. In both countries – as well as in other Central East European states with large national minorities – the process of the socialist nation-building proved to be a painful one. It was believed that only through a totalitarian rule was it possible to contain old national conflicts. And to construct a totalitarian political apparatus it was necessary to lift one nationality above the others to act as the main carrier of the new non-ethnic identity. In the Soviet Union this role was adopted by Russians and in Yugoslavia by Serbs. It is a curious fact that, in spite of the formal leadership of Russians and Serbs, the process of 'socialist nationalization' was led by a Georgian (Josef Stalin) and by a Croatian (Josip Broz Tito). While they were able to prevent the outbreak of national tensions, in both cases the collapse of the totalitarian rule almost immediately revitalized national sentiments.

It is not a coincidence that national conflicts have been aggravated in almost all former multinational socialist states. It was one of the basic beliefs of Marxism-Leninism that in the new socialist society national (ethnic) identity disappeared and that its place was to be taken by a new non-national identity, where affection was directed to the international proletariat instead of one's own national group.[2] National sentiments were defined as harmful residues of the bourgeois past for which there was no room in the socialist society. National differences were expressed only in politically harmless cultural activities like folk dances, dress, music, etc.[3]

In the West, nationalism was, in the same way, seen as a negative phenomenon that should somehow be contained to avoid crises like the Second World War. The solution was to construct such a union of nation states that their mutual conflicts could be negotiated beforehand without letting them develop into armed violence. The formation of the European Economic Community and NATO can be explained, in addition to the Cold War conflict between United States and Soviet Union, in terms of an effort to prevent the worsening of relations between Western European countries and especially in terms of preventing the restoration of national chauvinism in Germany. From that perspective, both organizations have so far been successful.

successful.

2. WESTERN EUROPE

At the end of the 1980s it seemed obvious that the (nation) state was about to lose its former central role in the European state system. The European integration process was meant to lead to a situation, where the role of the (nation) state would be transferred to all-European organs on one hand and to the regional (local) level inside (nation) states on the other. In other words, it was believed that in the future Europe the (nation) state would become less and less important when its former duties were transferred to all-European and regional decision makers.

However, several countertendencies against all-European integration have emerged since 1990. First, the formation of the European Union has run into difficulties. In three separate referenda, carried out in 1992, the anti-integration alternative has been surprisingly strong. In Denmark a slight minority voted against the Maastricht Treaty, while in France only a slight majority voted for it. In Swizerland, a small majority decided, in the November 1992 referendum, to oppose Swiss membership in the European Economic Space (EES). In countries where the referendum has not been on the agenda (especially in the United Kingdom), various opinion polls have clearly shown that there is a large amount of scepticism of and even opposition towards further European integration.

Second, an increasingly critical attitude towards Europeanization has already led to the emergence of a phenomenon called regional or provincial identity. Its social basis is territorial rather than ethnic. Provinces inside nation states have started to claim wider autonomy and in some cases even for independence. So far the consequences of these efforts have remained rather modest, but it is clear that the atmosphere can change. Some concrete examples are worth mentioning here. In the United Kingdom, Scottish (and Welsh) identity has become a notable political force. During the election campaign in 1992, Scottish nationalists strongly defended their case. Although their electoral gains were still quite limited (they even lost one seat), much an independent Scottish state but rather to have more influence in decision-making and resource allocation, especially in issues dealing with regional economic policies. They seem to be quite convinced that their existence alone has a certain influence on the way the British government allocates funds and resources to Scotland.

A similar situation can be found in some other Western European countries as well. In France, Bretons and Corsicans have rebelled against the central authority. Their cases can also be interpreted as territorial expressions of provincial interests, although again some linguistic factors are prevalent as well. In Spain, on the other hand, both Catalans and Basques have for decades demanded wider autonomy and even independence. The existence of the Basque ETA terrorist movement has kept these cases in the news. Their opposition towards central rule is obvious, but it does not mean that the majority of the Basque population would be for national independence. In the same way, in Catalonia, the Olympic Games of 1992 in its capital Barcelona offered a unique opportunity for the Catalans to present their national case. But again, it is rather a wider regional autonomy than independence they are striving for.[5]

The latest concrete example comes from Italy, where in the April 1992 election the wealthy North lifted its banner for larger local autonomy and demanded that taxes collected there should not be allocated to the less well-to-do Southern Italy in such amounts as before. The Northern League received 55 seats and became the fourth largest group in the new parliament.[6] The popularity of the Northern League can be seen as one of the examples of the new provincial identity in Europe. The difference to the former situation only is that this time it is those who are wealthy that have lifted the banner of rebellion against established economic practices.

Third, a new kind of national (ethnic) spirit has started to grow in some European countries, notably in Germany. This new spirit is strongly racist by nature and is especially directed against foreigners emigrated to the relatively wealthy Western Europe during the last years and decades. In the German case, the main factor to explain the outbreak of traditional national hatred is, at least partly, the problems connected to unification.

hatred is, at least partly, the problems connected to unification. After autumn 1989 it was believed that German unification would rapidly lead to the emergence of a politically and economically viable German state, within which the living standard of the East would soon reach the level of the more advanced West. These expectations proved to be over-optimistic, however. The backwardness of the East could not be overcome in the very near future. The disappointment about the slow economic recovery has made the Eastern parts of the country the main area of a number of violent racist clashes which not only have divided the German nation but have also violated her international image and brought back memories of the Nazi period.

Similar racist conflicts have not yet broken out in other European countries in the same quantity. It is clear, however, that, especially if integration fails and economic crisis continues, there is a great risk that the German development will be repeated in some other Western European countries as well. Today organizations basing their activities and ideology on racial hatred are still small and weak, but in due time they can develop into centrally led political units that can have a great negative influence on European unity.

3. EASTERN EUROPE

In Eastern Europe the question of the nation state must be stated in a completely different way. While in the West the nation state was already established during the nineteenth century and the states became homogeneous ethnically, in the East the process was carried out first during the twentieth century. Two different types of nation states can be found in Eastern Europe. In most cases, the nation state was created in the Versailles Peace Treaty of 1919.[7] On the ruins of the Habsburg empire, several nation states were formed. The aim was to draw the borders between these states on the basis of the national principle. Because of the long existence of large multinational empires (Austria-Hungary, Russia, Ottomans), this task proved to be more or less impossible to carry out. Because of the territorially scattered be created. Even Poland, today a homogeneous nation state, had at that time large German, Ukrainian, Belorussian, Lithuanian and Jewish minorities.[8] Communities of Hungarians, on the other hand, could be found in today's Slovakia, Rumania and Yugoslavia. Three nation states – Estonia, Latvia and Lithuania – were, right from the beginning, under such strong pressure from the Soviet Union that their national states proved to be quite short-lived: in 1940 they were reannexed.

In addition to the efforts to create homogeneous nation states, three states with at least two national groups of about the same size were created. Two of them – Czechoslovakia and Yugoslavia – were formed according to the plan of the victors of the war, while the third – the largest of them – was created on the ruins of the Russian Empire under the name of the Soviet Union. After the collapse of the socialist system, these three multinational states have all disappeared from the map of Europe. In all cases, the re-emerged ethnic identity has been one of the main factors to cause this.

Czechoslovakia has been dissolved into two nation states – the Czech Republic and Slovakia. The former has already reached a high level of industrialization and technology, while the latter is based rather on heavy industry and agriculture. It also has some unresolved disputes with its neighbours, mostly with Hungary.[9] It is therefore widely believed, that while the Czech Republic has some prospects of a rapid economic recovery, Slovakia will have great difficulties in both her domestic and foreign policy, which makes the whole area politically and militarily unstable.

The formation of Yugoslavia was based on the belief that the existence of a multinational state would cut off the tradition of the Balkan wars which during the last quarter of the nineteenth century and at the beginning of the twentieth century destabilized the whole European state system. The discrepancy between different national groups in the new state were so deep, however, that they could only be contained through force and centralization. As soon as *perestroika* in the Soviet Union was launched, the dissolution of Yugoslavia started as well.[10] The consequences have been extremely violent, as if the efforts to contain the war there would have been completely useless. The contain the war there would have been completely useless. The war in Yugoslavia has also shown that the possibilities of the international community to prevent hostilities are extremely limited, if the opponent (in this case the Serbs) is determined and unscrupulous enough.

The Soviet Union was created as a new type of multinational state, where national differences would gradually wither away. The negation of people's ethnic identity was not, however, based on people's personal emotions but on orders from above. The forced Soviet national identity was never properly rooted in the Soviet Union even though in February 1986 Mikhail Gorbachev still declared that the Communist Party had solved the national question permanently.[11]

As we now know, the national question was not solved but only supressed for the time being. When the possibility of pluralist thinking emerged along with *glasnost,* the national identity was also re-awakened. With the disappearance of the supressive political apparatus, the mechanisms of the national supression disappeared as well. After the failed coup attempt in August 1991, it took less than four months for the centrally ruled unitary Soviet state to be replaced by a number of semi-independent nation states, although their formation processes are not yet completely over. One of the largest problems in the former Soviet Union is that the process of national homogenization can become a very violent one, as already now can be seen in numerous violent ethnic conflicts in different parts of the country.

The question of the future of the nation state in Europe is not, as can be seen on the basis of the remarks above, a simple one. Neither can this collection offer any simple answers. The best we can do is to analyse the concepts of 'nation' and 'nation state' in different contexts and in that way clarify its content. What is evident on the basis of recent historical development is that the possibilities to anticipate future events are today especially limited. One thing is clear, however. The thesis of the disappearance of ethnic identity in modern times has already now proved to be incorrect. Along with the present crisis of political ideologies, old forms of identity have been revitalized, national identity among them.

NOTES

1. On emergence of a nation state in France, see, e.g., Fernand Braudel, *The Identity of France*. 2 vols (New York: Harper & Row, 1990).
2. On the Marxist-Leninist notion of national self-determination, see Jyrki Iivonen, *Independence or Incorporation? The Idea of Poland's National Self-Determination and Independence within the Russian and Soviet Socialism from the 1870s to the 1920s* (Helsinki: The Finnish Institute of International Affairs, 1990).
3. This has been especially true with most of the national minorities in former Soviet Russia. It is the Fenno–Ugric minorities that in particular struggle for the survival of their cultural identitites. (See, e.g., Seppo Lallukka, *The East Finnic Minorities in the Soviet Union. An Appraisal of the Erosive Trends*. Helsinki: Suomalainen tiedeakatemia, 1990.)
4. The small number of nationalist members from Scotland in the British parliament is due to the electoral system that strongly favours two main parties.
5. An important factor in the Basque and Catalan cases is the linguistic one. Their national languages are clearly different from Spanish. In addition, the years of the Franco dictatorship created such a dislike of the central rule that it has survived even in the democratic Spain, which already has enlarged the regional autonomy in many ways. (See Kari Sulevo, Baskimaa ja Katalonia – erilaisinta Espanjaa. *Ulkopolitiikka*, no. 2/1991, pp. 24–30.)
6. Philip Daniels, The Democratic Party of the Left and the 1992 Italian General Election. *The Journal of Communist Studies,* vol. 8, no. 3, September 1992, p. 131. The deepening political crisis during spring 1993 has only added to the discontent against the Christian-Democratic government.
7. As a general outline of the Versailles Peace Treaty, see, e.g., Robin Okey, *Eastern Europe 1740–1980. Feudalism to Communism* (London: Hutchinson, 1982), pp. 58–63.
8. It must be remembered here, of course, that Poland's present ethnic homogeneity is due to extensive ethnic 'cleansing' during and after the Second World War: the Jews were destroyed, the Germans were emigrated and the Ukrainians together with Belorussians became Soviet citizens.
9. See, e.g., Karoly Okolicsanyi, Slovak-Hungarian Tension: Bratislava Diverts the Danube. *RFE/RL Research Report,* vol. 1, no. 49/1992, pp. 49–54.
10. On the dissolution of Yugoslavia, see e.g. Hugh Poulton, *Balkans. Minorities and States in Conflict* (London: Minority Rights Publications, 1991), Michael W. Weithmann, *Krisenherd Balkan. Ursprünge und Hintergründe des aktuellen Konflikts* (Munich: Wilhelm Heyne, 1992) and Yrjö Lautela & Jyrki Palo, *Jugoslavia – Kansakunta, jota ei ollut* (Helsinki: VAPK-kustannus, 1992).
11. Jyrki Iivonen, *Neuvostovallan viimeiset vuodet* (Helsinki: Gaudeamus, 1992), p. 106.

2. NATION STATE: SOME BASIC CONCEPTS AND DEFINITIONS

Paavo Väyrynen

1. INTRODUCTION

The revolutionary changes in Europe have derived from an array of factors during recent years. One of the most striking phenomena of this development is the rise of nationalism. This has been a surprise for many observers because the dominating trend has been the increase of economic and ecological interdependence, not nationalism. Yet this perception has not fully matched the realities.

Scholars as well as political decision-makers face a puzzle when trying to predict whether the international system in general is in a real transition from a state-centric system to a global village or something else. It would be realistic to predict that any transformation would last years or even decades. Nations and nationalism will remain driving forces both for progress and for conflicts. The era of nation states, therefore, has not ended.

Consequently, it would be a great mistake to assume that nationalism would be in decline as a result of increasing transnationalism and integration. Both nationalism and integration or globalism will be contending forces in the 1990s. On one hand, transnational technological changes in communications and transportation are making the world smaller than before. On the other hand, nationalism is becoming stronger in most of the world, not weaker.

In the following I would like to deal with the conceptual problems of nationalism and then have a glance at the future of the European nation state.

2. THE NATION STATE SYSTEM IN TRANSITION

The nation state as an international experiment has European roots. The nation state system was to a great extent established with the Peace Treaty of Westphalia, ending the Thirty Years' War in 1648. The hereditary monarchs maintained absolute mastery over their territories in this system. In the eighteenth century, the age of Enlightenment promulgated rationalist, liberal and humanitarian principles of governance that could be applied universally. This development triggered off national sentiments and nationalism, with ordinary people demanding their human rights and democratic freedoms in the following century.

Unfortunately, European nationalism also fostered imperialism. As we know, the two world wars have been seen as extreme repercussions of the national rivalries of the twentieth century. In fact, many observers are now afraid that the old contest between nations will be repeated in the future again, as the Yugoslav crisis and many civil wars in the former Soviet Union clearly indicate. The question is, therefore, whether Europe will fall 'back to the future', because there is a great difference between the democratically tamed nationalism of Western Europe and the revival in Eastern Europe of untamed nationalism.[1]

The collapse of communism has released nationalism from its guarded camps in Eastern Europe and in the former Soviet Union. In these parts of the continent, nations are seeking their identities and would like to strengthen their sovereignty. The concept of 'union' is anathema to these neo-states.

For years to come, the security of Europe will be at stake as a result of questions related primarily to nationalism. These 'new nations' have deflected – if not reversed – the course of contemporary European history in western parts of the continent where the nations are pooling their sovereignties for economic and political integration.

It is crucial, however, to make a clear distinction between different kinds of nationalistic problems in Europe. Although Czechs and Slovaks were divorced at the beginning of 1993, Czechoslovakia will not become another Yugoslavia. Unlike the former Yugoslavia, there are no border or minority problems of a serious kind between Czechs and Slovaks, nor any tradition of ancestral violence between them.

3. A CONCEPTUAL CLARIFICATION

Nationalism has certain features which are common to all national sentiments and nation states. In order to analyae the theme properly, I would like to deal briefly with the concepts of 'nation', 'state' and 'nation state'. The following authoritative definitions are taken from the *International Encyclopedia of Social Sciences*.[2]

> **Nation**: 'A portion of mankind may be said to constitute a nationality, if they are united among themselves by common sympathies, which do not exist between them and any others – which make them cooperate with each other more willingly than with other people, desire to be under the same government, and desire that it should be governed by themselves or a portion of themselves, exclusively.' (John Stuart Mill, Considerations on Representative Government, Chapter 16, 1861)
> 'A state's boundaries may not coincide with the limits of national self-consciousness; the state may include ethnic minorities that do not feel the same national allegiance and exclude national groups beyond the borders that do.' [The subjective characteristics of nationhood, according to the *Encyclopedia*, are, e.g., consciousness, loyalty and will.]
> **State**: 'The state is a geographically delimited segment of human society united by common obedience to a single sovereign. The term may refer either to the society as a whole or, more specifically, to the sovereign authority that controls it.'
> **Nation state**: 'The modern nation state is one particular

> form of the territorial state. The size of the territory must reconcile the imperatives of unity, which impose upper limits, with the requirements of a modern division of labour, which impose lower limits.'

These basic definitions may help us to approach the core of the complex problems before us.

A 'nation' can be formed in two different ways. In some cases, different national and linguistic groups living in the same area may share a sense of unity and therefore form a nation (e.g., Switzerland). It is also possible that people living in different areas and yet belonging to the same ethnic group have a sense of unity and form a nation (e.g., Germany, Italy). In politics, these two manifestations of national feeling lead to very different results.

The concept of 'nation state' is subject to a number of interpretations. It can without question be applied to a state which is relatively homogeneous with respect to nationality and language, and whose population shares a sense of unity. However, states with heterogeneous population structures, but which are nevertheless united by national feelings, can be and often are referred to as nation states.

In order to obtain scientific support for solutions to Europe's difficult national disputes, we should, in my opinion, analyse national sentiments and their manifestations in different societies. A national sentiment or consciousness, bringing together people of various ethnic and linguistic groups living in the same area or state, is generally a positive phenomenon. The results are negative only when this leads to an attempt to establish hegemony over other nations or nationalities. However, this risk is a minor one because a multinational nation does not usually become chauvinistic.

National sentiment based on ethnic and linguistic ties may under some circumstances have positive consequences and under others negative ones. The history of Finland is a good example of the positive effects of national feeling based on ethnic factors. The emergency of national sentiment and consciousness was a prerequisite for the independence of the country, which in turn created favourable conditions for the well-being of the people and had a positive impact on the overall development of

Northern Europe.

However, national consciousness based on ethnic and linguistic factors frequently seems to lead to conflict, violence and even war. There are many examples of how different peoples have long lived in harmony with each other, but subsequently become involved in disputes and violent confrontations.

In Europe, solutions to national conflicts have been sought by increasing the rights of minorities and by providing self-government and autonomy for them. Such arrangements, however, do not always suffice, because there are often one or more other ethnic minority groups living in the territory inhabited by a national minority.

A durable solution should be sought in the gradual abatement of the ethnic sentiment that arouses antagonisms and its replacement by a national feeling that would unite people living in the same area. In order to achieve progress in this direction, we must define the factors that promote the growth of local, regional and national understanding and integration.

We should be able to see relations between people as communities at different levels, communities that supplement each other. The size of human communities has increased gradually: from families and kin to local and regional communities and eventually to the national level. Politics, or joint conduct of the affairs of a community, has expanded through the same phases.

The condition for the emergence of a nation state and its activities is that it forms a genuine national society, comprising its constituent communities. In a nation state, there should be exercised a popular sovereignty, at all levels of decision-making. Wherever there has been an effort to replace social communities with the activity of the state, the state itself has come to the brink of disaster or has been destroyed.

4. THE CHANGING ROLE OF THE NATION STATE

Mankind is now experiencing a new dynamic stage in its development. Nations are undertaking closer cooperation, which will lead to both regional and world-wide integration. Some have predicted that integration will mean the demise of the nation state. On one hand it is believed that supranational decision-making will increase, and on the other it is surmised that nation states will break up into more independent regions.

A determined effort to promote regional and world-wide cooperation is important. Our problems are increasingly international, and most often global by nature. Consequently, communities at new levels will arise, such as the European Community/Union, and a world community comprising all of mankind. Effective decision-making will also be required at these levels.

The United Nations Conference on Environment and Development (UNCED) started a process that will lead mankind to sustainable development. Environmental and development concerns require the UN system to be reformed in such a way that its economic and social sectors will develop into an effective instrument to realize sustainable and socially just development in the whole world. The global community is gaining effective instruments for decision-making and action.

The emergence of more extensive communities and the decision-making related to them, however, cannot replace the nation state, which will still be needed to manage the affairs of each nation. The intensification of global cooperation and the strengthening of the role of the UN will not weaken the position of the nation state. The UN consists of nations that agree on mutual cooperation; and the executers of that cooperation are usually nation states.

In the development of the European Community, the principle of subsidiarity will be applied. This principle should be observed consistently and rigorously at all levels, from local policy to the whole of mankind. True democracy, tolerance and justice are needed at all levels of decision-making and activity. Fortunately, both the Maastricht and the Lisbon summit meetings of the European Community in 1992 have made progress in this respect. A Europe of nations is gaining ground again.

In this way, we would create conditions in which people could best identify with all the communities to which they belong as individuals and citizens, and in which people and nations could live in peace and prosperity.

5. THE NATION STATE IN A NEW EUROPE

The single most remarkable macropolitical phenomenon of the past generation has been the global crisis of authoritarianism, and the spread of liberal democracy in its wake. Many of the countries that have become democracies in the past few years are very unstable or have an uncertain commitment to liberal values, and it would not be surprising to see a number of them lapse back into some kind of authoritarian rule in the near future. None the less, the trend is there.

Since the Paris CSCE Summit in November 1990, the number of the CSCE participating states has increased from 34 to 52. In addition to Albania (joined in June 1991), Estonia, Latvia and Lithuania (joined in September 1991), eleven former Soviet republics have been accepted as participants in the CSCE. Slovenia, Croatia, Georgia and Bosnia-Herzegovina have been the latest newcomers. This group of CSCE states will probably further enlarge in the future.

Nationalism is frequently held to be the major competitor of democracy, and many are of the opinion that the new world order, emerging after the Cold War, will be one of nationalist conflict rather than one of democratic peace. A sense of national unity, as I stated earlier, is, however, the only truly necessary precondition for the emergence of stable democracy. Liberal democracy does not seem to be very good at adjudicating the claims of longstanding linguistic or ethnic communities living on their traditional territory within multi-ethnic societies. In this sense, the American model cannot be imported into societies like Yugoslavia or the former Soviet Union, where national disintegration is a necessary precursor to democratization. National struggles at present seem to be a necessary first step towards the emergence of stable democracy in the future, just as they were in Western Europe in the nineteenth century. Now we have to work together to speed up the development of these societies towards harmony and national unity.

From the point of view of European security, the future role of the nation state will remain central. The strengthening of democratic values, a market economy and the rule of law as agreed in the Paris Charter of the CSCE constitute the basis for the controlling of change in the new Europe. The old and new nations have to adjust themselves to the emerging post-Cold War security architecture.[3]

The Helsinki process was designated to bridge the East–West division. It played an immense role in the evolution of relations across the dividing line. During the difficult years it helped to preserve dialogue while other channels failed. The CSCE made it possible for smaller states to be heard. Now the question is whether the CSCE can provide a channel for a number of national minorities everywhere in the Euro-Atlantic community from Vladivostok to Vancouver.

The ongoing century can also be seen – as some observers have stated – as a struggle between the legacies of two men, namely, Woodrow Wilson and Vladimir Ilich Lenin. Both of them wanted to promote internationalist goals. The former spoke about the need to make the world safe for democracies by promoting democratic values worldwide. The latter spoke about the need to make the world just for the working class by promoting a workers' revolution worldwide. Now we are approaching the end of the century and we are more aware of the ideas that have survived. Democracy has been one of them, and the world really is becoming a world of nations. This development started from Europe, and has not yet reached its end even there.

NOTES

1. The notion 'back to the future' is from John Mearsheimer. (See John Mearsheimer, Back to the Future: Instability in Europe after the Cold War; in Sean Lynn-Jones (ed.), *The Cold War and After: Prospects for Peace*. Cambridge Mass.: The MIT Press, 1991, pp. 141–92.)
2. *International Encyclopedia of the Social Sciences.* (The Macmillan Company and the Free Press, 1968 [no place]), vol. 11, pp. 7–8 and vol. 15, p. 150.
3. See, e.g., Alpo Rusi, *After the Cold War. Europe's New Political Architecture* (Basingstoke: Macmillan, 1991).

3. NATIONALISM AND THE DEVELOPMENT OF EUROPEAN SOCIETIES

Ernest Gellner

1. INTRODUCTION

If I have understood it correctly, my task here is to talk about nationalism, of the beast that we all have to contain. I think that the first point to make is that to contain nationalism one has to understand it. The difficulty about understanding nationalism is that there is almost virtually an inverse relationship between the self-image and self-presentation of nationalism and the actual reality. Most social phenomena may have a touch of false consciousness, of not presenting themselves quite correctly. Nationalism is unusual in that its self-presentation is actually inverse of the true reality. What is said of itself is the opposite of what is the case, and this self-misrepresentation of nationalism is, alas, also accepted by its critics as well as by its adherents. I think that it is important first of all to get it straight.

The self-image of nationalism is a kind of a mistaken piece of philosophical anthropology, a kind of a basic vision of man. It begins with the assumption that men simply have a nationality, an assumption which is, of course, built on the past documents rather in the same way as they have an age, a gender and other basic features. Now this simply is not the case.

Nationality, though very important in certain circumstances, which have prevailed for the past two centuries, is not a universal characteristic of human beings. Nationalism in a sense recognizes this fact, because it has noticed that nationality was not an important political principle until somewhere around the turn of the eighteenth and nineteenth centuries. But instead of drawing the correct inference from this, namely that nationality and nationalism is a powerful force operating under modern circumstances, it rather adopts the rhetoric of awakening (*"Deutschland erwache"*).

2. THE FEATURES OF AN AGRARIAN SOCIETY

The characteristic stance of nationalists in Europe has been that of awakeners of nationalities or national sentiments, which were dormant but which were a kind of 'Sleeping Beauty', needing to be awakened by the tender kiss of the awakener. Now this kind of a theory happens to be rubbish, and I will try briefly to sum up what I take to be the true state of affairs.

What it all has to do with is the relationship of political structure and of culture in human society. I will allow myself a very simple generalization about agrarian society. Agrarian society, as I define it, is a society which knows food production and food storage, but is based on a stable technology, where growth occurs occasionally, but is not a systematic principle. The technology is basically simple. The kind of agrarian society with which one has to deal in Europe can further be described as agroliterate: it also knows writing. It knows not only how to store food, but also how to store and codify ideas. These are the main facts which define it.

Now comes the generalization and there is a number of various generalizations one can allow oneself about agroliterate society. First, it is Malthusian society. An agroliterate society values offspring, or to be more precise, male offspring because it needs them for labour power and defence power. But because it is not a growth-based society, it periodically faces starvation, one in which people do not starve at random but rather in accordance with their rank. What follows from this is that the most important concern for members of agroliterate societies is to improve their position within the society, rather than to augment its production. They do not do that because, first of all, the idea of sustained growth is absent and, secondly, because work is despised in agroliterate society. It is hierarchical and values honour and pious learning, but does not value work. To be one of the producers is to earn contempt within such a society.

The result of all this has a number of consequences for the relationship of polity and culture. An agrarian society tends to have complicated political structures. There are no very sharp boundaries. You very seldom get very neat political units. Political units in agrarian societies are either imperial, large units which lack the communication and other technology for really controlling outlying territories, and which have to delegate power to local centres, with their own local power bases: complex empires which delegate much of the activity to local units and local power. Alternatively, these are local communities which generally do not stretch to the limits of the culture, but share it with other similar units. In other words, there is nothing in that kind of society to lead to the merging of political and cultural boundaries: the satisfaction of the nationalist principle is that the political unit and the cultural unit should be congruent, that the state should be an expression of culture.

On the contary, the main role of culture in an agrarian society is to be the expression, in speech, in dress, in food, in marital patterns and everything, of a person's status in an intricate hierarchical organization. The culture underwrites a complex role system, hierarchically inegalitarian and fairly stable. Agrarian society has no reason to be mobile. Culture does not delimit political units; partly because the political units themselves are not very sharp, and partly because there is not the slightest reason for such a fusion. There is a good deal of reason for the disparity of culture and polity, and indeed this is what one finds.

In the agrarian age, nationality was not an important political fact. It is not a kind of feature to be used even today. If you ask a Himalayan peasant what is his nationality, he does not know what you are talking about, are you asking about his caste or his religion or his political sovereign? For him all this will be complex, they won't all converge, they may even be seasonal, they won't be tidied up. It is only the age of nationalism which has tidied up these questions into one single question.

3. FROM AGRARIAN TO INDUSTRIALIZED SOCIETY

Agrarian society is replaced by an industrial and industrializing society, which is different in a number of ways. First of all, it is committed to economic growth: bribery by promise of material improvement has become the main principle of political legitimacy and the main principle of binding people to their units. Industrial society is committed to growth. Growth, in turn, implies occupational mobility, and occupational mobility implies the erosion of the old hierarchy.

The second feature is that work ceases to be physical and becomes semantic. In advanced societies, virtually nobody works with their muscles any more. Even the man handling the bulldozer is a man basically controlling quite a complex control mechanism which he has to understand; he has to be able to read the manual of instruction. In other words, he has to be able to maintain it with the help of a manual written for him. Basically people manipulate symbols, ideas and other people, but they do not manipulate matter. They only do that as a part of their recreation during the weekend, when they go to their gardens, but they do not do it as a part of their working lives.

Now, the consequence of this, not generally noticed, is that for the first time in human history, High Culture becomes a universal culture of the entire society. Here I don't use High Culture in any evaluative sense, but in the technical and sociological sense. High Culture is a culture transmitted by an educational system, which codifies the marks and the tokens used in communication, so that they are identical over the entire society. The ability to emit and to understand context-free messages is the central requirement for work. This is something which cannot be learned in the old way, at mother's knee, but only in the *'ecóle maternelle'*. The shift from the mother to the *'ecóle maternelle'* is the difference in the socialization of pre-industrial and industrial man.

Industrial man only acquires effective right of citizenship if he can communicate in a school-transmitted, literate culture, which is also the idiom of the economic, political and other bureaucracies within which he lives. The consequence is by far the most important investment, unlike agrarian man with his role in this stable hierarchy, in his membership in a culture. This has two preconditions: that he can operate that culture, and that his general characteristics are acceptable and compatible with the self-image of that culture. Given those two conditions, his life is quite agreeable. If, on the other hand, those conditions are not satisfied, his life is a long series of humiliations and insults and unpleasantnesses. The main consequence is that he must either live in a unit whose bureaucracies operate in the culture which he himself has mastered or, if he does not, he must assimilate or migrate or change the political map, and that he should henceforth live in a political unit which does operate in the idiom which he has mastered, and which defines and legitimates itself as a protector of that culture. In other words, he becomes a nationalist.

To resume, nationalism presents itself and is seen by its enemies as the expression of activistic deep forces of *'Blut und Boden'* and of the atavistic striving for kinship and territoriality, of *'Gemeinschaft'*. In fact, of course, as if my argument is correct, it is the expression of the modern *'Gesellschaft'*, of unanimous but culturally *'gleichgeschaltet'* society, which is *'gleichgeschaltet'* not because of some kind of a mania of its rulers, but because of quite objective economic necessities. This is a rather materialist, though by no means a Marxist, theory of nationalism, which relates it to the way in which modern society makes its living.

4. STAGES IN THE DEVELOPMENT OF THE INDUSTRIALIZED SOCIETY

My next step in the argument is to postulate five stages by which an agrarian society, where the nationalist principle is absent, moves to an industrialized or industrializing society, where nationalism is one of the principles of sovereignty. This does not, of course, happen overnight, and there are various stages through which it passes.

The first stage will be called a 'Congress of Vienna stage'. It is the stage where the old principle of dynastic, religious and local basis of power still operates. It ignores the principle of nationality, but the snake has already entered the Garden of Eden. During this stage, the snake is present, but not yet very effective.

The second stage follows very rapidly. This is the stage of nationalist irredentism, where the new force is making itself felt, but on the whole does not yet prevail. It is a curious fact that, if you take Eastern Europe, which is at the moment our main concern, you find that in the period between 1815 and 1918 nationalism, so conspiciously present, nevertheless made a very limited impact on the map of Eastern Europe, which had been carved up between three empires in 1815. By 1914, the only real change produced on that map was the emergence of a few buffer states in the Balkans. This was due more to the weakness of the Ottomans than to the strength of nationalism. In spite of that, stage two was the age of irredentism, but not yet of successful nationalism.

Stage three, from 1918 to 1939, was an age when nationalism was triumphant but self-defeating. In 1918 the new principle of sovereignty, of self-determination, under the auspices of Woodrow Wilson, was accepted, and produced a new system of states in Eastern Europe, totally replacing the pattern imposed by the Congress of Vienna. This pattern was also totally self-defeating: the states so created were pathetically feeble. They suffered from all the weaknesses of their predecessors because they were just as haunted by minorities. They also suffered from some additional weaknesses: they were inexperienced, small and weak. In addition to that, the minorities included members of the previously dominant groups, who did not like being in this new situation, and had means of resisting it. They did not need to invent a glorious past, because they had living memories of it. The system was pathetically feeble. Come Hitler and Stalin, and the system collapsed with virtually no effective resistance.

When discussing stage four, I would like to use a term the Nazis used of some of their war-time operations, namely that of *'Nacht und Nebel'*. Under the cover of the war-time secrecy, and also under the protection of the post-war victor's licence and retaliatory indignation, methods are employable which supplement the old methods for enforcing the nationalist imperative, the marriage of state and culture, namely genocide, enforced transplantations of populations. These are added to the old and more benign forms of assimilation. That is roughly speaking the story of the 1940s.

Stage five means the diminution of nationalism for various reasons, some of which were already mentioned by other authors. I will come to that later. Anyway, stage five may be a mixture of perception and wish fulfilment. Anyway, this is the kind of theory of the stages, of the transition from a non-nationalist world to a nationalist one. Stage five, of course, interests us most.

5. EUROPEAN TIME ZONES

The next thing I would like to do is to indicate briefly the way in which these five stages operate. They operate rather differently in the different time zones of Europe. I shall work against the sun, and will here proceed from West to East. The westernmost time zone of Europe, the Atlantic coastline, has been least affected by nationalism because – I think – by historical accident it was divided into strong dynastic states which roughly, even if only very roughly, correlated with cultural zones. The states based on Lisbon, Madrid, Paris and London correlated with cultural zones. The only major change in the map produced by nationalism within this zone has been the establishment of the Republic of Ireland, but otherwise the map looks much the same as it did before. The spirit of this area has best been expressed by one of the most interesting ancestors of nationalism, namely Ernest Renan, when he preached to the French, and opposed the use of ethnology or ethnography for political purposes. He preferred consent and will. You cannot have it both ways. In other words, he counselled the French against what might be called Central or East European populist-nationalist, or ethnographic-nationalist, propaganda.

The second time zone of Europe, immediately east of the Atlantic one, is roughly coextensive with the erstwhile Holy Roman Empire. Its interesting characteristics are that it was well-endowed with normative high cultures – in other words, with the Germans and Italians – which from the Reformation or Renaissance, and perhaps even earlier, possessed well-defined national cultures. All they needed, in order to implement the nationalist marriage of state and culture, was to provide the culture with a political roof as powerful as that of their neighbours. This could be done in a relatively humane way, with few battles and with much diplomatic activity. A great deal of cultural engineering was not required. Such a kind of alliance of nationalism and liberalism was possible.

The third zone to the east is, of course, the one where the five stages were played out to the full, not aided by the existence of prefabricated states with more or less national boundaries, nor aided by the existence of high cultures ready for the new order. This zone further east, consisted of a kind of Habsburg area plus the Ottoman Balkans plus certain areas to the north of them. It was marked by the absence of both nationalist states and of effective national cultures. The distinction between historic and non-historic states, which is often presented by historians, does not amount to very much, because both of them had to recreate the High Culture and the political unit to serve it. There the five stages played themselves out to the full.

Finally there is, of course, the fourth time zone of Europe, further east still. It shared the two first stages with the third time zone. But then something very strange happened. All the three empires which had carved up Eastern Europe in 1815 were losers in the First World War. One of them was, however, rapidly re-established under a new ideocratic management, which was effective, ruthless and committed. It was able to suppress nationalism for the next seventy years in an even more effective way than the *ancien régimes* had done between 1815 and 1914 in other parts of Europe. The fourth time zone was of course extended in 1945 to include some territories included in the third zone, due to the westward advance of the Red Army.

The main question we are facing at the moment is whether the fourth time zone will slot itself into the other development stages three, four and five, providing I am right about the five stages, and in saying that the fourth time zone has only gone through the first two, and that the further developments were frozen by a very powerful ruthless ideocracy for seventy years. Now that this ideocracy has collapsed and the lid has been taken off, the question is: will it create a Balkanized pattern of pathetically feeble small states haunted by minorities, including previous members of the dominant group now put into an inferior and irritating position? Or will they reach the stage of *'Nacht und Nebel'*, and proceed to tidy up the map in the light of the nationalist principle by massacres, and more or less forced movements of population? Or will they move to stage five, where under the mixture of various factors, such as relative affluence, late industrialism, convergence of industrial cultures and other considerations, the appeal of ethnicity is diminished?

The evidence we have so far is inconclusive. Obviously all three things have happened. There have been some massacres, but not nearly as many as one might have expected. A good deal of migration of people from areas where they are in a minority has taken place. There has also obviously been Balkanization and fragmentation and the creation of feeble and questionably viable political units. There is also a certain amount of desire to reach the stage five. However, I am not going to give any pointless prophecy as to which of these elements will prevail.

6. THE FUTURE OF EUROPE

Now I shall finish with some general conclusions about the overall political situation. There is a general trend towards both supranational and subnational political units. In other words, the great marriage of a generalized High Culture with the political unit, which marks the age of nationalism, is now followed by a countertrend to divorce, which is very much to be desired.

Let me now specify some of the factors which are making for supranational units. It seems to me obvious that the age of late industrialism based on a very advanced, very powerful technology, makes a supranational authority imperative for at least two related reasons: the avoidance of ecological disaster and the avoidance of blackmail by very powerful but increasingly cheap and increasingly accessible weapons. National units are not going to refrain from either ecologically disastrous policies or from the arms race simply as a response to some kind of an abstract morality. There will always be the 'drug traders argument' that because it is being done anyway, why should we impoverish ourselves by refraining from it. The only way of stopping this is by some effective supranational authority. There is a hope that, informally or otherwise, this supranational authority will emerge.

The reasons are the following. There is a kind of club of developed or semi-developed societies which share a number of desirable features. After 1945 the old dominance of the agrarian ethos which linked glory and power to territory – this might be called aristocratic-peasant thinking, the notion that power depends on land, or that survival depends on land – has been broken. The perception that power is more effectively based on industrial might than on territoriality has become very persuasive through the economic history of the post-1945 period. The shift from honour values to production and consumption values has been very marked. The year 1945 marked the defeat of the last attempt to impose 'martial values' at the cost of productive values. Those who represented honour and martial values were defeated on the ground of their own choosing, namely in war.

The year 1989 marked the defeat of the ideological or ideocratic values. The one great world religion which was articulated in formally secular terms foolishly put its money on the claim that it would constitute a short cut to affluence. It was also defeated on the ground of its own choosing, namely economic competition. It is really a kind of a *'Krakh'* of ideology. The end of ideology was vindicated by an inprecedented self-dismantling from above of a new major world religion. The survivors and victors in this economic war were a kind of alliance of non-believing pragmatic consumerists, who have everything to fear from the non-members of the club who might pursuit policies of military blackmail and ecological catastrophy. They themselves are not likely to go to war against each other. I might be too optimistic in this.

Right now it looks as though this club of the powerful is free of missionary zeal for some ideology. Its members are, on the whole, consumerist unbelievers. Nor do they believe in power through territoriality. They prefer to be powerful through economic growth, rather than through geographic expansion. They can naturally form a kind of alliance which informally existed at the time of the Gulf War in 1990–1991, but – somewhat to my regret – nobody pointed out the logic of the situation, nor codified it to some kind of case law, nor created any institutional base for it.

Basically this seems to be the way in which world government can come about: through the shared interests of consumerist unbelievers in avoiding ecological disaster and blackmail from societies which are still not production and consumption orientated, societies which often know nothing other than clientilistic *mafioso* politics. These societies have leaders who have come up the hard way, through the conflict of clientilist cliques, and who know nothing else and understand nothing else or, alternatively, societies which have not yet been secularized like the affluent ones, and which take an absolutist missionary belief only too seriously. Or, indeed, there may be societies where the *mafiosi* and the believers are conflated into one person. This creates a genuine danger.

Presumably the curve of development of technology as such (I am not an expert in this field) indicates that very, very nasty weapons will get smaller and smaller and cheaper and cheaper and will sooner or later inevitably fall into the hands of potential blackmailers. The logic of the ethos of the consumers and their shared interest and the dangers which they face from the ecological or military blackmail situation may create a kind of world government, informal or other. Anyway, that is my prediction.

How does that development fit in with the logic of

nationalism? Well, this is, as far as I can see, the only way to square the two, because nationalism will continue to operate through all the factors which make for the pervasiveness of a High Culture. The only hope I can see is some kind of a divorce between the political unit and cultural identification. It won't be easy, but I think it is feasible.

In the past Europe has benefited enormously from political pluralism, which ensured that the same mistake was not committed by everyone at the same time. It was very fortunate for Europe that neither Charles V nor Napoleon nor Hitler managed to unify it. The mistakes were never generalized. If my argument is correct, insurance through political pluralism will no longer be available in a technologically very powerful age. It can perhaps be replaced by cultural pluralism, which benefits from the fact that the demagogues tend to be culture-specific, so that a kind of culturally pluralist system arises where all cultures that desire it are endowed with their own national museum, national theatre, national television, mass media network, etc. This is the kind of cultural infrastructure which is not linked to the functional political infrastructure.

The kind of diminution in the significance of geographic boundaries is already highly visible in some parts of Europe. When you for example drive from Belgium to Holland it is extremely hard to tell where the frontier is, because it is no longer marked. Some other frontiers, which once upon a time were very potent, are no longer marked either. This kind of reduction of the significance of political boundaries, a cultural pluralism combined with a political centralism, seems to me to be the hope for the future.

4. PATRIOTISM AND NATIONALISM

Aira Kemiläinen

1. MEANING OF 'PATRIOTISM', 'NATIONALISM' AND 'NATION STATE'

Patriotism and nationalism belong to the subject matter of the future nation state because (1) 'patriotism' has since the eighteenth century been connected with the state, and (2) 'nationalism' concerns both a nation (nationality) and a national state (nation state). The meaning of 'nation state' will be discussed below.

Originally, '*patria*' had the meaning of 'home country' or 'native place', or literally 'the land owned by one's father' (in English '*fatherland*', in German '*Vaterland*', in Swedish '*fäderneslandt*', in Finnish '*isänmaa*'). In the seventeenth century, the word '*patria*' was used to refer to a country, such as France; with regard to an individual, '*patria*' meant his or her native country. The word 'patriotism', which came into being later, was used when speaking about the 'love of one's own country'.[1] Originally 'nation' (Latin '*natio*') – from the Latin word '*nascor*' (I am born) – meant a tribe or a group of people who had the same ancestors. In ancient Rome, the citizens did not form a nation (*natio*) because that word was used for foreign tribes. In the Middle Ages, ancient Teuton peoples and also heathen tribes were called nations. At the beginning of the Modern Age, 'nation' already had the meaning of a civilized nation such as the Italians, French or English, and in general the inhabitants of certain European countries. At first, the characteristics of a nation were considered to be common language, common origin, common inheritance and traditions and the same history. In the eighteenth century, nation was often, especially in France and England, identified with state although the original meaning of the word, i.e., indicating a common language and the same ancestors, was kept alive at the same time.[2] So even the term 'nation' could be used when one spoke about a state. '*Patria*' and '*natio*' ('*patrie*', '*nation*' in French) could both mean a country or a state.

Later, and especially nowadays, other meanings were developed for these words. Both 'isms', 'patriotism' and 'nationalism', have often merged, meaning the same attitude to one's own national state (love of or pride in this state or even fanaticism about one's own country or people).

Recently, people who have been dedicated to internationalism and cosmopolitanism have considered even patriotism to be a hateful feeling or a negative way of looking at things.[3] People have usually made a distinction between patriotism and nationalism. In some countries – such as France and Germany – nationalism was regarded as chauvinism or an aggressive attitude to other nations.[4] Patriotism, on the other hand, was often considered to be a positive attitude to one's own state or society. In the Soviet Union nationalism was an unfavourable and bourgeois attitude while Soviet patriotism meant the solidarity of Soviet people with each other and – at the same time – cosmopolitanism in their relation to the rest of mankind.[5] The meaning of important words can change during hundreds of years, and even during a short time.

As we have seen, patriotism and nationalism are associated with the state, even a nation state, but not only a nation state. We can be patriotic towards many kinds of home places, such as our home town or village, province or country, sometimes an autonomous state or an American state, and finally a federal state or even an empire. For instance, it is possible to be a Pennsylvanian patriot and an American patriot at the same time, and perhaps to be a Philadelphian patriot, too. We speak also of local patriots, we may love a village or a suburb like patriots. I shall give some other examples. When Finland was a part of Sweden, until 1809, the inhabitants of Finland regarded both Finland itself and the Swedish state as their fatherland. When Finland belonged to Russia in 1809–1917, Finland was the fatherland, but for most Finns Russia was not a fatherland.[6] In the newspapers they had to speak about Moscow in terms of the 'home country', but they did not feel that Russians were their fellow citizens. The Finns had citizenship in Finland, but the Russians were not citizens of Finland. A geography text-book from 1904 first described Finland in 41 pages and after that Russia in 21 pages.[7] Beyond the borders of Finland are – according to the book – to the west Sweden, to the north Norway and to the east Russia. Outside the Russian borders there lay to the west Norway, Finland, the Baltic Sea, Germany, Austria and Romania. The book was published at the time of the so-called Russification, and the Finns were eager to emphasize their autonomous position. Probably the Scots feel patriotism towards both Scotland and the United Kingdom. Slovenians were expected to be Slovenian and Yugoslavian patriots, but now probably the latter patriotism has disappeared. It is possible to love both one's own autonomous state and an empire, but if the latter is not friendly, it may be regarded as an oppressor and be hated. In regard to Austria-Hungary, which was a multinational empire, there were times when even other nationalities than Germans felt themselves to be Austrian patriots or loved the Habsburg Monarchy. This happened especially during the Napoleonic Wars.

In the eighteenth century patriotism was a popular word.[8] Patriots were expected to love their country, and according to the humanitarian ideology of the Enlightenment, people were encouraged to be good citizens so that their behaviour and activities would profit the whole society. Even in antiquity people knew that a patriot had to defend his or her country in times of war. The eighteenth-century patriots gradually began to think of their country and their society as a state and themselves as citizens of this state. In the Modern Age, the state became even more important. The inhabitants of a country were no longer only the king's subjects, but they began to be citizens who had human rights, and they insisted on a good government and a good administration. The French revolution proclaimed the idea of popular sovereignty. The revolutionary patriots accepted only a democratic state, and during the first years of the French Revolution patriotism meant, in the first place, a revolutionary attitude.[9] The supporters of other political systems were called 'antipatriots'. In fact, everybody from fanatics to conservatives claimed the title of patriot. Finally, the 'true' patriots were the most fanatical 'friends of the people' or, as is now said, the 'friends of the nation'. A democratic people who had the rights of citizens was called a nation. When the terror was over, patriotism gradually began to take on old connotations. The country of a patriot was, however, a modern state which was often centralized and uniform. The love of one's own state was patriotism.

What had nationalism to do with the nation state? First we have to clarify the meaning or meanings of nationalism. These mainly derive from the root word 'nation' as well as 'national', 'nationalist' and 'nationalistic'. At the end of the eighteenth century, 'nation' had at least four important senses:

1. People who spoke the same language and had the same ancestors (the old meaning of the word).
2. The population of a country, living under the same government, having the same laws, speaking the same language and having the same religion. As time went by, this population became more and more homogeneous.
3. The population of a state, also a state.
4. A population which claimed popular sovereignty and democratic political rights (a parliament) in their state. This conception originated when the French Revolution broke out.[10]

Sense (1) covered two groups. The first consisted of large or small peoples having a political unity, i.e., forming a state, such as the Portuguese and Dutch. These states were unilingual and had a Portuguese or Dutch national consciousness. The second group consisted of peoples without political unity living in several states such as Germans and Italians, or being a small nation within a state where the majority belonged to another nation, such as Finns in Sweden, Estonians in Russia and Czechs in Austria. These unpolitical nations began to be called nationalities (*Volkstümer* in Germany).

Sense (2) concerns the modern states which were so homogeneous and uniform that their populations had some kind of a feeling of solidarity towards the other members of the 'nation' and towards the state, e.g., France, England, Denmark and Spain.

Sense (3) is based on sense (2). 'Nation' and 'state' became identified with respect, for instance, for the French and English nations. The fact that the meanings of the words in question came nearer to each other may explain the later term 'national state'.

The famous German historian Friedrich Meinecke divided nations into two types, cultural nation and state nation ('*Kulturnation*', '*Staatsnation*'). These terms corresponded to our sense (1) and sense (2). Both could be preliminary phases of a national state, if, (a) a nationality could form a state, and if, (b) the state covered one nationality, or a great majority of the population consisted of one and the same nationality. The famous historical term of a European national state or nation state was the result of these types of national consciousness.

The word 'nationalism', in fact, concerns the nations of senses (1), (2) and (3). The populations in question have a strong feeling of solidarity and share sympathies and interests with each other, although class interests or religions may weaken their solidarity. In these cases, nationalism means that these nationalities are national-minded, i.e., they love the common language and the same traditions and customs. Further, they appreciate both their popular culture and their High Culture. If someone tries to prevent them using their own language and following their own habits, or offends their economic interests, they may revolt and raise a national struggle which often has the purpose of making them independent political units or throwing off a foreign yoke.

Often these nationalities have a national pride; in any case, they share a feeling of solidarity which can be called national feeling or national consciousness. If linguistic minorities live in a multinational state, the majority may oppress them. These attitudes can be seen in the homogeneous nations which form a state; they share the feeling of solidarity, they are proud of their nation and they perhaps think that they should spread their better philosophy of life; i.e., they have a missionary idea (the French during the Revolution, the Soviet Union in regard to socialism and Leninism), they may oppress the national minorities and try to amalgamate them with their nation (and language). Both of these types (a political nation or a nationality on the cultural basis) can have the same kind of nationalism. However, the political nations do not need to fight for their independence or for their language, because there are no obstacles to overcome in this respect.

As to nation states, they remind us of the above-mentioned senses (2) and (3). France and England have been considered nation states because they are quite strong and homogeneous and have one official language. The citizens of these states also share the same interests, sympathies and actions. There is national pride and even aggressiveness in their relations to foreign nations, especially during the time they were colonial powers and sought to dominate the seas.

During the past century, the dissolution of multinational empires (universal monarchies) and the birth of nation states (senses (2) and (3) above) have been typical of the modern international system in Europe. National consciousness has been strong in the new states. In the First World War, German social democrats supported the government although they were supposed to be internationalists. During the Winter War between the Soviet Union and Finland (1939–1940), most of the Finnish communists were brave defenders of their country. This attitude can be called patriotism. Was it also nationalism? In Germany it certainly was nationalism because the great majority of soldiers defended the German nation, which was understood to form a German state as well as to be a German nationality.

In regard to Finland most people would say that the Finnish army was nationalistic because it did fight for the Finnish nation. However, Finland is a bilingual state, and especially the Swedish-speaking inhabitants stress that they form a different Swedish nationality in Finland. If a nation state is considered to be a homogeneous population which speaks a common language, then Finland is not a nation state – at least, not a typical one. In this sense the Finnish soldiers would have been patriotic but not nationalistic! Nowadays, however, even the Swedes of Finland speak about the Finnish nation state. Yet, as a student of nationalism I still hesitate if I am asked whether Finland is a nation state. Aren't Finns nationalistic when defending the rights of the Finnish-speaking population, and aren't the Swedish-speaking citizens of Finland nationalistic when they try to improve the position of their nationality (language)? These examples indicate that there are many problems in defending 'nation state' and 'nationalism'.

2. WHAT IS OR WAS A NATION STATE?

I now turn to the question of what is a nation state or a national state. France has been considered a typical nation state. The French language was from the sixteenth century onwards the only official language in France. The French Academy gave the model of the French language, and this was followed all over the country. The kingdom was strengthened from the Middle Ages on, while the power of the dukes became weaker and finally the duchies were united with the kingdom. The administration became more and more centralized, but only later did the French Revolution develop a really uniform state. This type of state was suited to increase feelings of solidarity, especially when the state became gradually democratic. In fact, France was unilingual only officially because the languages or dialects of the *langue d'oc* (Provençal) and *langue d'oil* were kept alive, and people spoke Basque in the South, Breton in Brittany, and German in some border districts and particularly in the territories which belonged to the German empire.

When a state in which the government was very strong, or even had unlimited power as in France under absolutist rule, had only one official language, the minor languages were forgotten. States of this type were nevertheless considered uniform nation states. In Eastern Central Europe and in multinational empires this situation caused wars of independence and often gave birth to new nation states such as Greece, Hungary and Bulgaria, although even these states were, in fact, usually not quite uniform nor unilingual. After the Second World War Eugen Lemberg, in his book on European nationalism, supposed that the age of nationalism would belong to history, because super-powers had replaced nations.[11] Yet, during the last few decades we have been surprised by the rising nationalism of small populations that had been national minorities, i.e., populations speaking a language which had been regarded as a dialect or as an inferior language. They have begun to claim rights for their national groups and national languages, for instance the Celtic languages of Wales and Brittany, Basque and Catalonian in Spain, Lappish in Finland, Sweden, Norway and Russia as well as Eskimos in North America.

What then is a nation state and what is the relation of those small national groups (nationalities) to a ruling nation state or to the state to which they belong? The League of Nations and the United Nations tried to establish rights for minorities, but it seems that this attempt was not successful. The Slavonic federal state of Yugoslavia consisted of several states which were not satisfied with their rights although the languages were related to each other. Now Slovenia and Croatia in particular have been feeling oppressed by Serbia, which did not want to allow Croatia to separate because there are a great number of Serbians in the Croatian state. What is the fatherland of those different parts? For whom do these people have patriotic feelings? What is in that case the position of nations or nationalities?

3. CHANGING MEANING OF NATION STATE: WHAT ARE PATRIOTISM AND NATIONALISM NOW?

It is obvious that the meaning of the term 'national state' or 'nation state' has changed during the last hundred years. At the same time, the object of patriotism and nationalism has probably also changed.[12] The state has become extremely important in the modern world; it is expected to be homogeneous, and it is often rather uniform and centralized. A patriot loves and defends this state. When people nowadays speak about a 'Europe of fatherlands' they specifically mean the states of which they are citizens. What then is a nation or a nationality? Most often a state has already formed a feeling of coherence and solidarity among the citizens, so that they feel they belong to a special nation.

Nowadays language is perhaps no longer the essential factor it was previously. The state with its political system and ideology may now be more important than language as a uniting force. After 1871 the inhabitants of Alsace-Lorraine seem to have felt that way. Switzerland, consisting of four nationalities, has not been a national state either. But there is a special Swiss national consciousness. It is a political national consciousness connected with old traditions and interests going back to the Middle Ages. These can be just as important as language. We realize that the ideology of political administration and human rights may be a more important factor for the feeling of solidarity than language and popular culture. So even Finland could therefore be called a national state. The factors which unite the Finnish-speaking and Swedish-speaking populations are more important than the languages themselves. Finland could, therefore, be a nation state consisting of two quite large nationalities. In this respect, nationality could not be identified with nation, which would be a broader term including culture, form of government and administration and the whole general way of looking at things.

In this new situation, people would then be both patriotic and nationalistic towards their own nation state, a homogeneous political and cultural unit. This means that the role of language has changed. However, this happened only in a few states which have a common history. We shall see that language can be a very important and also dividing factor in some countries, if it is the true sign of the local (national) culture and the real implement of communication. We may draw the conclusion that a nation state should give its citizens a real national consciousness, but we realize at the same time that the factors of this feeling of solidarity can vary widely and change in the long run when the circumstances change. The twentieth-century nation state may, therefore, have a different basis from its precursor in the nineteenth century. But there can still be major problems.

The German *Fischerlexicon* gives a modern definition of nation state (*Nationalstaat*) and nation. A nation state is a state which consists of a relatively homogeneous people in contrast to multinational states. A nation according to this lexicon is a politically organized society in which the majority of the population is coherent in respect of the basic cultural features, i.e., language, religion and common political tradition. A nation state is regarded as the legitimate expression of these common features, in contrast to older dynastic forms of government.[13]

On one hand, this definition precisely emphasizes homogeneity as the basis of a national state without mentioning the different factors, and on the other hand, the characteristics of a nation are considered to be both cultural and political. The language, the traditions and the national legal system – the factors of the age of Romanticism – are not the only characteristics, but the political organization of the society is regarded as central. This new development explains why the Swedes, i.e., the minority in Finland, nowadays speak about the nation state of Finland, though they previously considered themselves to be a special nationality. It also explains why the people of Switzerland are considered to form a political nation. It means that the non-linguistic factors of national consciousness have been so important that they surpass the language factor as the cohesive force. The quality of the society, the administration, the culture, the political and social system of the country do not depend on the language if the position of the language is satisfactory. The new development is also caused by the improvement of education; children are now taught several languages, including the national languages. A knowledge of several languages also makes it possible to think of some kind of a union between several independent states, such as the union of European states.

4. ETHNIC AND NATIONAL MINORITIES

The new situation described above seems to be the opposite of the new phenomenon of national struggles initiated by so-called national minorities in states which were formerly regarded as unilingual nation states as France, Spain and the United Kingdom. This phenomenon shows another side of nationalism. The new democracy justifies the claims of very small ethnic groups like Lapps or Basques about using their own languages in culture and administration. If they are large enough and live in a distinct territory they may continue national struggles of the nineteenth century in order to form a state, like the Slovenians. Iceland became independent as late as the 1940s. If independence turned out to be impossible, they wanted more rights for their own language. Today the improvement of education would make this possible, because national minorities could also learn the state language which would be necessary for a prosperous individual career.

When nation states came into being they included other nationalities. It is a matter of opinion whether these groups are called nationalities or ethnic groups. Flemish people in Belgium and Swedish-speaking people in Finland may be called nationalities in the same way as Hungarians in Romania, while Lapps living in Norway, Sweden, Finland and Russia, speaking different dialects (almost languages) are perhaps ethnic groups. However, the Lappish language itself is a different Fenno-Ugrian language, not a dialect. The League of Nations and the United Nations affirmed the rights of minorities but were very careful about questions of nationality.

There are several national minorities in Europe:

1. Catalonian and Basque nationalities in Spain that under the Franco regime were oppressed.
2. Provençals, Basques, Bretons of Brittany and Germans of Alsace-Lorraine in France. Inhabitants of Alsace-Lorraine accepted the state of France, although their language was originally German. Provençals (*langue d'oc*), Basques and Bretons have been discontented because their languages have been neglected. According to the ideology of the French

Revolution, the sovereign nation (popular sovereignty) was of primary importance. All inhabitants of France were obliged to choose revolutionary France as their fatherland. French had already become the official language of France in 1539. Other languages had no importance in the state.

3. The inhabitants of Scotland (not only Gaelic people) and the Cymric people of Wales. The Cymrics have very eagerly defended their language, and many Scots would prefer independence. They cannot be said to be oppressed, but for instance some Scots think that they would do better as an independent state than in the union with the United Kingdom. With regard to Scottish nationalism, the Gaelic language hardly has any meaning except as the old basis of Scottish individualism. What is the object of their patriotism and nationalism? Both Wales and the United Kingdom, both Scotland and the United Kingdom, or only Wales and Scotland? Or perhaps they are nationalistic towards the nationality of Wales/Scotland and the nation of the United Kingdom?
4. The Ladins (Rheto-Romanic people) in Italy and Austria. In Switzerland they are not a national minority because their language is one of the national languages.
5. Germans in Belgium. Walloons and Flemings are the two main nationalities of Belgium.
6. The new minorities in Estonia, Latvia and Lithuania. In Estonia there is a great number (more than 30 per cent) of Russians, while in Latvia nearly half of the population consists of non-Latvians. In Lithuania there are Russian and Polish minorities.
7. In Scandinavian countries and in Northern Russia there are Lapps. Only recently they have received the right in Finland to use Lappish officially and to be educated in Lappish.
8. In Sweden there are also original Finns who were not emigrants after the Second World War. They do not have rights which could be comparable with the rights of Swedes in Finland.
9. The Swedish-speaking inhabitants of Finland are actually not a national minority because their language is the second national language although Swedish Finns total less than 6 per cent of the population.[14]

National minorities are different from nation states because their populations are small and because they are perhaps not prominent in any cultural, economic or social field. Further, they are often living among other nationalities or amidst the majority of the state. From the viewpoint of internationalism, one could say that the form of government, the political ideology, the wellbeing of the inhabitants and the culture ought to be more important than national language, folklore and traditions. In reality, however, there are many other factors which count more than those mentioned above. Perhaps the most important is the language, which is the means of communication. Individuals cannot manage in everyday life if they do not understand the language of the administration. Their thinking and education cannot be improved if they do not use a cultivated language. In a wealthy modern state, the members of a minority can be taught the language of the majority, but perhaps they do not feel themselves to be as fortunate as the other members of society. If the state is wealthy and the school education is good, bilingualism can solve the problem and remove the feeling of inferiority. It is interesting that the Swedish-speaking inhabitants of Finland can say that they identify with the state. This can be explained by the fact that their language is the second national language and a great many members of the minority and majority are bilingual.

Language is a very important factor of national consciousness, but it is not the only one. Religion, legal traditions and economic interests may also create the feeling of solidarity. Irish and Scottish people speak mostly English, but their Irish and Scottish national consciousness is very strong.

Why are there no national minorities in Switzerland? It was explained above why the Swedes of Finland do not feel themselves to be a national minority. The four languages of Switzerland are national and official languages. So their patriotism can be directed towards the Swiss state just as their nationalism may concern the political nation of Switzerland, as well as their own nationalities. The situation in Belgium is not as clear. The anthropologist William Z. Ripley said in 1900 that Walloons and Flemish-speaking citizens of Belgium have a very intense sense of Belgian nationality, but the Flemings have not always been satisfied with their position, and there are a great many people who probably would like to separate the two nationalities and form new states.[15]

When the modern world admired cosmopolitanism and internationalism, the nationalism of national or ethnic minorities was considered an obstacle and an anachronism. Nationalities which felt oppressed were called 'object nations' (in contrast to the old nation states or 'subject nations'), as Milan Kundera put it in *Le Nouvel Observateur* in 1991,[16] or 'the nations of the shadow'. Are they rebels and reactionaries who do not understand the new spirit of the European Union? Or are they modern supporters of the Enlightenment who demand human rights and equality with the 'subject nations' or old nation states? They may feel patriotism and nationalism towards their home territory and nationality as well as towards the state and towards Europe. This phenomenon might be a new phase in the history of Europe.

5. OPPRESSED NATIONS AND NATIONALITIES IN THE EASTERN PART OF EUROPE

The nation states were assumed to have reached their goal. The contemporary world has been shocked by nationalistic claims and struggles, but the fact that there are nation states which seem to be homogeneous does not mean that the historical development has come to an end. The situation today is a consequence of at least two reasons. First, some nations and nationalities were oppressed even after the First World War and especially after the Second World War. Second, as we have seen, the development of the national movements of the nineteenth century was interrupted. Even in the nation states, there remained national minorities which were not satisfied with their national rights.

The First World War liberated only some nations, namely Poland, Finland, Estonia, Latvia, Lithuania and Bessarabia which was united with Romania again. All these nations suffered much in the Second World War, lost their independence or were more or less patronized by the Soviet

Union. Hungary, Czechoslovakia, Romania and Bulgaria got into the same situation as Poland. In the Soviet Union the nations and national/ethnic minorities were allowed an apparent autonomy only. The centralized administration frustrated their autonomy, and some minorities were almost destroyed or moved from Europe to Asia. These events are some of the worst examples of the oppression of nationalities. One can compare them with the fate of Armenians in Turkey. The internationalistic attitude of the Soviet Union meant in reality an active Russification, although the non-Russian peoples were taught in their own languages at school in order to be able to read communist publications.

In Eastern Central Europe new problems arose when a great number of Hungarians and their territory were transferred to Romania. The federal state of Yugoslavia was created. Many nationalities and ethnic groups were not satisfied with the new state. The same was true of Slovaks in the then new Czechoslovakia. These relations came to light during the Second World War, when Slovaks and Croatians used the help of Germans against their compatriots. For modern politicians, it is extremely difficult to understand that Slovenians, Croatians and even Macedonians are in earnest in wanting to shake off the Serbian yoke. To Americans it is very strange that minor – as they think – controversies can kindle a civil war. Linguistic and cultural differencies still have great significance even today, especially if they are connected with economic problems and ideological and political discontent.

The character of the new nation states, to be formed in Eastern and Central Europe, will be unclear. They came into being as a result of their own national consciousness, i.e., nationalism. Their birth is compared with the old nation states. They have the same weak points as those, namely the problem of national minorities.

Ukrainians, Belorussians, Armenians etc. were national minorities in the Soviet Union in spite of the fact that it was a federal state. In the name of socialism and internationalism, this federal state practised an efficient Russification. The new so-called 'Independent States' are large enough to become similar to old nation states such as France, Hungary and Denmark.

The patriotism of these new 'nation states' is unclear. In the Ukraine it concerns the Ukraine and its people. Do they feel the Commonwealth of Independent States (CIS) to be their fatherland and the populations of this federation to be their nation? Probably not. The object of patriotism and nationalism of the Slovenians is Slovenia and the Slovenian nationality – or nowadays that nation – but not Yugoslavia. At the moment, they are Eastern Europeans, but not yet Europeans like the nations of Western Europe.

Catalonians may be Catalonian and Spanish patriots and nationalistic towards the Catalonians and – some of them – towards the Spanish nation state. The Basque population seems to be hostile towards Spain. The Germans in Belgium are perhaps Belgian patriots, and they probably think that they belong to the German nationality and to the Belgian nation state – if Belgium can be called a nation state! For all of these minorities the Union of Europe is perhaps a uniting force. We may therefore say that the old mature nation states and their national minorities are – all of them – good European patriots. Poland, Czechoslovakia and Hungary are close to this Union. The parts of the former Yugoslavia and the new states of Old Russia are continuing the course of development of nation states which was interrupted during the first half of the twentieth century. Their patriotism and nationalism has not yet taken shape, except for the consciousness of solidarity to their own nationality or nation.

Nation states and nationalities which did not form a state mostly had a common history because nationalities strove for political independence incited by their national feeling and according to the doctrine of national self-determination. Usually they had to struggle for their freedom. The law of nations in fact concerned sovereign states, and there was no superior power to settle a disagreement between a sovereign state and a nationality living in this state but differentiated from the dominating nation. At the end of the nineteenth century, some political philosophers claimed for national minorities the right to influence parliamentary decisions as a national group because they could never gain a majority when voting with other members of the parliament. This procedure would have been especially important in Austria-Hungary, which consisted of several nationalities.[17]

Even J. V. Snellman defended an idea introduced by Ferdinand Lassalle, who had insisted that nationality ought to be a legal principle in the law of nations. A nationality ought to have the right to form a state of its own. Such an idea could not have been put into practice in nineteenth-century Europe, and certainly not in Snellman's Finland.[18] States in the twentieth century are still sovereign, but the new supranational councils like the United Nations Security Council and the General Assembly, and other international organizations (European Community, Conference on Security and Cooperation in Europe) have begun to give directives to sovereign states and to use sanctions against them. From this viewpoint, these councils could also interfere in conflicts between a sovereign state and a national minority. A supra-national organization may therefore strengthen the position of minor nationalities in a sovereign state which may be unilingual but in reality is multinational.

6. PATRIOTISM AND NATIONALISM IN THE FUTURE NATION STATE

The European Union will be composed of several states. It will not be a federation of provinces as some adversaries of the centralized states now predict. If the future states are rather homogeneous in regard to their administration, they may be called nation states even if they comprise different nationalities or national minorities. The object of the patriotic feelings of their citizens will be expected to be their own nationality and the state to which they belong, and even the European Union itself. Even today a European may have a feeling of solidarity towards this continent when he or she lives or travels in America, Asia or Africa. European patriotism will probably also grow stronger if we begin to feel more solidarity towards the rest of mankind. However, at present the Islamic world, China, Japan, the African states and perhaps even the United States may still differ so much from the European way of looking at different things that a true European patriotism is possible.

Unlike patriotism, however, there will be no European nationalism because there exists no European nation, although most of the inhabitants of Europe speak languages related to each other and even if they do not have common ancestors in the immediate past, their gene patterns show common features with their neighbours more often than, for instance, with Asian or African populations. The existence of nation states will be a common characteristic in Europe for at least a hundred years. In Russia and in the CIS the government could plan the Russification of minor peoples and ethnic groups because the main population, the Slavs or Russians – including Ukrainians and Belorussians – were the repository of an old Byzantine civilization and an old Christian religion. The small tribes and nationalities, apart from the Poles and Islamic nations, could not compete with Russians in this respect. The Ukraine and Belorussia were too close to Russia or lacked the power to resist Russian dominance.

In the 'melting pot of nations', the United States, the new nation of 1776 was in principle English, and the immigrants had to merge into the American nation. They could be interested in their native languages and they perhaps searched for their roots, but for them it was necessary – and even a point of honour – to become American.

Europe is formed of old and glorious nations and cultures. Even the small nations may have a famous history, and they have their share of the old European civilization which is also called Western civilization. Once Europeans thought that they were the leaders of mankind. None of the big nations – French, English, Germans, Italians, Spaniards – and not even the small nations will give up their language and culture in order to submit to a European nation the language of which would be other than its own. The Danish referendum against the Maastricht Treaty (2 June 1992) may be a good example of a European nation which will not transfer power to the supranational parliament of the European Union or to its leaders, the important ministers of the great powers. Even the small Finnish nation is fond of its history, so that the Finns, too, want to belong to their own country, Finland, although in reality they are already good Europeans.

NOTES

1. Aira Kemiläinen, 1700-luvun nationalismi ja patriotismi. *Academica Scientiarum Fennica*. Yearbook 1977, pp. 155–6, 160–2.
2. Aira Kemiläinen, Nationalism. Problems Concerning the Word, the Concept and Classification. *Studia Historica Jyväskyläensia,* III. (Jyväskylä 1964), pp. 13–46.
3. Simo Talvitie (ed.), *Minun isänmaani* (WSOY: Porvoo-Helsinki, 1974) and Simo Talvitie (ed.), *Entä minun isänmaani?* (WSOY: Porvoo-Helsinki, 1975).
4. Cf. *Der Grosse Brockhaus* (1955): 'Nationalismus': die übersteigerte, intolerante Erscheinungsform des Nationalgedankens und des Nationalbewusstseins; and Paul Robert, *Dictionnaire alphabetique et analogique de la langue française* (1959): 'Nationalisme' Exaltation du sentiment national... (Cf. chauvinismus).
5. Ks. *Aakkosellinen tietokirja Neuvostoliitto* (Otava: Helsinki, 1967), p. 455.
6. Cf., for instance, articles in the journal *Tidningar utgifne af et Sällskap i Åbo* in 1771–1772 and the minutes kept at the diets from 1863 until 1906, especially the minutes of the Peasants' Estate in 1863–1864.
7. Elis Lagerblad, *Maantiedon oppikirja,* 5. painos (WSOY: Porvoo, 1904).
8. On eighteenth-century patriotism, see Kemiläinen, 1977.
9. Aira Kemiläinen, The Idea of Patriotism during the First Years of the French Revolution. *History of European Ideas*, vol. 11, 1989, pp. 11–19.
10. Cf. Abbé Sieyés, *Qu'est-ce que le tiers état?* (1789).
11. Eugen Lemberg, *Geschichte des Nationalismus in Europe* (Stuttgart: Schwab, 1950), p. 12.
12. Hugh Seton-Watson criticized the belief that every state is a nation, or that all sovereign states are national states. He said that states can exist without a nation, or with several nations. In his opinion, a state is a legal and political organization, while a nation is a community of people, whose members are bound together by a sense of solidarity, a common culture, a national consciousness. He examined the processes by which nations have been formed and the types of political movements which sought to achieve a national purpose and were influenced by the relations of states with each other. (See Hugh Seton-Watson, *Nations and States. An Enquiry into the Origins of Nations and the Politics of Nationalism.* London: Methuen, 1982, pp. 1–2.)
13. *Das neue Fischerlexicon in Farbe,* Band 6. Fischer Taschenbuch Verlag, 1981.
14. In addition, there are numerous small nationalities and language groups like the Slavic Sorbs or Wends in Germany and the Kasubi in Poland.
15. William Z. Ripley, *The Races of Europe. A Sociological Study* (London: Kegan Paul & Co., 1900), pp. 157–8. In *Time* (16 December 1991, p. 8), two letters dealt with the Belgian national identity. Marc Deschrijvere (Brussels) said: "You report that just as Brussels is becoming the capital of a more united Europe, serious rivalries between

French and Dutch Belgians have erupted." According to him, however, no Belgian identity has ever existed. Patriotism is an unknown term there, because this small land has been Roman, Spanish, Austrian, French, Dutch and German. His family members speak French, Dutch and English, and this fact does not create any problems. Another letter was written by Vicky Schotte (Bonheiden), who blamed the fanatics on both sides of political Belgium. She said that before the Second World War Belgium was a proud little nation, whose inhabitants were neither French, Dutch nor German. They had been taught to love their mixed country. Both writers seem to think that their Dutch-, French- or German-speaking compatriots form a Belgian people or 'a proud little nation' without a linguistic Belgian identity.

Donald L. Horowitz says that according to Lijphart (in his *Democracy in Plural Societies*) Switzerland, Austria, Belgium and the Netherlands have attained democracy in spite of considerable heterogeneity. Their success has depended on cooperation by the leaders of different groups, which transcends the segmental cleavages. He advocates this model for developing countries. There are thus suprasegmental sentiments that tie group members to the Swiss or the Dutch nation. (Donald R. Horowitz, *Ethnic Groups in Conflict*. London: University of California Press, 1985, pp. 571–2)

16. *Helsingin Sanomat*, 5 January 1992.
17. E. Viefhaus, Die Minderheitenfrage und die Entstehung der Minderheitenschutzverträge auf der Pariser Friedenskonferenz 1919; in *Eine Studie zur Geschichte des Nationalitätenproblems im 19. und 20. Jahrhundert*. (Würzburg: Holzner, 1960), pp. 19–34.
18. Aira Kemiläinen, The Idea of Nationalism. *Scandinavian Journal of History*, no. 9/1984, p. 50.

Part II

HISTORICAL PROCESSES

5. THE THREE HEGEMONIES OF HISTORICAL CAPITALISM

Giovanni Arrighi

1. THE ORIGINS OF THE MODERN INTERSTATE SYSTEM[1]

World hegemonies are a phenomenon of the modern interstate system which emerged out of the decay and eventual disintegration of the system of rule of medieval Europe. As argued by John Ruggie, there is a fundamental difference between the modern and the medieval (European) systems of rule. Both systems can be characterized as 'anarchic' but anarchy, in the sense of 'absence of central rule', means different things according to the principles on the basis of which the units of the system are separated from one another.[2]

The medieval system of rule consisted of chains of lord–vassal relationships based on an amalgam of conditional property and private authority. As a result, 'different juridical instances were geographically interwoven and stratified, and plural allegiances, asymmetrical suzerainities and anomalous enclaves abounded.'[3] In addition, ruling elites were extremely mobile *across* the space of these overlapping political jurisdiction being able 'to travel and assume governance from one end of the continent to the other without hesitation or difficulty'. Finally, this system of rule was 'legitimated by common bodies of law, religion, and custom that expressed inclusive natural rights pertaining to the social totality formed by the constituent units.' In sum, this was quintessentially a system of segmental rule; it was anarchy. 'But it was a form of segmental territorial rule that had none of the connotations of possessiveness and exclusiveness conveyed by the modern – of sovereignty. It represented a heteronomous organization of territorial rights and claims – of political space.'[4]

In contrast to the medieval system of rule, 'the modern system of rule consists of the institutionalization of public authority within mutually exclusive jurisdictional domains'.[5] Rights of private property and rights of public government become absolute and separated from one another; political jurisdictions become exclusively and clearly demarcated by boundaries; the mobility of ruling elites across political jurisdictions slows down and eventually ceases; law, religion, and custom become 'national', that is, subject to no political authority other than that of the sovereign.

This becoming of the modern system of rule has been closely associated with the development of capitalism as a mode of accumulation on a world scale. This close association is at the heart of Wallerstein's conceptualization of the modern world-system. In this conceptualization, the rise and expansion of the modern interstate system is held to have been both the main cause and an effect of the endless accumulation of capital: 'Capitalism has been able to flourish precisely because the world-economy has had within its bounds not one but a multiplicity of political systems.'[6] At the same time, the tendency of capitalist accumulators to mobilize their respective states so as to enhance their competitive position in the world-economy has continually reproduced the segmentation of the political realm into separate jurisdictions.[7]

The segmentation of the world-economy into competing political jurisdictions does not necessarily benefit capitalist accumulators. It largely depends on the form and intensity of competition. For example, if interstate competition takes the form of intense and long-drawn-out armed struggles, there is no reason why the costs of interstate competition to capitalist accumulators should not exceed the costs of centralized rule that they would have to bear in a world-empire. On the contrary, under such circumstances the profitability of capitalist enterprise might very well be undermined and eventually destroyed by an ever-increasing disruption of the networks of production and exchange through which capitalist enterprises appropriate surpluses and transform them into profits.

At the same time, competition among capitalist accumulators does not necessarily promote the continual segmentation of the political realm into separate jurisdictions. It largely depends on the form and intensity of competition, in this case among capitalist enterprises. If capitalist accumulators are enmeshed in dense trans-state networks of production and exchange, the segmentation of these networks into separate political jurisdictions may bear negatively on the competitive position of each and every capitalist enterprise relative to non-capitalist enterprises. Under these circumstances, capitalist accumulators may well mobilize their respective states to reduce rather than to increase or reproduce the political segmentation of the world-economy. And this tendency can be expected to be stronger, the more intense is intercapitalist competition.

More generally, interstate and interenterprise competition can take different forms, and the form that they take has important consequences for the way in which the modern world-system functions or does not function. It is not enough to emphasize the historical connection between interstate and inter-enterprise competition. We must also specify the form they take and how they change over time. Only in this way can we fully appreciate the evolutionary nature of the modern world-system and the role played by successive world hegemonies in making and remaking the system so as to resolve the recurrent contradiction between an endless accumulation of capital and a comparatively stable organization of political space.

Central to such an understanding is the definition of 'capitalism' and 'territorialism' as opposite modes of rule or logics of power. Territorialist rulers identify power with the extent and populousness of their domains and conceive of wealth/capital as a means or a byproduct of the 'endless' pursuit of territorial expansion. Capitalist rulers, in contrast, identify power with the extent of their command over scarce resources and consider territorial acquisitions as a means and a byproduct of an 'endless' accumulation of capital.

The difference between these two logics can be expressed in terms of the metaphor that defines states as 'containers of power'.[8] Territorialist rulers tend to increase their power by expanding the size of the container. Capitalist rulers, in contrast, tend to increase their power by piling up wealth within a small container and increase the size of the container only if it is justified by the requirements of the accumulation of capital.

The essential feature of the modern world-system has been the constant opposition of these two logics and the recurrent resolution of their contradictions through the innovative reorganization of world political-economic space by the leading capitalist state of the epoch. This dialectic between capitalism and territorialism antedates the establishment of the modern interstate system. Its origins lie in the formation within the medieval system of rule of a regional subsystem of capitalist and protocapitalist states in northern Italy.

Initially, this region was nothing but one of the 'anomalous enclaves' that abounded in the political space of the medieval system of rule. But as the decay of the medieval system of rule widened and deepened, the northern Italian capitalist enclave became organized into a subsystem of separate and independent political jurisdictions held together by the principle of the balance of power and by dense and extensive networks of residential diplomacy.

This subsystem of city-states – centred on Venice, Florence, Genoa and Milan – anticipated by two centuries or more many of the key features of the modern interstate system. Four such features stand out for comment.

First, this subsystem of city-states constituted a quintessentially capitalist system of war and state-making. The most powerful and leading state in the subsystem (Venice) is the true prototype of the capitalist state, in the double sense of 'perfect example' and 'model for future instances' of such a state. A merchant capitalist oligarchy firmly held state power in its grip. Territorial acquisitions were subjected to careful cost-benefit analysis and, as a rule, were undertaken only as mere means to the end of enhancing the profitability of the traffics of the capitalist oligarchy that exercised state power.[9]

If there has ever been a state whose executive met the *Communist Manifesto*'s standards of the capitalist state ('but a committee for managing the common affairs of the whole bourgeoisie'),[10] it was fifteenth-century Venice. From this standpoint, the leading capitalist states of future epochs (the United Provinces, the United Kingdom, the United States) appear as increasingly 'diluted' versions of the ideotypical standards realized by Venice centuries earlier. This is no accident. Although Genoa, Florence and Milan (in that order) did not meet the ideotypical standards of the capitalist state as well as Venice had, they all did by the lower standards of later epochs.

Secondly, the operation of the 'balance of power' played a crucial role at three different levels in fostering the development of this enclave of capitalist rule within the medieval system. The balance of power between the central authorities (pope and emperor) was instrumental in the emergence of an organized capitalist enclave in northern Italy – the geopolitical locus of that balance. The balance of power among the northern Italian city-states was instrumental in preserving their mutual separateness and autonomy. And the balance of power among the emerging dynastic states of Western Europe was instrumental in preventing the logic of territorialism from nipping in the bud the rise of a capitalist logic within the European system of rule.[11]

The balance of power was thus integral from the start to the development of capitalism as a mode of rule. In fact, the balance of power can be interpreted as an instrument by means of which capitalist rulers can, individually or as a group, reduce protection costs absolutely and relative to competitors. For the balance of power to be or become such an instrument, however, the capitalist state(s) must be in a position to manipulate the balance of its (their) advantage instead of being cog(s) in a mechanism which no one or someone else controls. If the balance of power can only be maintained through endless and costly wars, then participation in its working defeats the purpose of the capitalist state(s), because the pecuniary costs of such wars inevitably tend to exceed their pecuniary benefits.

The secret of capitalist success is to have one's wars fought by others, if feasible for free or, if not, at the least possible cost.

Thirdly, by developing wage-labour relations, the Italian city-states managed to transform at least part of their protection costs into revenues, and thus make wars pay for themselves. 'Enough money circulated in the richer Italian towns to make it possible for citizens to tax themselves and use the proceeds to buy the service of armed strangers. Then, simply by spending their pay, the hired soldiers put these monies back in circulation. Thereby, they intensified the market exchanges that allowed such towns to commercialize armed violence in the first place. The emergent system thus tended to become self-sustaining.'[12]

The emergent system could become self-sustaining only up to a point – that is, up to the point where cost inflation and changes in the social composition of the city-state undermined the capability of the dominant capitalist oligarchy to pursue effectively the endless accumulation of capital. In situations of permanent war, the ever-expanding circulation of money within the narrow territorial domains of the city-states sooner or later was bound to, and generally did, raise the price of supplies (means of livelihood, means of protection, means of production) more rapidly than their productivity. Alternatively, or in addition to cost inflation, endless wars tended to increase the social power of artisans (as in Florence) or of military personnel (as in Milan) with negative repercussions on the capitalist predispositions of the city-state.

Fourthly and last, the capitalist rulers of the northern Italian city-states took the lead in developing dense and extensive networks of residential diplomacy. Through these networks they acquired knowledge and information concerning the predispositions and capabilities of other rulers that were necessary to manage the balance of power so as to minimize protection costs. Just as the profitability of long-distance trade developed crucially on a quasi-monopolistic control of information over the largest economic space possible, so the capacity of capitalist rulers to manage the balance of power to their own advantage depended crucially on a quasi-monopolistic knowledge of, and capacity to monitor, the decision-making process of other rulers.[13]

The accumulation of capital through long-distance trade, the management of the balance of power, the commercialization of war, and the development of residential diplomacy thus complemented one another and, for a century or two, promoted an extraordinary concentration of wealth and power in the hands of the oligarchies that ruled the northern Italian city-states. Circa 1420 the leading Italian city-states not only functioned as great powers in European politics but had revenues that compared very favourably with the revenues of the most successful dynastic states of Western and North-western Europe.[14] They thereby showed that even small territories could become huge containers of power by pursuing onesidedly the accumulation of riches rather than the acquisition of territories and subjects. Henceforth, 'considerations of plenty' would become integral and central to 'considerations of power' throughout Europe.

The Italian city-states, however, never attempted individually or collectively a purposive transformation of the medieval system of rule. They had neither the predisposition nor the opportunity to undertake such a transformative action. Two more centuries had to elapse – from circa 1450 to circa 1650 (the so-called 'long' sixteenth century) – before a new kind of capitalist state (the United Provinces) would actually be presented with, and seize, the opportunity to transform the European system of rule to suit the requirements of the accumulation of capital on a world scale.

2. DUTCH HEGEMONY AND THE BIRTH OF THE WESTPHALIA SYSTEM

The new situation arose as a result of a quantum leap in the European power struggle precipitated by the attempts of territorialist rulers to incorporate within their domains, or to prevent others from incorporating, the wealth and power of the Italian city-states. As it turned out, outright conquest proved impossible primarily because of the competition among the territorialist rulers themselves. In this struggle for the impossible, however, select territorial states (Spain and France in particular) developed new war-making techniques which gave them a decisive power advantage *vis-à-vis* other rulers, including the supra- and sub-statal authorities of the medieval system of rule.[15]

The intensification of the European power struggle was soon followed by its geographical expansion, because some territorialist rulers sought more roundabout ways to incorporate within their domains the wealth and power of the Italian city-states. Instead of, or in addition to, seeking the annexation of the city-states, these rulers tried to conquer the very sources of their wealth and power. These sources were circuits of long-distance trade.

More specificially, the fortunes of the Italian city-states in general and of Venice in particular rested primarily on a monopolistic control over a crucial link in the chain of commercial exchanges that connected Western Europe to India and China via the House of Islam. No territorial state was powerful enough to take over the monopoly, but select territorialist rulers could and did attempt to establish a more direct link between Western Europe and India/China so as to divert money flows and supplies from the Venetian to their own trade circuits. Portugal and Spain, assisted by Genoese agents crowded out by Venice from the most profitable traffics of the Mediterranean, took the lead in these attempts. While Portugal succeeded in the purpose, Spain failed but stumbled across an entirely new source of wealth and power, the Americas.

The intensification and the global expansion of the European power struggle engendered a vicious/virtuous circle (vicious for its victims, virtuous for its beneficiaries) of more and more massive resources and of increasingly sophisticated and costly techniques of state- and war-making deployed in the power struggle. Techniques which had been developed in the struggle within Europe were deployed to subjugate extra-European states and peoples, and the wealth and power originating from the subjugation of extra-European states and peoples were deployed in the struggle within Europe.[16]

The state that initially benefited most from this circle was Spain, the only state that was a protagonist of the power struggle simultaneously on the European and on the extra-European fronts. Throughout the sixteenth century, the power of Spain exceeded that of all other European states by a large margin. This power, however, far from being used to oversee a 'smooth' transition to the modern system of rule, became an instrument of the Habsburg imperial house and of the papacy to save what could be saved of the disintegrating medieval system of rule.

In reality, little or nothing could be saved because the quantum leap in the European power struggle since the middle of the fifteenth century had taken the disintegration of the medieval system beyond the point of no return. Out of that struggle new realities of power had emerged in North-western Europe which, to varying degrees, had subsumed the capitalist logic of power within the territorialist logic. The result was the formation of compact mini-empires (best exemplified by the French, English and Swedish dynastic states) which, individually, could not match the power of Spain, but collectively could not be subordinated to any old or new central political authority. The attempt of Spain, in conjunction with the papacy and the Habsburg imperial house, to unmake or subordinate these new realities of power, not only failed, but created the conditions for the rise of Dutch hegemony and the final liquidation of the medieval system of rule.

For conflict quickly escalated beyond the regulative capacities of the medieval system of rule and turned its institutions into so many new causes of conflict. As a consequence, the European power struggle became an ever-more-negative-sum game in which all or most of the European rulers began to realize that they had nothing to gain and everything to lose from its continuation. The most important factor in this realization was the sudden escalation of system-wide social conflict into a serious threat to the collective power of European rulers.

This system-wide intensification of social conflict was a direct result of the previous and contemporaneous escalation of armed conflicts among rulers. The escalation of protection costs led to a sharp increase in the fiscal pressure on subjects which, in turn, triggered many of the seventeenth-century revolts.[17]

Alongside this escalation in protection costs, there had been an escalation in the ideological struggle. The progressive breakdown of the medieval system of rule had led to a mixture of religious innovations and of religious restorations from above – following the principle *cuius regio eius religio* – which provoked popular resentments and rebellions against both.[18] As rulers turned religion into an instrument of their mutual power struggles, subjects followed suit and turned religion into an instrument of insurrection against rulers.

Last but not least, the escalation of armed conflicts among rulers disrupted the trans-European networks of trade on which rulers depended to obtain the means of war and subjects depended to obtain the means of livelihood. The costs and risks of moving goods across political jurisdictions increased dramatically and supplies were diverted from the provision of the means of livelihood to the provision of the means of war. It is plausible to assume that this disruption and diversion of trade flows contributed far more decisively than climatic factors (the Little Ice Age) to the worsening problem of vagrancy and to the 'subsistence crisis' which constitute the social and economic backdrop of the general crisis of legitimacy of the seventeenth century.[19]

It was under these circumstances that the United Provinces became hegemonic by leading a large and powerful coalition of dynastic states toward the liquidation of the medieval system of rule and the establishment of the modern inter-state system. In the course of their previous struggle for national independence from Spain, the Dutch had already established a strong intellectual and moral leadership over the dynastic states of North-western Europe, which were among the main beneficiaries of the disintegration of the medieval system of rule. As systemic chaos increased during the Thirty-Year War, Dutch proposals for a major reorganization of the pan-European system of rule found more and more supporters among European rulers until Spain was isolated completely. With the Peace of Westphalia in 1648, a new system of rule was thus born.[20]

This system had a social purpose as well. As rulers legitimated their respective absolute rights of government over mutually exclusive territories, they also placed under international guarantee the principle of religious equality. Participation in the newly created interstate system was thus made conditional upon certain domestic social practices (religious tolerance). A more general principle was thus established which complemented the principle of the separation of political jurisdictions – the principle, that is, that civilians were not included in quarrels between sovereigns.

Besides religious tolerance, the most important application of this principle was in the field of commerce. In the treaties that followed the Settlement of Westphalia a clause was inserted that aimed at restoring freedom of commerce by abolishing barriers to trade which had developed in the course of the Thirty-Years War. Subsequent agreements introduced rules aimed at protecting the property and commerce of non-combatants. An international regime was thus established in which the effects of war-making between sovereigns on the everyday life of subjects were minimized.[21]

The systemic chaos of the early seventeenth century was transformed into a new anarchic order. The considerable freedom granted to private enterprise to organize commerce peacefully across political jurisdictions even in time of war reflected not only the general interest of rulers and subjects in dependable supplies of the means of war and the means of livelihood, but the particular interests of the Dutch capitalist oligarchy in an unfettered accumulation of capital. This reorganization of political space in the interest of capitalist accumulation marks the birth, not just of the modern interstate system but also of capitalism as a world-system. The reasons it took place in the seventeenth century under Dutch leadership instead of in the fifteenth century under Venetian leadership are not far to seek.

By the early seventeenth century increasing systemic chaos had created both a general interest among European rulers in a major rationalization of the power struggle and a capitalist oligarchy with the motivations and the capabilities necessary to take the lead in serving that general interest. The Dutch capitalist oligarchy was in important respects a replica of the Venetian capitalist oligarchy. Like the latter, it was the bearer of a capitalist logic of power and, as such, a leader in the management of the balance of power and in diplomatic initiatives and innovations. Unlike the latter, however, it was a product rather than a factor of the quantum leap in the European power struggle prompted by the emergence of capitalist states in northern Italy. This difference had several important implications.

First, the scale of operation, and hence the power, of the Dutch capitalist oligarchy in European and world politics was much greater than that of Venice. The wealth and power of Venice rested on a circuit of trade that was itself a link in a much longer circuit which Venice did not control. This link could be and was superseded by more roundabout and new circuits of trade. The wealth and power of Holland, in contrast, was based on commercial and financial networks that the Dutch capitalist oligarchy had carved out of the seaborne and colonial empires through which the territorialist rulers of Portugal and Spain had superseded the wealth and power of Venice.

The wealth and power of the Dutch capitalist oligarchy rested more on its control over world financial networks than on commercial networks. This meant that it was less vulnerable than the Venetian capitalist oligarchy to the establishment of competing trade routes or to increased competition on a given route. As competition in long-distance trade intensified, the Dutch oligarchs could recoup their losses and find a new field of profitable investment in financial speculation. The Dutch capitalist oligarchy therefore had the power to rise above the competition and turn it to its own advantage.

Secondly, the interests of the Dutch capitalist oligarchy clashed far more fundamentally with those of the central authorities of the medieval system of rule than the interests of the Venetian capitalist oligarchy ever did. As the history of the Long Sixteenth Century demonstrated, the wealth and power of Venice were threatened more fundamentally by the waxing power of the dynastic states of South- and North-western Europe that were emerging out of the disintegration of the medieval system of rule than they were by the waning power of the papacy and the imperial house. In contrast, the Dutch capitalist oligarchy had a strong common interest with the emerging dynastic states in the liquidation of the claims of pope and emperor to a supra-statal moral and political authority as embodied in the imperial pretensions of Spain.

The Dutch became thus champion and organizer of the protonationalist aspirations of dynastic rulers and of popular aspirations for religious self-determination. At the same time, they constantly sought ways and means to prevent conflict from escalating beyond the point where the commercial and financial foundations of their wealth and power would be seriously undermined. In pursuing its own interest, the Dutch capitalist oligarchy thus came to be perceived as the champion not just of independence from the central authorities of the medieval system of rule but also of a general interest in peace which the latter were no longer able to serve.

Thirdly, the war-making capabilities of the Dutch capitalist oligarchy far surpassed those of the Venetian oligarchy. The capabilities of the latter were closely related to the geographical position of Venice and had little use outside that position, particularly after the great leap forward in war-making techniques of the Long Sixteenth Century. The capabilities of the Dutch oligarchy, in contrast, were based on successful front-line participation in that great leap forward. As a matter of fact, the Dutch were leaders not just in the accumulation of capital but also in the rationalization of military techniques.

Long-forgotten Roman military techniques were rediscovered and brought to perfection by the Dutch army in the early seventeenth century.[22] Siege techniques were transformed (a) to increase the efficiency of military labour power, (b) to cut costs in terms of casualties, and (c) to facilitate the maintenance of discipline in the army's ranks. Marching and the loading and firing of guns were standardized and drilling was made a regular activity of soldiers. The army was divided into smaller tactical units, the number of officers and non-combatants was increased, and lines of command were rationalized so that 'in this way an army became an articulate organism with a central nervous system that allowed sensitive and more or less intelligent response to unforseen circumstances.'[23]

The significance of this innovation is that it neutralized the advantages of scale enjoyed by Spain and thereby tended to equalize relative military capabilities within Europe. By actively encouraging the propagation of the new techniques among its allies, the United Provinces created the conditions of substantive equality among European states that were the premise of the future Westphalia system. By so doing, it strengthened its intellectual and moral leadership over the dynastic rulers who were seeking the legitimation of their absolute rights of government.

Fourthly, the state-making capabilities of the Dutch capitalist oligarchy were far greater than those of the Venetian oligarchy. The exclusiveness of capitalist interests in the organization and management of the Venetian state was the main source of its power but was also the main limit of that power. For this exclusiveness kept the political horizon of the Venetian oligarchy within the limits set by cost-benefit analysis and double-entry bookkeeping. It kept Venetian rulers aloof from the political and social issues that were tearing apart the world within which they operated.

The state-making capabilities of the Dutch capitalist oligarchy, in contrast, had been forged in a secular struggle of emancipation from Spanish imperial rule. In order to succeed in this struggle, it had to forge an alliance and share power with dynastic interests (the House of Orange) and had to ride the tiger of popular rebellion (Calvinism). As a consequence, the power of the capitalist oligarchy within the Dutch state was far less absolute than it had been within the Venetian state. But for this very reason the Dutch ruling group developed much greater capabilities than Venetian rulers ever had to pose and solve the problems around which the European power struggle raged. The United Provinces became hegemonic in virtue of being less rather than more capitalist than Venice.

3. BRITISH HEGEMONY AND FREE-TRADE IMPERIALISM

The Dutch never governed the system they had created. As soon as the Westphalia system was in place, the United Provinces lost control of the European balance of power and soon lost their previous world-power status as well. In terms of power, the great beneficiaries of the new system of rule were its former allies France and England. For the next century and half – from the outbreak of the Anglo-Dutch wars in 1652 to the end of the Napoleonic Wars in 1815 – the inter-state system came to be dominated by the struggle for world supremacy between these two great powers.

This secular conflict developed in three partly overlapping phases which replicated in some respects the phases of struggle of the Long Sixteenth Century. The first phase was once again characterized by the attempts of territorialist rulers to incorporate within their domains the leading capitalist state. Just as France and Spain had attempted in the late fifteenth century to conquer the northern Italian city-states, so in the late seventeenth century England and France attempted to conquer the United Provinces.

As these attempts failed – due to the competition between the would-be conquerors – the struggle entered a second phase in which the efforts of the two rivals increasingly focused on incorporating the sources of the wealth and power of the capitalist state rather than the capitalist state itself. Just as Portugal and Spain had struggled for control over the traffic with the East, so now France and England struggled for control over the Atlantic. Differences between these two struggles, however, are as important as the analogies.

Both France and England were late-comers in the global power struggle. This had some advantages. The most important was that by the time France and England entered the business of territorial expansion in the extra-European world the spread of Maurician 'scientific management' to the European armies had turned their comparative advantage over the armies of extra-European rulers into an unbridgeable gulf.[24]

Nevertheless, the comparative advantage *vis-à-vis* extra-European rulers was of little help to the latecomers in displacing the Portuguese, the Spaniards and, above all, the Dutch from established positions at the crossroads of world commerce. In order to catch up with and overtake the early-comers, the latecomers had to restructure radically the political geography of world commerce. This is precisely what was achieved by the new synthesis of capitalism and territorialism brought into being by French and British mercantilism in the eighteenth century.

This new synthesis had three major and closely interrelated components: settler colonialism, capitalist slavery, and economic nationalism. All three components were essential to the reorganization of world-political economic space, but settler colonialism was probably the leading element in the combination. British rulers in particular relied heavily on the private initiative of their subjects in countering the advantages of early-comers in overseas expansion.[25]

Capitalist slavery was partly a condition and partly a result of the success of settler colonialism. For the expansion in the number and industriousness of the colonists was continually limited, and continually recreated, by shortages of labour power that could not be satisfied by relying exclusively, or even primarily, on the supplies engendered spontaneously from within the ranks of the settler populations or extracted forcibly from the indigenous populations. This chronic labour shortage enhanced the profitability of capitalist enterprises engaged in the procurement (primarily in Africa), transport and productive use (primarily in the Americas) of slave labour. The development of capitalist slavery, in turn, became the leading factor in the expansion of the infrastructure and of the outlets necessary to sustain the settlers' productive efforts.

Settler colonialism and capitalist slavery were necessary but insufficient conditions for the success of French and British mercantilism in radically restructuring the global political economy. The third key ingredient (economic nationalism) had two main aspects. One was the endless accumulation of monetary surpluses in colonial and interstate commerce – an accumulation with which mercantilism is often identified. The other was national- or better, domestic-economy-making. As underscored by Schmoller, 'in its inmost kernel [mercantilism was] nothing but state-making – not state-making in a narrow sense, but state-making and national-economy-making at the same time'.[26]

National-economy-making brought to perfection on a

greatly enlarged scale the practices pioneered by the Italian city-states three centuries earlier of making wars pay for themselves by turning protection costs into revenues. By spending greater tax revenues within their domestic economies, new incentives and opportunities were created to establish ever new linkages between activities and thus make wars pay for themselves more and more.

What was happening, in fact, was not that wars were 'paying for themselves', but that an increasing number of civilians were mobilized to sustain indirectly and often unknowingly the war- and state-making efforts of rulers. War- and state-making were becoming an increasingly roundabout business which involved an ever-growing number, range and variety of seemingly unrelated activities. The capacity of mercantilist rulers to mobilize the energies of their civilian subjects in undertaking and carrying out these activities was not unlimited. On the contrary, it was strictly limited by their ability to appropriate the benefits of world commerce, of settler colonialism, and of capitalist slavery, and to turn these benefits into adequate rewards for the entrepreneurship and productive efforts of their metropolitan subjects.

In breaking out of these limits British rulers had a decisive comparative advantage over all competitors, the French included. This comparative advantage was geopolitical and resembled the comparative advantage of Venice at the height of its power.[27] The channelling of British energies and resources toward overseas expansion, while the energies and resources of its European competitors were locked in struggles close at home, generated a process of circular and cumulative causation. British successes in overseas expansion increased the pressure on the states of continental Europe to keep up with the United Kingdom's growing world power. But these successes also provided the United Kingdom with the means necessary to manage the balance of power in continental Europe so as to keep its rivals busy close at home. Over time, this virtuous/vicious circle put the United Kingdom in a position to eliminate all competitors from overseas expansion and, at the same time, to become the undisputed master of the European balance of power.

When the United Kingdom won the Seven-Years' War (1756–1763), the secular struggle with France for world supremacy was over. But the United Kingdom did not thereby become world-hegemonic. On the contrary, as soon as the struggle for world supremacy was over, conflict entered a third phase characterized by increasing systemic chaos. Like the United Provinces in the early seventeenth century, the United Kingdom became hegemonic by creating a new world order out of this systemic chaos which was the result of the intrusion of social conflict into the power struggles of rulers. There were, however, important differences between the two situations. The most important was the much greater degree of autonomy and effectiveness demonstrated by the rebellious subjects in the late eighteenth and early nineteenth centuries in comparison with the early seventeenth century.

The United Kingdom became hegemonic by leading a vast array of primarily dynastic forces in the struggle against the infringements upon the absolute rights of government and for the restoration of the Westphalia system. This restoration was successfully accomplished with the Settlement of Vienna of 1815 and the subsequent Congress of Aix-la-Chapelle of 1818. Up to this point British hegemony was a replica of Dutch hegemony. Just as the Dutch had successfully led the about-to-be-born interstate system in the struggle against the imperial pretensions of Habsburg Spain, so the British had successfully led the about-to-be-destroyed interstate system in the struggle against the imperial pretensions of Napoleonic France.[28]

Unlike the United Provinces, however, the United Kingdom went on to govern the interstate system and, in doing so, it undertook a major reorganization of that system aimed at accommodating the new realities of power released by the ongoing revolutionary upheaval. The system that came into being is what Gallagher and Robinson have aptly called Free-Trade Imperialism – a world-system of rule which both expanded and superseded the Westphalia system.[29] This expansion and supersession is noticeable at three different but interrelated levels of analysis.

First, the interstate system came to include a much greater number and variety of states, while the balance of power came to operate above rather than between states. A new group of states joined the group of dynastic and oligarchic states that had formed the original nucleus of the Westphalia system. It consisted primarily of states controlled by national communities of property holders which had succeeded in gaining independence from old and new empires. Interstate relations thus began to be governed not by the personal interests, ambitions and emotions of monarchs but by the collective interests ambitions, and emotions of those national communities.[30]

This 'democratization' of nationalism was accompanied by an unprecedented centralization of world power in the hands of a single state, the United Kingdom. It alone was simultaneously involved in the politics of all the regions of the world and, more importantly, held a commanding position in each and every one of them. For the first time, the objective of all previous capitalist states to be the master rather than the servant of the global balance of power was fully (if temporarily) realized by the leading capitalist state of the epoch. In order to manage more effectively the global balance of power, the United Kingdom took the lead in tightening the loose system of consultation between the great powers of Europe. The result was the Concert of Europe which, from the start, was primarily an instrument of British overrule in continental Europe.

Secondly, the disintegration of colonial empires in the Western world was accompanied and followed by their expansion in the non-Western world. The territorial scope of the modern interstate system thus expanded manyfold but through a resurgence of imperial rule in its midst. This resurgence of imperial rule is indeed the main reason for designating the new system as Free-Trade *Imperialism*.

No territorialist ruler had ever before incorporated within its domain so many, so populous and so far-flung territories as the United Kingdom did in the nineteenth century. Nor had any territorialist ruler ever before forcibly extracted in so short a time so much tribute – in labour power, in natural resources, and in means of payments – as the British state and its clients did in the Indian subcontinent in the course of the nineteenth century. Part of this tribute was used to buttress and expand the coercive apparatus through which more and more non-Western subjects were added to the British territorial empire. But another, equally conspicuous part was siphoned off in one form or another to London to be recycled in the circuits of wealth through which British power in the Western world was continually reproduced and expanded. The territorialist and the capitalist logics of power thus cross-fertilized and sustained one another.

The recycling of imperial tribute extracted from the colonies into capital invested all over the world enhanced London's comparative advantage as a world financial center *vis-à-vis* competing centers such as Amsterdam and Paris. This comparative advantage made London the natural home of *haute finance* – a closely knit body of cosmopolitan financiers whose operations and networks had grown in scale and scope ever since the Westphalia system had placed under international guarantee the property and commerce of noncombatants. And as the organic links between the British government and *haute finance* grew tighter, the networks of world finance were turned into yet another instrument of British overrule in the interstate system.

Last, the expansion and supersession of the Westphalia system found expression in an entirely new instrument of world government. The Westphalia system was based on the principle that there was no authority operating above the inter-state system. Free-Trade Imperialism, in contrast, established the principle that the laws operating within and between states were subject to the higher authority of a new metaphysical entity – the 'world market' – allegedly endowed with supernatural powers greater than anything pope and emperor had ever mastered in the medieval system of rule. By presenting its world supremacy as the embodiment of this metaphysical entity, the United Kingdom succeeded from the 1820s onward in expanding its power in the interstate system well beyond what was warranted by the extent and effectiveness of its coercive apparatus.

This power was the result of the adoption by the United Kingdom of a free-trade practice and ideology. To be sure, the principle of universal free trade was never applied, nor did the

United Kingdom ever try to impose on the interstate system anything more than a very limited measure of free trade. Nevertheless, by the middle of the nineteenth century the principle became dominant through the progressive opening up of the British domestic market.[31]

By opening up their domestic market, British rulers thus created world-wide networks of dependence on, and allegiance to, the expansion of wealth and power of the United Kingdom. This control over the world market, combined with mastery of the global balance of power and a close relationship of mutual instrumentality with *haute finance*, enabled the United Kingdom to govern the interstate system as effectively as a world-empire. The result was 'a phenomenon unheard of in the annals of Western civilization, namely, a hundred years' peace – 1815–1914'.[32]

The appeal and credibility of the British hegemonic claim were based on systemic circumstances created by the revolutionary upheavals of 1776–1848. For the national communities that had risen to power in the Americas and in many parts of Europe in the course of these upheavals were primarily communities of property holders, whose main concern was with the pecuniary value of their assets rather than with the autonomous power of their rulers. It was the ensemble of these communities that formed the 'natural' constituency of British free-trade hegemony.

At the same time, the revolutionary upheavals had promoted changes within the United Kingdom itself that enhanced the capabilities of its rulers to satisfy this system-wide demand for 'democratic' wealth. The most important of these changes was the Industrialist Revolution which took off after the American Revolution of 1776 and was practically completed during the subsequent renewal of the Anglo-French rivalry. For our present purposes, the main significance of this revolution was twofold.

On the one hand, it greatly enhanced the relationship of complementarity that linked the enterprises of British subjects to the enterprises of subjects of other states, particularly of the states that had emerged out of the settlers' rebellion against British rule in North America. As a result of this development,

British rulers began to realize that their lead in domestic-economy-making gave them a considerable advantage in the use of subject–subject relations across political jurisdictions as invisible instruments of rule over the subjects of other sovereign states. It was this realization more than anything else that induced British rulers after the end of the Napoleonic Wars to sustain and protect the forces of democratic nationalism against the reactionary predispositions of its former dynastic allies.

On the other hand, the Industrial Revolution transformed the British state by changing its structure of representation and, hence, its predispositions and capabilities in world politics. This transformation was the result of the emergence of a new class of capitalist and proto-capitalist entrepreneurs engaged primarily in domestic production, trade and banking and dependent upon the state and the older and better-established class of capitalist merchants and financiers for the procurement of inputs and the distribution of outputs in foreign markets.

It was in this context that the British national bourgeoisie became 'internationalist' and spearheaded a powerful social movement aimed simultaneously at a reform of the structures of representation of the British state and at a more radical opening of the British domestic market to foreign wage goods and raw materials. In struggling for these objectives, the British national bourgeoisie was pursuing its class interest, that is, it was seeking relief from the pressure of overcrowding in the domestic economy. But this interest could be presented truthfully and credibly as being the motor force of the expansion of British world power and of the wealth of all nations. The victory of the British national bourgeoisie in its struggle for representation within the dominant bloc of the United Kingdom thus put the final touch on the making of British world hegemony.

4. US HEGEMONY AND THE FREE-ENTERPRISE SYSTEM

The United Kingdom exercised world governmental functions

up to the end of the nineteenth century. From the 1870s onward, however, it began to lose control of the European balance of power and soon afterward of the global balance of power as well. The capacity of the United Kingdom to hold the centre of the world market was undermined by the emergence of a new national economy of greater wealth than its own. The United States developed into a sort of 'black hole' with a power of attraction for the labour, capital and entrepreneurship of the world-economy with which the United Kingdom, let alone less-wealthy states, had few chances of competing. Another new rival was Germany. The US and German challenges to British world power strengthened one another, lessened British capabilities to govern the interstate system, and eventually led to a new struggle for world supremacy of unprecedented violence and viciousness.

In the course of this struggle, conflict went through some, but not all, of the phases that had characterized the previous struggle for world supremacy. The initial phase in which territorialist rulers attempted to incorporate the leading capitalist state was skipped altogether. As a matter of fact, the fusion of the territorialist and capitalist logics of power had gone so far among the three main contenders for world supremacy (the UK, Germany, and the US) that it is difficult to say which rulers were capitalist and which were territorialist.

Throughout the confrontation, German rulers showed much stronger territorialist predispositions than the rulers of either the UK or the US But these stronger predispositions reflected their late arrival in the business of territorial expansion. As we have seen, the United Kingdom had been all but parsimonious in its territorial acquisitions, and empire-building in the non-Western world had been integral to its world hegemony. As for the US, its development into the main pole of attraction for labour, capital and entrepreneurial resources of the world-economy was closely connected with the continental scope attained by its domestic economy in the course of the nineteenth century.

Neither Germany nor the US ever tried to incorporate within their domains the leading capitalist state, as France and Spain had tried to do in the fifteenth century and France and

England in the seventeenth century. The world power of the leading capitalist state had grown so much in comparison to its forerunners and to its contemporary challengers that the struggle could only start with what had previously been the second phase – the phase, that is, in which the challengers tried to supersede the comparative wealth-and-power advantage of the leading capitalist state. Even though control over world commerce and finance continued to play an important role in determining relative capabilities in the interstate system, in the course of the nineteenth century the most decisive advantage in the struggle for world power had become the comparative size and growth potential of the domestic market. The larger and the more dynamic the domestic market of a state relative to all others, the better the chances of that state replacing the United Kingdom at the centre of the global networks of patron–client relations that constituted the world market.

From this point of view, the US was far better positioned than Germany. Its continental dimension, its insularity and its extremely favourable endowment of natural resources, as well as the policy followed by its rulers of keeping the doors of the domestic market closed to foreign products but open to foreign capital, labour and enterprise, had made it the main beneficiary of British Free-Trade Imperialism. By the time the struggle for world supremacy began, the US domestic economy was well on its way to being the new centre of the world-economy – a center connected to the rest of the world-economy not primarily by trade flows but by more or less unilateral transfers of labour, capital and enterpreneurship flowing from the rest of the world to its political jurisdiction.

Germany could not compete with the US on this terrain. Its history and geographical position made it a tributary rather than a beneficiary of these flows of labour, capital and enterpreneurship. At the same time, its secular involvement as a front-liner in the European power struggle endowed its rulers with a comparative advantage in the incipient 'industrialization of war'. From the 1840s onward, military and industrial innovations began to interact more and more closely within the region that was in the process of becoming Germany. It was precisely this interaction that sustained both the spectacular industrialization and the ascent to world-power status experienced by Germany in the second half of the nineteenth century.[33]

The growing obsession with *Lebensraum* ('vital space') induced German rulers to follow in the footsteps first of the UK and then of the US These attempts prompted defensive reactions which made interstate conflict escalate quickly into major confrontations. Right from the start, however, the escalation of interstate conflict was followed by increasing systemic chaos. Here lies a second important difference between this struggle for world supremacy and the previous one between France and England. In the previous struggle, it took more than a century of armed conflict among the great powers before anarchy provoked a major wave of popular rebellions which, in turn, precipitated systemic chaos. But in the twentieth century anarchy turned into systemic chaos almost as soon as the great powers faced one another in an open confrontation.

Under British hegemony, non-Western peoples did not qualify as national communities in the eyes of the hegemonic power and of its allies, clients and followers. While the right of Western nations to pursue wealth was elevated above the absolute rights of government of their rulers, non-Western peoples were deprived of their customary rights to self-determination. At the same time, the nations that had become the constituent units of the interstate system were as a rule communities of property holders from which the propertyless were more or less completely excluded. The right of propertied subjects to pursue wealth was thus elevated, not just above the absolute rights of government of rulers, but also above the customary rights to a livelihood of the propertyless masses. Like Athenian democracy in the ancient world, nineteenth-century liberal democracy was an 'egalitarian oligarchy' in which 'a ruling class of citizens shared the rights and spoils of political control'.[34]

The process of socialization of war- and state-making, which in the previous wave of struggle for world supremacy had led to the 'democratization' of nationalism, was carried a step further by the industrialization of war. The productive efforts of the propertyless in general, and of the industrial proletariat in particular, became a central component of the war- and state-making efforts of rulers. The social power of the propertyless increased correspondingly and so did the effectiveness of their struggles for state protection of their livelihoods.[35]

Under these circumstances, the outbreak of war among the great powers was bound to have a contradictory impact on ruler–subject relations. On the one hand, it enhanced the social power of the propertyless masses directly or indirectly involved in the military-industrial efforts of rulers. On the other hand, it curtailed the means available to the latter to accommodate that power. This contradiction became evident in the course of the First World War, when a few years of open hostilities were sufficient to release the most severe system-wide wave of popular rebellion ever experienced by the modern world-system.

The focal point of this wave of rebellion was the Soviet Revolution of 1917. By upholding the right of all peoples to self-determination ('anti-imperialism') and the primacy of rights to livelihood over rights of property and government ('proletarian internationalism'), its leaders raised the spectre of a far more radical interference in the operation of the interstate system than anything previously experienced. Initially, the impact of the Revolution of 1917 was similar to that of the Revolution of 1776; it fostered the revanchism of the great power that had just been defeated in the struggle for world supremacy (Germany, this time) and thereby led to a new round of open conflict among the great powers.

The interstate system was polarized into two opposite and antagonistic factions. The dominant faction (headed by the UK and France) was conservative, that is, orientated toward the preservation of Free-Trade Imperialism. In opposition to this faction, upstarts in the struggle for world power who had neither a respectable colonial empire nor the right connections in the networks of world commerce and finance, coalesced in a reactionary faction led by Nazi Germany. Rulers who coalesced in this faction had an even greater interest than rulers of the conservative faction in the annihilation of the Soviet Revolution. Yet, rightly or wrongly, they reckoned that their counter-revolutionary objectives were best served by a preliminary or contemporaneous confrontation with the conservative faction. Under the joint impact of war and revolution, Free-Trade Imperialism collapsed, leaving the interstate system in a state of apparently irremediable disorganization.

Like the UK in the early nineteenth century, the US first became hegemonic by leading the interstate system toward the restoration of the principles, norms and rules of the Westphalia system, and then went on to govern and to remake the system it had restored. This capability to remake the interstate system was based on a generalized perception among the rulers and subjects of the system that the national interests of the hegemonic power embodied a universal interest.

This perception was fostered by the capacity of US rulers to provide solutions to the problems around which the power struggle among revolutionary, reactionary and conservative forces had raged since 1917. From the start, the most enlightened factions of the US ruling elite showed a much greater awareness than the ruling elites of the conservative and reactionary great powers of what these issues were.[36]

After the Second World War every people whether 'Western' or 'non-Western' was granted the right to self-determination, to constitute itself into a national community and, once so constituted, to be accepted as a full member of the interstate system. In this respect, global 'decolonization' has been the most significant correlate of US hegemony.

At the same time, the provision of a livelihood to all subjects became the most legitimate of objectives for the members of the interstate system to pursue. Just as the liberal ideology of British hegemony had elevated the pursuit of wealth by propertied subjects above the absolute rights of government of rulers, so the ideology of US hegemony has elevated the welfare of all the subjects ('mass consumption') above absolute rights of property and absolute rights of government. If British hegemony had expanded the interstate system so as to accommodate the 'democratization' of nationalism, US hegemony has completed the expansion so as to accommodate the 'proletarianization' of nationalism.

Once again expansion has involved supersession. The supersession of the Westphalia System by Free-Trade

Imperialism was real but partial. The principles, norms and rules of behaviour restored by the Congress of Vienna left considerable leeway to the members of the interstate system on how to organize their domestic and international relations. Free trade impinged upon the sovereignty of rulers, but their ability to 'delink' from trade networks if they so chose remained considerable. Above all, war and territorial expansion remained legitimate means for members of the interstate system to resort to in the pursuit of their ends.

At the same time, there were no organizations with autonomous capabilities – autonomous, that is, from state power – to rule over the interstate system. Under British hegemony, international law and the balance of power continued to operate, as they had since 1650, between rather than above states. As we have seen, the Concert of Europe, *haute finance* and the world market all operated above the heads of most states. Nevertheless, they had little if any organizational autonomy from the world power of the United Kingdom. They were instruments of rule of a particular state over the interstate system rather than autonomous organizations overruling the interstate system.

In comparison with Free-Trade Imperialism, the institutions of US hegemony have considerably restricted the rights and powers of sovereign states. The principles, norms, and rules to which states must submit have increased in number and have become tighter, while a growing number of supranational organizations have acquired an autonomous power to overrule the interstate system.

From the first point of view, sovereign states under US hegemony have been far less free than under British hegemony to organize relations with other states and with their own subjects as they see fit. In particular, sovereign states have been far less free than they ever were to use war and territorial expansion as legitimate means in the pursuit of their ends. From the second point of view, the contemporaneous development of international organizations and transnational corporations has created an extensive and dense network of pecuniary and non-pecuniary exchanges which no single state can control unilaterally and, more importantly, from which no state can 'delink' except at exorbitant costs.

To be sure, from about 1948 to about 1968 these networks were instruments of world government wielded by the US and, as such, they parallel the instruments of world government wielded by the United Kingdom in the nineteenth century. The United Nations, with its Assembly, Security Council, and specialized agencies and bureaucracies, came to perform functions analogous to those performed by the Concert of Europe. The Bank of International Settlements, the IMF and the World Bank came to perform functions analogous to those performed by *haute finance*. And the organizational networks of US-centred multinational corporations came to perform functions analogous to those performed by UK-centred commercial networks.[37]

However, the analogies are more formal than substantive. For one thing, the organizational scope and complexity of the institutions of US hegemony are a world apart from those of British hegemony. This greater organizational scope and complexity has in itself been a major factor in enhancing the autonomy of the institutions of US world hegemony from each and every member of the interstate system, including the hegemonic state itself. In addition, and more decisively, from circa 1968 onward, transnational corporations have developed into an integrated system of production, exchange and accumulation which is subject to no state authority and has the power to subject to its 'laws' each and every member of the interstate system.

The emergence of the Free Enterprise System – free, that is, from all previous vassalage to state power – has been the most distinctive result of US hegemony as well as its ultimate limit.[38] It marks the end of the process of supersession of the Westphalia system and the beginning of the withering away of the interstate system as the primary locus of world power.

5. SOME PRELIMINARY CONCLUSIONS

What has been said concerning the past recurrence of world hegemonies is sufficient for us to draw some preliminary conclusions concerning the conditions under which new world hegemonies can be expected to rise or not to rise. Three main points in particular deserve to be emphasized.

First, what has made the United Provinces, the United Kingdom and the United States hegemonic in the past has not been their military might or superior command over scarce resources, but their predispositions and capabilities to use either or both to solve the problems over which system-wide conflict raged. These predispositions and capabilities reflected the will and intelligence of the would-be hegemon, but this will and intelligence was itself largely shaped by the systemic chaos that created a general demand for order.

If the past is any guide to the future, we should expect that future hegemon(s) will emerge out of a new situation of social conflict and systemic chaos, the contours of which, however, are for now still hazy and difficult to predict. In any event, it is not sufficient to focus on the actual or prospective military might and command over scarce resources of the present competitors for world power in order to decide which one(s) is (are) the most likely to become hegemonic and remake the world-system so as to turn future systemic chaos into a new (anarchic?) order. Military might and/or superior command over economic resources may continue to be necessary conditions of world hegemony, but they are even less likely to be sufficient conditions than they have been in the past.

This brings us to our second point: the pitfalls of excessive reliance on past patterns of hegemonic recurrences to predict future patterns. The modern interstate system has been an essentially evolutionary system, just like its historical correlate – capitalism as world-system of accumulation. World hegemonies have been rising and declining not in an unchanging system, but in a system which they have themselves created, expanded and superseded. As a consequence of this evolution, the conditions of the rise and decline of world hegemonies have changed from one hegemony to the next in significant ways.

The most important change has been what we may call the 'speeding up of (social) history' as the obverse of Raymond Aron's 'slowing down of (political) history'. In all three instances of world hegemony, the intensification of interstate conflict has engendered system-wide waves of rebelliousness of subjects which, in turn, were instrumental in the transformation of systemic anarchy into systemic chaos. Nevertheless, from one hegemonic cycle to the next it has taken less and less time for interstate conflict to engender system-wide social conflict, and more and more time to bring social conflict back under control once the acute phase of interstate conflict has come to an end. This speed-up in the reaction time of popular rebellion to interstate conflict has been due to the increasing socialization of the state- and world-making efforts of rulers. As wider and wider circles of subjects have been mobilized directly or indirectly in these efforts, the more quickly has interstate conflict aroused popular rebellions over the distribution of the costs and benefits of these efforts.

The obverse of the speeding-up of social history has been the slowing-down of political history. The socialization of war- and state-making has greatly increased the costs and risks to rulers of their mutual antagonisms. If this is the case, the next struggle for world hegemony may take an even more condensed form than the previous one and skip the phase of armed conflict among the great powers altogether. As a matter of fact, for all we know a new period of struggle for world hegemony may have already begun, a struggle in which systemic chaos is the result, not of heightened interstate conflict, but of the on-going crisis of the interstate system and of its supersession by suprastatal organizations.

In this connection a third and last provisional conclusion can be drawn from the analyses developed above. In all three historical instances of world hegemony, the hegemon was also the leader in the organization of global processes of capital accumulation and, in this sense, it was the leading capitalist state of this epoch. But the three states were 'leading capitalist states' to different degrees and in different ways. If we focus on the representation of interests within the executive of the three states, then we reach the conclusion that each successive hegemonic state has been less capitalist than the previous one. However, while the hegemonic state has become less and less capitalist in this sense, the interstate system has become more and more capitalist in the sense that each and every one of its members has been subjected more and more closely to the capitalist logic of power.

If this progression were to continue, the next hegemon would have to be less capitalist in its inner structures of representation than the post-Second World War US, and at the same time it would have to make the world-system even more capitalist than it already is. This sounds very much like world social democracy but could be something quite different. In any event, the road from here to there is quite rough, and it is hard to predict what kind of human race will emerge out of the next round of systemic chaos. Nor is it clear whether the progression of the last 500 years, on which our prediction is based, will continue into the next 50 or 100 years. In order to assess how likely that is, we need to carry our analysis much further than has been possible here.

NOTES

1. This is an abridged version of the original article that was published in *Review*, vol. XIII, Number 3, Summer 1990, pp. 365–408.
2. John Ruggie, Continuity and Transformation in the World Polity: Toward a Neorealist Synthesis. *World Politics*, vol. XXXV, no. 2, January 1983, p. 274.
3. Perry Anderson, *Lineages of the Absolutist State* (London: New Left Books, 1974), pp. 37–8.
4. Ruggie, op. cit., p. 275.
5. ibid., p. 275.
6. Immanuel Wallerstein, *The Modern World System, I: Capitalist Agriculture and the Origins of the European World-Economy in the Sixteenth Century* (New York: Academic Press, 1974), p. 348.
7. Immanuel Wallerstein, *The Modern World System, III: The Second Era of Great Expansion of the Capitalist World-Economy, 1730-1840s* (New York: Academic Press, 1974), p. 402. The strength of Wallerstein's conceptualization is in its emphasis on the fundamental unity of capitalism and the modern system of rule. Its weakness is in its tendency to blur all analytical distinctions between the two terms of this relationship. 'Capitalism and the world-economy (that is, a single division of labor but multiple policies and cultures) are obverse sides of the same coin. One does not cause the other. We are simply defining the same indivisible phenomenon by different characteristics.' (ibid., p. 391). In my view, the close historical connection between capitalism and the modern interstate system does not warrant this blurring of their separate analytical identities. For the relationship between the two is just

as much one of contradiction as it is one of unity.

8. See Anthony Giddens, *The Nation-State and Violence* (Berkeley: University of California Press, 1987).
9. Fernand Braudel, *Civilization and Capitalism 15th-18th Century. Vol. III: The Perspective of the World* (New York: Harper & Row, 1984), pp. 120–1; George Modelski and Sylvia Modelski (eds), *Documenting Global Leadership* (Seattle: University of Washington Press, 1988), pp. 19–32.
10. Karl Marx and Friedrich Engels, *The Communist Manifesto* (Harmondsworth: Penguin, 1967), p. 82.
11. William McNeill, *The Pursuit of Power: Technology, Armed Force, and Society since A.D. 1000* (Chicago: University of Chicago Press, 1984), chapter 3.
12. Ibid., p. 74.
13. See Fernand Braudel, *Civilization and Capitalism 15th–18th Century. Vol. II: The Wheels of Commerce* (New York: Harper & Row, 1982).
14. McNeill, op. cit., p. 78; Braudel, 1984, p. 120.
15. McNeill, op. cit., pp. 79–95.
16. Ibid., pp. 94–5, 100ff.
17. Niels Steensgaard, The Sevententh-Century Crisis; in Geoffrey Parker and Lesley Smith (eds), *The General Crisis of the Seventeenth Century* (London: Routledge & Kegan Paul, 1985), pp. 42–4.
18. Parker and Smith, op. cit., pp. 15-18.
19. Cf. Fernand Braudel and Frank Spooner, Prices in Europe from 1450 to 1750; in E. E. Rich and C. H. Wilson (eds), *The Cambridge Economic History of Europe,* vol. IV (London: Cambridge University Press, 1967) and Ruggiero Romano, Between the Sixteenth and the Seventeenth Centuries: The Economic Crisis of 1619–22. In Geoffrey Parker and Lesley Smith (eds), *The General Crisis of the Seventeenth Century* (London: Routledge & Kegan Paul, 1985), pp. 165–225.
20. 'The idea of an authority or organization about sovereign states is no longer. What takes its place is the notion that all states form a world-wide political system or that, at any rate, the states of Western Europe form a single political system. This new system rests on international law and the balance of power, a law operating between rather than above states and a power operating between rather than above states' (Leo Gross, The Peace of Westphalia, 1648-1948; in R. A. Falk and W. H. Hanrieder (eds), *International Law and Organization.* Philadelphia: Lippincott, 1968, pp. 54–5).
21. Carr writes: 'The 18th century witnessed many wars; but in respect of the freedom and friendliness of intercourse between the educated classes in the principal European countries, with French as the recognized common language, it was the most "international" period of modern history, and civilians could pass to and from and transact their business freely with one another while their respective sovereigns were at war' (E. H. Carr, *Nationalism and After.* London: Macmillan, 1945, p. 4).
22. McNeill, op. cit., pp. 127–39 and Jacques van Doorn (ed.), *Armed Forces and Society* (The Hague: Mouton, 1975), pp. 9ff.
23. McNeill, op. cit., p. 130.

24. The power of the Ottoman Empire had begun to decline irreversibly. McNeill writes: 'Further East, the new style of training soldiers became important when European drillmasters began to create miniature armies by recruiting local manpower for the protection of French, Dutch, and English trading stations on the shores of the Indian Ocean. By the 18th century, such forces, however minuscule, exhibited a clear superiority over the unwieldy armies that local rulers were accustomed to bring into the field' (ibid., p. 135).
25. 'What English colonies in America lacked in natural resources and uniformity, they made up for in the number and industriousness of the colonists themselves' (George Nadel and Perry Curtis (eds), *Imperialism and Colonialism.* New York: Macmillan, 1964), pp. 9–10).
26. Charles Wilson, *Mercantilism* (London: Routledge & Kegan Paul, 1958), p. 6.
27. Britain gained supremacy, because she was favoured by two interacting factors: her island position and her role of intermediary between two worlds. Unlike the continental powers, Britain could direct her undivided strength toward the sea; unlike her Dutch competitors, she did not have to man a land front (Ludwig Dehio, *The Precarious Balance: Four Centuries of the European Power Struggle.* New York: Vintage, 1962, p. 71).
28. Cf. ibid.
29. John Gallagher and Ronald Robinson, The Imperialism of Free Trade. *Economic History Review,* vol. VI, no. 1, August 1953, pp. 1–15.
30. Carr, op. cit., p. 8.
31. Ibid., pp. 13–14.
32. Karl Polanyi, *The Great Transformation: The Political and Economic Origins of Our Time* (Boston: Beacon, 1957), p. 5.
33. See McNeill, op. cit., chapters 7–8 and Robert Gilpin, *U.S. Power and the Multinational Corporation* (New York: Basic Books, 1975).
34. R. M. MacIver, *The Modern State* (London: Oxford University Press, 1932), p. 352.
35. Cf. Carr, op. cit., p. 19.
36. 'In many ways the most significant feature both of Wilson's programme and of Lenin's is that they were not European-centered but world-embracing: that is to say, both set out to appeal to all peoples of the world, irrespective of race and colour. Both implied a negation of the preceding European system, whether it was confined to Europe or whether it spread...over the whole world... Lenin's summons to world revolution called forth, as a deliberate counter stroke, Wilson's Fourteen Points, the solidarity of the proletariat and the revolt against imperialism were matched by self-determination and the century of the common man' (Geoffrey Barraclough, *An Introduction to Contemporary History.* Harmondsworth: Penguin Books, 1967, p. 121).
37. Cf. Carr, op. cit., p. 49.
38. Cf. Giovanni Arrighi, A Crisis of Hegemony. In S. Amin, G. Arrighi, A. G. Frank and I. Wallerstein (eds), *Dynamics of Global Crisis* (New York: Monthly Review, 1982), pp. 55–108.

6. THE NATION STATE AND NATIONALISM WITH DIFFERENT FORMS OF TECHNOLOGY

Erik Allardt

1. INTRODUCTION

A nation state has to fulfil two conditions: a capacity for the enforcement of authority within its territorial boundaries, and a prevalence of fairly uniform sentiments of national solidarity.[1] There may exist societies which do not satisfy either of these two conditions, but more important is that there are many societies which meet only one of them. There are states consisting of many nations, and there are nations which have not, at least not yet, developed into states. Nationalism consists of strong sentiments of identification with, and a consciousness of belonging together in, a nation. Nationalism according to this definition is not confined to the nation state, and not even to the aspiration of becoming a nation state, but it exists as soon as there are unitary national groups, here called nations.

Both the importance of the nation state and the strength of nationalism are related to the dominant forms of technology in the society. Following Ernest Gellner it can be maintained that the whole way of life in the typical agrarian society militates against the constructing of political units such as states in terms of cultural boundaries. In the industrial society, political and cultural boundaries begin to coincide.[2] Gellner defines nationalism as a political principle which holds that the political and cultural unit should be congruent.[3] From this definition, and his observation about the coincidence of political and cultural boundaries in the industrial society, it also follows that nationalism is primarily a phenomenon of an industrial society. Whereas Gellner's observations about the patterns of coincidence of political and cultural boundaries are agreed with here, nationalism is defined in a different and admittedly looser way.

As we have said, nationalism consists of sentiments of identification and of a consciousness of belonging together, and it can occur also in societies other than an industrial one. Yet the fact that political and cultural boundaries tend to coincide in the industrial society gives its nationalism a special flavour. One reason for abandoning Gellner's definition of nationalism is the wish to say something about the society which has recently been succeeding the industrial one, the so-called information society. The term 'information society' may be questioned, but it seems nevertheless to be a fact that the nationalism today observed in most advanced societies is of a different kind than during the heyday of industrialism.

The points of departure in this chapter are hypotheses about the nation state rather than about nationalism, the nature of which will be discussed here as a consequence of prevailing political and societal forms. It is argued that the nation state fits particularly well with and reaches its greatest strength in the industrial society. As a political form the nation state is less important and weaker in the types of societies preceding and succeeding the industrial society. Nationalism exists in all types of societies, but in the industrial society nationalism is sustained by the state much more than in other types of societies.

2. THREE DIFFERENT TYPES OF SOCIETIES

It was assumed above that during a historically fairly short time span there have existed three types of societies, namely the *agrarian, industrial and information societies.* Such a tripartite classification implies, of course, a crude oversimplification. Nevertheless, it seems useful in describing how the importance of the nation state and the nature of nationalism are related to technology and the conditions of production.

The three societies are ideal types, and they should be described rather than sharply defined. Nevertheless, they might be preliminarily defined by differentials in the occupational structure. A customary division for analysing social structure in terms of occupational structure has been the three-sector model consisting of agriculture or the primary sector, processing industry or the secondary sector, and the service industries or the tertiary sector. With the spread of the ideas of the information society a quaternary sector consisting of information occupations has begun to be identified as a separate entity.[4] At any rate, the three types of society are distinguishable on the basis of a four-sector model. *The agrarian society* prevails when the huge majority of the labour force is working in the primary sector and the processing industry has not yet started to grow. *The industrial society* emerges as soon as the industrial or secondary sector is starting to grow, and it is fully fledged when the secondary sector is clearly the largest of the different sectors. *The information society* emerges when the service or tertiary sector becomes larger than the primary and secondary sectors, and prevails when the quaternary sector employs more people than any other sector.

It has to be admitted that the so-called information society still has many features in common with the industrial society. Even if the number of employees used for the production of goods has declined in the information society, the industrial enterprise is still the main model of production. Yet the new technology, and especially the information technology, enables and speeds up international contacts on an entirely different scale than was earlier the case.

Even if the basic position here is that the nation state is of particular importance in an industrial society, the differences between the three types of society are observable on many counts. The societal types differ from each other as regards the degree of cultural conformity and homogeneity demanded and required. As a corollary of the importance of the nation state in an industrial society, it is contended that the industrial society in particular is the societal type in which cultural conformity and homogeneity is demanded. In comparing the three societal types there will be a special emphasis on how the position of ethnic minorities, relations in working life and the problems of mass communication are approached in the three different societies.

The Agrarian Society

In discussing the agrarian society, the focus is here on its most developed forms. According to Gellner, in the typical agroliterate society there was a great variety of cultural forms. He emphasizes how in such a society the ruling class is rigidly separated from the majority of peasants. Furthermore, the administrative and military elite is usually clearly separated from the main bearers of culture, the clergy. The worldly rulers concentrate on collecting taxes and keeping order, but as a rule they are not interested in imposing shared cultural norms or in producing cultural unity. The clergy as the cultural ruling class imposes a cultural uniformity but the efforts are restricted to religious forms and religiously relevant behaviour.

Below the ruling class the great majority, the peasants, live in widely different local communities. The cultural differentiation is marked but in a very different way than within the ruling class. Local communities are self-sufficient, inwardly oriented and strongly dependent on the surrounding natural environment. The core of Gellner's argument is that in the typical agrarian society political units are not constructed in terms of cultural boundaries. Gellner goes on to say that if nationalism had been invented in a period with the agroliterate society as the predominant societal form, its prospects of general acceptance would have been very slender. The marked cultural heterogeneity in the typical agrarian society can be clearly observed in its treatment of ethnic minorities, working life and problems related to mass communication.

That ethnic and cultural distinctions are of minor importance in the agrarian society can be observed in its patterns of state-building. The size of the state in agrarian societies varied considerably. Both large empires and city states were common, whereas culturally uniform nation states formed a clear exception. If small states started to grow they usually became, if not always empires, then at least multi-cultural states. Of course, it happened that linguistically and ethnically distinct groups were mistreated, but this was rarely in order to impose cultural unity and uniformity.

Work was, of course, hard in the agrarian society, but no uniform system of working-life rules were superimposed throughout the society. It is self-evident that a doctrine such as Taylorism would have been unthinkable in the agrarian society, but the implication of this observation is not without importance. Working life was strongly dependent on conditions imposed by nature. Authority relations were mainly patriarchal, allowing for expectations and human differentials. A bureaucracy in Max Weber's sense, with an emphasis on cold rationality and on equal treatment of everybody according to universalistic rules, did not exist. It cannot be denied that working life in the agrarian society was often full of hardships and injustices, but the point here is that uniformity was not demanded and that there was much more leeway than in the industrial society to allow for regional and individual variations.

As regards mass communication, it is natural and common to conclude that there simply were no technical possibilities for mass communication and mass media in the agrarian society. While this is true, it also appears reasonable to say that neither did there exist a need for mass media. The codes for meaning and understanding in the agrarian society were related to experiences and economic necessities in the local community. Raymond Williams has convincingly argued that technical inventions do not spread automatically and by themselves, but that their wider application is always based on needs and demands of social significance.[5] He refers to the rise of radio broadcasting. Its basic technology was found in Heinrich Herz's discovery of radio waves, but it took a long time before the needs for machines and mass entertainment reached private homes and made it natural to use his discovery for broadcasting. At first, radio transmission was mainly thought of as a new way of signalling and as a substitute for the system of wired telegraph and telephone. Even if the agrarian society basically lacked the technique for uniform mass entertainment, it seems right to reason that it did not feel any need for such a form of entertainment.

The Industrial Society

The emergence of an industrial society produces waves of new demands for cultural unity and uniformity. As argued above, the nation state with its emphasis on the convergence of political and cultural boundaries is the typical state form of the industrial society. The number of states, first in Europe and then over the whole world, increases almost dramatically during the era of the industrial society. In the formation of states, there is a clear tendency to build nation states, although this admittedly is often very difficult because nationalities and ethnic groups are almost like mosaics intertwined and inlaid within the same regions.

The birth of the industrial society is, of course, a very multifaceted and complicated process. It is, as already hinted at, related to the rise of a rational bureaucracy trying to impose universalistic rules. In particular, it is related to the forms of production in the industrial society. It becomes common and natural to impose a work ethic with a strict time-bound discipline and a sharp division between work and leisure. Wage labour becomes a way of life. The imposition of a strict working discipline and rules also presupposes a great amount of uniform schooling and education. In many states, such as the Scandinavian countries, uniform rules are imposed over the whole system of primary and secondary education. It becomes difficult to accept and politically defend the existence of schools with unique and divergent aims and deviant didactic means.

It goes almost without saying that many kinds of uniform demands, particularly prominent in the industrial society, have been greatly beneficial to the broad mass of the population. This is for instance true of the school system in the industrial society, with its demands for equal schooling of all children and for increasing the educational opportunities in the lower strata. It is also true in relation to the welfare system, especially in the form that has been developed in the Scandinavian countries. Typical of the Scandinavian welfare model have been three particular aims. The first of them is universalism: the welfare state should encompass the whole population. The second is equality: social policies should not only aim at raising the standards of the poor – they should also bring about a just redistribution. The third aim is that of comprehensiveness: social policy should be related to a great array of human needs.[6] It can hardly be denied that the large-scale welfare programmes have been greatly beneficial to the population of the Scandinavian countries.

Despite all these beneficial consequences of the welfare state in the modern industrial society, it has to be admitted, nevertheless, that many of the good and successful measures definitely presuppose a high degree of cultural conformity. They presuppose, for instance, a large public sector, a consensus about what is worthwhile to pursue, and strict rules for the distribution of material goods.

The era of the industrial society is also the era of the nation state and of state-supported nationalism. The nation state is the guarantor of the uniformity needed in the industrial society. In the agrarian society, such conformity was simply not needed. The industrial society is also the societal form during which it has been common to try systematically to erase and eliminate ethnic and linguistic minorities. Such a tendency prevailed during the second half of the nineteenth and the first half of the twentieth century in practically all European states. The most sinister treatment of minorities occurred, as we know, in the 1930s and early 1940s in Nazi Germany with the persecution and mass murder of the Jews and gypsies. However, nationalist policies with the aim of linguistically and culturally homogenizing national populations were current during the second half of the nineteenth and first half of the twentieth century in almost all European states. Mostly these were implemented by various educational means and by attempting to restrict the language of instruction to the dominant national one. A very typical case was France.

The French situation has been excellently and vividly described in Eugene Weber's book *Peasants into Frenchmen: The Modernization of Rural France 1870-1914*. France is an illuminating example of a state in which modernization definitely meant an imposition of cultural uniformity. In the chapter about the variety and richness of different languages in rural France Weber reports that in as many as 22 per cent of the communes no French was spoken in 1863. A quarter of the population of France actually lived in such communes. The Ministry of Popular Education found that about 10 per cent of the school children did not speak any French at all and that an additional 36 per cent spoke and understood French but were unable to write it. In fact, French was an alien language to many inhabitants of France. Half of all children who were to grow to adulthood around 1900 could have belonged to this category.[7]

In fact, the French authorities began very rapidly to Frenchify and unify the culture of France. For a long time, the common conception was that this linguistic uniformitization of French cultural life had also succeeded almost completely. The ethnic revival at the end of the 1960s has now opened up a reconsideration of the issue. As will be emphasized below, the ethnic revival with its mobilization of ethnic and linguistic minorities is one of the signs of passing from an industrial into an information society.

Many similar examples can be presented. In Sweden, for instance, there were systematic attempts at Swedification of the Finnish-speaking population in the Tornio valley in Northern Sweden. It is worth noting that this Swedification policy started in about 1870, and that it was definitely lessened and also deplored after the Second World War.[8]

From the first half of the twentieth century there is a plenitude of symbolic expressions emphasizing the need for national conformity. In Hitler's Germany this ideal was expressed in the phrase *'Ein Volk, Ein Reich, Ein Führer'*. Even in democratic countries, there existed expressions which, although less authoritarian, pointed in similar directions. The United States was innocently described as a melting pot, but the intention there was, nevertheless, that everybody should become American with English as his or her language. In Finland, with its language conflict between Finnish and Swedish speakers, a slogan used by the Fennomans advocating the sole use of Finnish was 'one mind, one language'. Owing to the decreasing birth rate, the fear of a declining population was felt and expressed in many West European countries in the 1930s. Not only in Germany but in many other countries too, the population policies had a strong nationalistic and racial-biological emphasis. Even in Sweden, where the social democrats Alva and

Gunnar Myrdal became the leading spokesmen for an active population policy, one of the central aims was to preserve the 'Swedishness' of the population.[9]

The electronic mass media were born in the industrial society. It is striking that during the initial period of mass communication, at least in the European countries, it became a tool for cultural unity and uniformitization. This tendency was, of course, strengthened during the Second World War, when radio broadcasting became one important part of warfare and a foremost tool in enforcing national unity. Yet the culturally uniformitizing patterns were evident and strong according to a number of national reports during several decades, from the 1920s through to the 1950s. Umberto Eco has summarized this type of broadcasting in the term *paleo-radio*. Broadcasting was national, paternalistic and inner-directed by nature and offered guidance for complying with standard patterns of behaviour in the industrial society.[10]

The Information Society and the Relative Decline of the Nation State

The present predicament in technologically advanced societies has been given many names, such as the post-industrial society, the service society, the high technological society, the information society, etc. None of these terms is entirely satisfactory, but because it enables us clearly to identify a quaternary sector the term 'information society' is used here. One new feature in technologically advanced societies during recent decades has been phenomenal increase in the speed of international communication. Through the new information technology, it has become increasingly possible to direct companies and projects in other countries. To use a war-like metaphor, conquests today do not have to be pursued by changing the borders of states. Rather, they are pursued by buying and creating enterprises and developing projects of various kinds in other countries, all of which have become possible through vast networks of electronic communication.

The trend towards internationalization is observable in many spheres of life. As already indicated, it is a typical feature of today's commercial life. There are multinational companies with headquarters spread all over the commercially and technologically advanced part of the world. Scandinavian companies also have many affiliated companies in other parts of Europe and even in other parts of the world. As regards enterprises concentrating on export, it is more or less taken for granted that they can survive only if they are able to control a sizeable part of the international market. Similar tendencies exist also in other arenas. For instance, the top sports teams in soccer, basketball and ice hockey have an international composition, and competitions between clubs within the so-called European cup tournaments are becoming just as important as competitions between national teams. In the field of science, there is an increasing number of huge European and international research institutes. Launching projects within the large science programmes of the European Community presupposes that they are developed and proposed by scientists from at least two and preferably several member countries. Similar tendencies are observable in working life, both in the boardrooms and on the shop floor. Reports show how workers in today's European industrial enterprises have workmates from other countries in much larger numbers than before the Second World War. This is not surprising, considering that in many European countries the number of foreign citizens among their residents is more than 5 per cent. In Germany alone, foreign citizens exceed today five million persons.

The new international contacts also create new solidarities and cultural meanings. The nation state has by no means disappeared from the West European scene, but its boundaries and especially its demands for cultural conformity are not as strong and rigid as in the typical industrial society. The nation state is still a very important societal unit, but increasingly it has to share its importance as a solidarity-forming entity with both regions and blocks of states.

Internationalization is almost flagrant in the field of mass communication and the electronic media. It has meant fierce international competition among TV companies, broadcasting stations and newspaper owners. A tendency towards the diffusion of an international mass culture is clearly observable and often lamented. Yet it is striking that the content of the international mass culture is continuously changing. Rather than producing any lasting forms of conformity, it creates an almost chaotic tendency to constant movement and change. It goes without saying that the present patterns of mass communication entail alienating tendencies. The point here is, however, that the developments in the mass media do not produce conformity but rather a great variety of cultural forms and code systems. If anything is typical of the present cultural situation all over Europe, it is the rise of a great number of different tastes and code systems for interpreting the world and for communicating with kindred souls. These code systems also extend to an increasing degree over the national borders. In public cultural life, schools of linguistic philosophy and TV channel audiences are living more and more a life of their own. The present predicament is not without its liabilities, but it certainly does not produce the kind and degree of conformity which prevailed in the industrial society.

In the world of work, tendencies towards an increasing flexibility are observable. The effects and consequences of the computerization of working life have been studied intensively from the moment this began to be a central feature of the world of work. The findings are varied, rich and somewhat confusing. Computerization seems to contain an abundance of both opportunities and risks. Nevertheless, work organizations are now characterized by an increasing flexibility and tendencies to change.[11] The problem does not seem to be rigidity but rather the question of how much flexibility human beings can endure. Even physically the organization of work is changing rapidly. Industrial sites with a traditional shop-floor organization are rapidly disappearing.

Studies of work content clearly indicate a moving away from the rigid Taylorism that characterized so much of the working life in the typical industrial society. The number of routine tasks has decreased in industrial work in particular, but the same trend is also observable among the white-collar workers in offices. In the industrial society, wage labour was indeed an all-encompassing feature. Typical wage labour in the industrial society was a strict time-bound discipline and there was a sharp division between work and leisure. There is now a tendency towards a disintegration of the traditional wage labour system.[12] The borderline between work and leisure begins to be blurred. The need for a strict time-bound discipline has disappeared. With these changes traditional means of supervision and reward have become inefficient, if not simply obsolete. Daily work routines are less and less controlled by strict rules, and more and more formed by objectives explicitly set and formulated. This pattern is clearly observable both in the work routines of management consultants and in the demands of the labour unions. The former are increasingly emphasizing how individual workers feel a need to discuss the objectives and meaning of their work. The labour unions in their turn are putting an increasing emphasis on the autonomy of workers and on their rights to take part in discussions of aims and objectives. It is interesting to note also that working-life research is putting an increasing stress on questions of autonomy and co-determination, and, as the title of a well-known book indicates, on a democratic rationality in working life.[13] The present developments contain many unresolved problems, but the rigidity typical of work organization, working-life rules and labour market relationships in the typical industrial society is gone.

One of the critical points in the present development towards an increasing dependence on high technology and on human capital – i.e., on human capacities and networks – is the risk of the marginalization of workers with very low qualifications living in communities with high unemployment. Together with such 'social quarantines' a disintegration of previous rigid forms can take place because of the decreasing importance of wage labour. Informal exchanges of services and the informal economy as a whole have revived, but not of course at the level it had in the agrarian society, but definitely at a level more intense than that typical of an industrial society.

Even if the long-time trends in the field of working life contain a bunch of unpredictable elements it seems obvious that today there is less rigidity, more flexibility and clearly much more variation of organizational arrangements than was the case with the industrial society.

3. WESTERN EUROPE: ETHNIC REVIVAL AND THE WEAKENING OF STATE-SUPPORTED NATIONALISM

In some realms of life, the tendency of the information society towards an acceptance of cultural diversity is particularly obvious. This is particularly true as regards the treatment of ethnic and linguistic minorities.

One of the crucial tendencies in the West European societies at the turn of the 1960s and 1970s was the recrudescence of ethnic mobilization. It was a time of revival for ethnic and linguistic minorities. Historical minorities which had been silent for centuries suddenly became aware of their ethnic identity and became politically alive. This was the case, for instance, on the Celtic fringe in the United Kingdom and in Occitania in Southern France. One of the crucial features of this ethnic and linguistic revival was the increasing responsiveness of governments to the needs and demands of ethnic minorities. Even if ethnic mobilization has weakened in the 1980s from its peak at the beginning of the 1970s, some features have prevailed. One of them is the comparatively benevolent attitudes of governments towards their ethnic minorities.

During the second half of the twentieth century, European ethnic minorities, often located on territorial peripheries, have been able to formulate their claims in terms of generally accepted policy goals. While in earlier times their demands were easily dismissed as obsolete and nationalistic fancies, governments now feel obliged to take them seriously. It is unnecessary to assume that governments act benevolently by free choice and without any demands from the minorities themselves. There is, however, an increasing pressure towards responsiveness. Even small movements can upset governments, both because today's economy is technically vulnerable and because internal disruptions are often devastating for a country's public and international image.[14] The public policy literature has emphasized how conflict management is a part of public budgeting and a key element in what is called incremental budgeting.[15]

The ethnic revival of the 1960s and 1970s was a typical

feature of such historical and territorial minorities as the Basques, the Frisians, the Bretons, the Alsatians, etc. At the same time, migratory workers over large parts of Europe formed new minorities. The predicament of the immigrants was, as is known, extremely difficult. The new waves of immigration were basically made possible because of the need to recruit new workers into the national workforce. Yet the large-scale acceptance of foreigners into the national labour forces is something fairly new. In the 1930s, alien elements were as a rule strongly rejected everywhere in Europe. The control of culturally and nationally defined borders is today much weaker than it was in the typical industrial society of the 1920s and 1930s. As already mentioned, the 1930s was everywhere in Europe a period of persecution and strong discrimination for ethnic and linguistic minorities. There were not only the atrocities committed by the Nazis but in all corners of Europe the social and language rights of minorities were curbed in the name of national consolidation.

In addition to the ethnic revival among the historical territorial minorities, the increasing benevolence of governments is also related to the pressures towards economic integration. Regions that for centuries have been arenas of combat, such as Alsace-Lorraine (Elsass-Lothringen), have become centres for cooperation between French- and German-speaking territories of continental Europe. Yet whatever the background and causal relationships, the fact remains that there exists nowadays a much greater acceptance of cultural diversity than in the industrial society and during the period between the two World Wars.

The changes described above do not imply that nationalism in Western Europe has disappeared. It has, however, changed very substantially. It has become, in a sense, marginalized and atomized. Nationalism and nationalistic feelings can occur anywhere people have different languages and different cultural backgrounds. Such nationalisms and conflicts are, however, less and less supported by the state. As pointed out above, states now focus more on conflict management than on emphasizing the congruence between political and cultural borders. As a general feature, the strong state-supported nationalism of industrial Western Europe is a phenomenon of the past. However, this does not mean that it cannot appear again. Ethnic boundaries and conflicts are always changing and hard to predict, but at least nowadays responsiveness to different demands is a prevailing tendency within Western European societies.

The present tendencies and mood can, of course, be described in terms of different concepts and formulations. One way to describe the present situation is to emphasize the present predilection for the 'civil society'. In the words of Ernest Gellner, 'civil society is based on the denial of ideological monopoly, on the acceptance of compromise on deep issues concerning the nature of things, on doubt, irony and all kinds of adjusments'.[16] People are permitted to have their ethnic and linguistic identities, but they are also expected to make compromises, and they will be helped to adjust by a state engaged in conflict management.

4. EASTERN EUROPE: A GREAT VARIETY OF CONDITIONS

Also in Eastern Europe, in the former socialist states, there are signs of increasing ethnic marginalization and atomization. Both the former Yugoslavia and the former Soviet Union are afflicted by a multitude of ethnic and national conflicts. These conflicts are small in the sense that they, at least so far, are regionally restricted, but they are also strong in the sense that they are very intensive.

The national conflicts in the former Soviet Union are usually described as reactions against the absolutist and oppressive nature of the former Soviet state. Typical of the Soviet policy *vis-à-vis* ethnic and linguistic minorities was a strange mixture of liberalism and absolutism. On one hand, a kind of emancipatory ideal was emphasized, with a desire for plurality and a wish for vernacular language maintenance; and on the other hand, there was a strong stress on unity and on the strong overriding dominance of the Russian language.

Actually, the aim of the Soviet language policy was a

very clear pattern of diglossia, in other words, bilingualism between a 'mother tongue' to be used in the private sphere, and a 'Soviet Russian' to be used in all official communication.[17] This dualism probably also laid the grounds for the present strong nationalistic and ethnic conflicts in the country. At any rate, such conflicts are very prevalent now at the beginning of the 1990s.

However, it cannot be overstressed that the observations and generalizations discussed above apply only to Western Europe. They are not as such valid in Eastern Europe, that is, the part of Europe which was socialist during the decades succeeding the Second World War. One reason for this is fairly obvious: none of these former socialist states yet has an occupational structure in which the quaternary sector is larger than the other sectors; none can, in other words, be labelled an information society.

The developmental differences between the countries in the former socialist part of Europe are, of course, very large. Some of the states, such as the Czech Republic, Hungary, Poland, and probably also the Baltic states, are approaching the occupational structure prevailing in the advanced Western European countries. Some other former socialist states are on the verge of being transformed from an agrarian into an industrial society. As regards state and nation-building there are also crucial differences. The above mentioned countries – the Czech Republic, Hungary and Poland – all have a long tradition as nation states, whereas countries like Moldova and the Ukraine are somewhere in the early stages of the state and nation-building development.

Despite the fact that the generalizations presented here apply only to Western Europe, they may, nevertheless, be relevant to observations about the new nation states in the former socialist part of Europe. It is apparent that some of the former socialist countries are already experiencing a strong trend towards internationalization, whereas in some other countries in Eastern Europe a state-supported nationalism is becoming increasingly prevalent.

NOTES

1. Juan Linz, Early State-Building and Late Peripheral Nationalisms against the State: The Case of Spain; in S. N. Eisenstadt and Stein Rokkan (eds), *Building States and Nations. Analysis by Region*, vol. II. (Beverly Hills and London: Sage Publications, 1973), pp. 34–5.
2. Ernest Gellner, *Nations and Nationalism* (Oxford: Basil Blackwell, 1983), pp. 8-18.
3. Ibid., p. 1.
4. Zoltan Kennesey, The Primary, Secondary, Tertiary, and Quaternary Sectors of the Economy. *Papers of the Nineteenth Conference of the International Association for Research in Income and Wealth* (Norwijkerhout, Netherlands, 1985) and Marc Uri Porat, *The Information Economy: Definition and Measurement* (Washington D.C.: US Department of Commerce, Office of Telecommunications, 1977).
5. Raymond Williams, *Towards 2000* (Harmondsworth: Pelican Books, 1985), p. 130.
6. Robert Erikson, Erik Jorgen Hansen, Stein Ringen and Hannu Uusitalo (eds), *The Scandinavian Model, Welfare States and Welfare Research* (Armonk and London: M. E. Sharpe, 1987).
7. Eugene Weber, *Peasants into Frenchmen. The Modernization of Rural France 1870–1914* (Stanford: Stanford University Press, 1976), p. 67.
8. Magdalena Jaakkola, Diglossia and Bilingualism among Two Minorities in Sweden. *International Journal of the Sociology of Language*, no. 10, 1976, pp. 9–10.
9. Ann-Katrin Hatje, *Befolkningsfrågan och välfärden. Debatten om familjepolitik och nativitetsökning under 1930- och 1940-talen* (Stockholm: Allmänna förlaget, 1974), pp. 237–45.
10. Umberto Eco, *La Guerre du faux* (Paris: Grasset, 1985).
11. Gunilla Bradley, *Psykosocial arbetsmiljö och datorer* (Borås: Akademilitteratur, 1986), pp. 248–51.
12. Hans de Geer et al., *In the Wake of the Future. Swedish Perspectives on the Problems of Structural Change* (Aldershot: Avebury, 1987), pp. 90–2.
13. John Fry (ed.), *Towards a Democratic Rationality. Making the Case for Swedish Labour* (Aldershot: Gower, 1986), pp. ix–xi.
14. Erik Allardt, *Implications of the Ethnic Revival in Modern Industrialized Society* (Helsinki: Commentationes Scientiarum Socialum, no. 12/1979), pp. 22–3.
15. Adam Wildavsky, *Budgeting: A Comparative Theory of Budgetary Processes*, 2nd edition (New Brunswick: Transactions Books, 1986), pp. 5–35.
16. Ernest Gellner, From the Ruins of the Great Contest. *Times Literary Supplement*, March 13, 1992.
17. Helen Liesl Krag, *Sovjetunionens mange sprog. Mål og midler i sovjetisk sprogpolitik* (Copenhagen: Institute of Slavonic Studies, 1982), pp. 79–80.

Part III

DIFFERENT CONTEXTS OF NATION STATE

7. THE FUTURE OF NATIONAL CULTURES IN EUROPE

Jaan Kaplinski

1. BASIC DEFINITIONS

My task is not an easy one, because I have to speak about three emotionally loaded concepts – 'nation', 'culture' and 'Europe'. By far the worst of these three is 'nation'. It has many meanings. It is difficult to explain to an Estonian or Georgian what this word means in Western Europe, and it is difficult to explain to an Englishman or Frenchman what the word '*natsionalnost*' – nationality – has meant in Soviet documents. Because of such difficulties and because of the unscrupulous exploitation of things national by such people as Adolf Hitler, there are some social scientists who deny nations any universality, considering them to be temporary phenomena, born under the influence of German romantic philosophy and the emergence of the industrial states.

I do not want to contest their conclusions, but when rereading for example Herodotus, who constantly talks about Lydians, Medes, Scythians, etc., having their own territory, their own kings and their own sense of identity, I cannot but wonder whether these peoples were nations or not. We can certainly refuse them this honour and call them ethnic groups or something similar; but this seems to be negativistic wishful thinking, a parallel to the nationalistic thinking where everything human is confined to national blocks without any no-man's-land between them. I would agree to call, for example, ancient Lydians, Sumerians or the twelve Jewish tribes proto-nations, but I would not want to deny them any nationality. I think that modern nations have a long prehistory: they have not come into being only in the eighteenth century. And this prehistory is worth some consideration; perhaps it will give us some indications about nations' future history and even post-history.

If there is ideological confusion about the word 'nation', there is probably even more confusion about the word 'culture'. The best definition of the word that I know comes from my famous Estonian compatriot Yuri Lotman, who once said that culture is everything that is not absolutely necessary, for instance art, poetry, religion, ethics, tablecloths, spoons and forks, etc. To put it in a different way, culture gives us a possibility of choice between several varieties of art, religion, ethics, tablecloths, including a zero choice. In culture, nothing is indispensable; in culture there is no absolute security.

Our third concept, 'Europe', has several meanings, too. It is, first of all, a continent, a geographical entity. But it is also a cultural concept, loaded with strong emotions and preferences. Right up to the present day there have been many people in Europe who are so convinced of the supremacy of their culture, especially their religion, that they propagate it abroad, trying to convert other people to Europeanism, to Europeanize themselves. This was done most efficiently in the nineteenth century, when the Europeans divided the whole world between them. During that time, the white men had so few doubts about their culture and mission that some of them even had a genuine interest in other cultures, giving birth to such phenomena as theosophy and oriental studies. This gave Europe some openness. European artists were influenced by African and Japanese art, oriental religions and philosophies were studied and admired, oriental literature translated. A culture that is self-confident often seems more interested in other cultures than in its own roots.

Now the situation has changed. Europe has lost much of its self-confidence. It has been nearly colonialized by the two superpowers – the United States and the Soviet Union – neither of which was purely European. New economic superpowers have emerged in the Far East, challenging the Europeans and Americans even in what they considered their field of activity *par excellence* – science and technology. All this has greatly undermined the Europeans' sense of security, not to mention superiority.

Europe has responded to this challenge in two ways. The pressure from outside contributed in a decisive way to Europe's increasing integration and a reconsideration of its European identity. But within this identity the main emphasis tends to be put on the strictly European elements. Europe is much less interested in other cultures, it is returning to its roots, to its history, to its Europeanness. A kind of isolationism is emerging in Europe. This tendency is reinforced by the tide of new rightism and conservatism that is sweeping the Western world.

This, in a few words, is the background against which I have to develop some of my thoughts about the future of national cultures in Europe.

2. THE EMERGENCE OF NATIONS

Both elementary particles and living beings behave in a strikingly similar manner. The world strongly wants to be a soup with plain dumplings, not a purée. Matter is condensed into atoms, molecules, crystals, stars and galaxies. Living beings are condensed into various groups as families, peer groups, kins, clans, nations and groups of nations.

Men are members of these groups by virtue of communication. The optimum size of a human group is determined by the necessity of communication and collaboration, but also by the ecological limitation imposed by the environment. A larger group gives men more security, but then they also need a larger territory and longer hunting and food-gathering expeditions. Such limitations were imposed on human beings for several hundred thousand years. It is extremely probable as well that the size of a group we can belong to and the number of people we can effectively communicate with is also genetically determined. It has something to do with the size of our brains and with the organization of our memory and language. In other words, we are determined by our natural communicative capacities to be members of a relatively small group consisting of no more than a couple of hundred people. Such groups exist now, too, for example as families, extended families, street corner societies, teams, classes, military units, groups of friends, etc., that is, groups within which we can effectively communicate verbally and non-verbally without the necessity of using writing or other modern means of communication. Such small groups are in close contact with each other and occupy a small territory, such as a house or some other building.

When the human population on the Earth started to increase rapidly during the so-called neolithic revolution, the size of human groups increased too and neighbouring groups often formed larger units, integrated into tribes and what I have already proposed calling proto-nations. The neolithic population explosion was also an explosion in complexity: human beings were suddenly facing social, environmental and technical problems they had not known before. We cannot say that they were entirely successful in coping with these problems. Some of them are far from being solved even in modern times. But our relative success in passing through the neolithic revolution proves that our communication potential is much greater than the use our ancestors made of it.

Living in an entirely new social and natural environment would not have been possible without great innovations in human communication. Security consisted of this in many groups who had to coordinate their activities in, for instance, building irrigation systems or forming armies to defend their newly won riches. Because of this, communication over large distances in space and time was needed. The answer to this challenge was the invention of writing, a symbol system that people could effectively use in transmitting and preserving information. It was writing that made education and the cumulative development of culture possible. For the first time, it was possible to preserve what was considered important and could not be preserved in the living memory in the same way as exact astronomical data or maps.

The integration of groups and societies soon reached its social and ecological limits. The first large empires of the Middle East were short-lived and even the Roman Empire did not last long. In ancient times, such a large state had to be a centralized monarchy, it had to be ruled from one location by one person or by a small group of persons. Other theoretical variants proved to be too cumbersome and precarious, as the history of the Roman Empire proves. But at the same time, a centralized monarchy tends to create more opposition than it can cope with. Its history degenerates into military history, relentless wars exhaust its economic and human resources. Efforts to reach a cultural, religious and linguistic unity create opposition and rebellion which, in combination with the attacks by external enemies and economic difficulties, finally lead to the disintegration of the empire. This scenario has been repeated many times in history, and it has shown that unless dramatic changes occur in statehood, economy and communication, there can be no long-lived states larger than the Roman Empire.

Seen from a distance, all these empire-building efforts are instances of the process of the unification of mankind. This is a percolation-type process. Its analogy is, for example, the formation of a continent from a large number of small islands emerging from the sea. As the land rises, land bridges are formed between separate islands until there is more land than water and every point is connected with every other via land. Nations are such continents, large groups of people who can communicate freely, having a common language and culture. This is, of course, a simplification – it is risky to talk about communication between, for example, a king and a beggar. But even such communication was easier than the communication between the Emperor of China and the envoys of the King of England.

Having a common or similar language and culture greatly contributed to the possibilities of integration. It was between such groups that 'land bridges' could easily develop. Linguistic and cultural diversity was an obstacle to human communication, to empire-building and the unification of mankind.

It is clear that both worldly and spiritual rulers having such aims understood this and tried to combat this diversity. An empire needed uniformity amidst diversity. Building up and maintaining an empire was an episode in the age-long war between universality and diversity, where neither succeeded in gaining the final victory. Despite the declaration by Tamerlane that the whole inhabited world did not merit having more than one ruler, and despite the efforts of Christian and Moslem missionaries and rulers to reach uniformity of religion, diversity fought back and often re-established itself forcefully.

3. FORMATION OF THE NATION STATE

When the Roman Empire collapsed, a multitude of new nations and cultures emerged from its ruins, giving birth to what was destined to become Europe. This peninsula of the Eurasian continent is interesting because of its stubborn resistance to the attempts of its leaders and rulers to unite it. This task was too much for emperors, popes and kings. Europe has preserved its diversity up to modern times, although it did a lot to abolish it in other places like America or Africa. We could perhaps say that in Europe the process of empire-building stopped at its medium stage, achieving the stage of nation-building. This meant the emergence of states based on some existing ethnic and cultural similarity. In the Middle Ages, this was often overshadowed by other factors, dynastic and religious.

Beginning with the age of Enlightenment, however, the national factor gained an increasingly essential role. The nation states became really national in the contemporary sense. This was greatly advanced by a factor that was not very important in the past – that is, the emergence of a real school system. At its cradle stand Martin Luther and other reformers with their emphasis on the necessity of reading and understanding the Bible. This meant also that emphasis was laid on the hitherto more or less neglected native tongues which often achieved a written standard precisely thanks to Bible translation, as was the case for example with German. Roughly during the same period we can observe the beginning of the modern science of pedagogy, introduced by such men as John Komensky (Comenius) and the Jesuits. In a sense only educated people can be citizens of a nation state; illiterate peasants or minorities speaking a different language are in a way outsiders in it. Sometimes they are tolerated, sometimes persecuted and assimilated.

In principle, a nation state is always somehow authoritarian. Its aim is to achieve more or less complete cultural, linguistic and often religious homogeneity. In this endeavour, three possible means were used – assimilation, deportation and genocide. Assimilation meant education in the 'national' language and culture, plus suppression of others. Deportation was used at an early date by most of the Catholic rulers of Spain to get rid of the Jews and the Moors and to confiscate their riches. Together with genocide it was also used against gypsies and some other minority groups. The cultural homogeneity in Europe has been achieved at the cost of the weaker nations (or proto-nations), who were assimilated or exterminated. Their list is a long one and includes the Provençals, most Celtic peoples, Jews, Basques and many others. Some of them have succeeded in remaining alive, but their cultures have not kept pace with their more fortunate neighbours.

This process of homogenization has spread from Northwestern Europe to other parts of Europe and to other continents. The ethnic purges now going on in the former Yugoslavia as well as similar processes in Armenia, Azerbaidzhan and other parts of the former Soviet Union can be seen as steps on the way Western Europe took several centuries ago, a way that has led to the formation of modern nation states.

The nation states have proved to be very effective politically, militarily and culturally. It is therefore no wonder that they are imitated in many parts of the world. In achieving a cultural homogeneity of population, these states in fact created a professional, well-disciplined labour force, a part of which could also become an armed force. For the first time, a state became an organization whose members were all, or almost all, people living on its territory.

The territory of a modern nation state is relatively large, which means that it has achieved ethno-cultural homogeneity on much larger territories than in earlier times. Then, the population map of Europe had more of a patchwork character, such as can nowadays be found in more remote areas such as the Balkans and Caucasia. This ethnic mosaic corresponded to the communication realities of the past, but became a hindrance to the development later.

As we have already mentioned, the European way out of this impasse was the creation of nation states with a homogeneous population. This would have been impossible to achieve without such advances in communication as a written language and a school system. In this way, modern nation states are children of books, literacy and schools. It may be worth mentioning that a similar development took place in China at a much earlier period. There the written language had a hieroglyphic character and in this way was able to unite many ethnic groups speaking very different dialects and languages.

4. THE FUTURE OF THE NATION STATE

Now the situation is changing once again. For the first time in history, it seems to be possible to achieve a remarkable degree of integration without abolishing diversity. This has been made possible by advances in transportation, communication, translation and education. Theoretically, a modern 'empire' can well be multilingual and multicultural; there is no longer a need for 'one tsar, one religion and one fatherland'. The European Union seems to be at least partly an attempt to put such ideas into practice. At the same time, it has borrowed much from European history and is trying to build up an ideology of 'Europeanism'.

But a united Europe can be no more than a step on the long path which finally leads to a real World Community of Nations. The unification of Europe can be evaluated against this background. Unfortunately, it is still far from clear whether the unification of Europe will contribute to the unification of the world or inhibit this process by adhering to an isolationist conception of Europe. This would in fact mean the creation of a super nation state with its own European nationalism. The local languages and cultures would be formally preserved and even supported, but in many cases their basis would be seriously weakened by integration and standardization. It would, for example, make little sense to support the position of the Swedish-speaking community on the west coast of Finland at the same time as the Common Agricultural Policy makes it impossible for them to continue their own way of life.

The European Community is basically an organization born of the necessity for economic effectiveness in a more and more competitive world. It can, of course, invest considerable funds in supporting culture, but, as we know, there can be a great difference between a genuine culture and a culture kept alive by donations and subsidies. Would, for example, the Estonians, Basques or Saamis in the Europe of the future receive some benefits for being Estonians, Basques or Saamis, preserving a kind of cultural pluralism in Europe? I think that there are many among them who would be against such a status as living exhibits in Europe's open-air museum.

In order to survive as a culture, culture must therefore be something serious, it must be a necessity, not luxury goods. I think that it is not at all improbable that the national cultures will survive in a united Europe as something secondary, as a decoration. The real Europe will become more and more homogeneous and will more and more resemble America, although its standards and images will be somehow different, perhaps even consciously different from those of the United States.

My view is also that Western Europe is too small a region to be culturally self-sufficient. In European history, the most creative periods were those during which, after a break, new contacts were established between Europe and other regions, for example with the Moslem world, with the Orient, with Russia, etc. The periods of isolationism have as a rule been culturally more sterile. Europe is like the Baltic Sea, which suffocates unless there is a flux of ocean water from the North Sea.

This means that for the future of European culture, the most welcome development would be a cultural renaissance in Russia and China. In these areas there seems to be enough autonomous thinking and creativity, and both influences proved to be very stimulating in the eighteenth and twentieth centuries.

To be creative, to be living, a culture needs contacts with other cultures with different paradigms. But, alas, there seem to be no different cultural paradigms in contemporary Europe. Even now there do not exist genuinely different cultures but only one European culture with local variations from the Elbe to the Atlantic. Europe does not, in fact, consist of separate national cultures but of parish cultures, that is, of local cultures that represent variations on the same themes. And it is hard to imagine that in such a situation numerous new ideas could be born. These ideas must come from somewhere else. I suggest that they could come from the East, where different paradigms really can be found. They could even be found in some places in Eastern Europe, e.g. in Finland or in Estonia, if people here had more courage to be themselves, not succumbing to influences from prestigious Western Europe.

My last point is that there is a danger inherent in the advancing integration of the world. This process can lead to a cultural impoverishment of the world. Even if, as seems to be the case, measures are taken to preserve the diversity of cultures and languages, they tend to lose some of their diversity and originality. They acquire the same paradigms and become local, provincial, rather than national. In such a case, contacts with other, basically different cultures have a special importance; they can revitalize a stagnating culture. Now, if the whole world becomes united, where do such revitalizing contacts come from, where is the fundamental otherness to be found?

I think that the answer to this question cannot be found in the European paradigm, in European attitudes towards culture and the spirit which are rather formalistic and rigid. Instead, an answer could be found outside Europe, in the Far Eastern understanding of creativity, freedom and uncertainty that has been able to preserve the creative impulse there, even at times of isolation and decadence. In China people understood that there is always something basically different, some otherness, in ourselves. We only have to discover it, to become conscious of it. This also means that we have to refuse to identify ourselves totally with any nation or group. The roots of culture lie deeper, they lie where there is no Europe, no Asia or no Africa.

8. A PROSPECTIVE VIEW ON THE EUROPEAN NATION STATE AND UNIFICATION

Ali Kazancigil

1. MAASTRICHT: A CAUTIOUS STEP TOWARDS POLITICAL UNION

Since Robert Schuman, then the French Minister for Foreign Affairs, made his celebrated declaration of 9 May 1950, calling for a common European authority on coal and steel, which set into motion the process of European integration, the fate of the nation state[1] in Europe has been a subject of controversy and speculation. This debate, which remained rather a theoretical, and at times a metaphysical one, for about four decades, has taken on more concrete and immediate overtones since the signing of the Maastricht Treaty on European Union. Public debates in many countries during the ratification process throughout 1992, the Danish *no* and the narrow French *yes* to the Treaty, mostly revolved around the issue of whether the nation state, and with it the national culture and identity, would survive the European Union or whether they are doomed.

Whatever its adversaries may claim, the Maastricht Treaty is not really a radical departure from the European Community as it has developed over the last four decades. Clearly set within the same process of mutually agreed gradual integration which has always characterized the Community, it is the companion document to the European Single Act of 1985, which as of 1 January 1993 establishes a single market between the twelve EC members. However, with the Maastricht agreement, the EC goes beyond its traditional economic, commercial, monetary and agricultural areas. In that way it ventures into the highly symbolic sphere of national sovereignty and makes provisions for a unique European currency and a European Central Bank to manage it.

New spheres included are common police and judicial actions on sensitive issues such as immigration, terrorism and drug traffic. The Treaty also foresees the establishment of a European citizenship, mainly through the right for nationals of the EC member states residing in another EC country to vote and be elected in municipal and European elections. As regards the Community institutions, the Council, consisting of the heads of states and governments, is given stronger powers. The European Parliament also obtains additional prerogatives, but much less than it claimed, while the executive powers of the Commission are not extended.

How far will the Maastricht agreement, if properly implemented, interfere in the sovereignty of the European nation states? The federalists, who favour complete integration, leading ultimately to a 'European state', would say: *'not much'*. In this they would be partly right, because Maastricht foresees full integration only in one respect, in creating the ECU, the unique European currency. In its provisions concerning the gradual development of common foreign and defence policies, as well as common internal security and judiciary actions, it basically remains within the inter-governmental framework through cooperation between states.

In foreign policy, the Council will determine the general policy guidelines unanimously, but if 'common actions' are to be taken it may decide to vote by qualified majority rule. It is also foreseen, rather vaguely, that in due course there will be a 'common defence'. The decision-making power rests with the Council, and the European Parliament is far from replacing the national parliaments and improving the situation which the critics of the Community institutions call 'Europe's democratic deficit'. A European citizenship doesn't involve any revolution, since Denmark and the Netherlands already grant residents who are nationals of other EC countries (and even those who are from non-EC countries) voting rights in municipal elections, while Italy does the same in European elections.

A contrario, the confederalists loudly announce the end of the sovereign state and declare that the nation is henceforth an endangered species in Western Europe, victimized by the EC technocracy. Their exaggerations aside, they too might be partly right in their forecasts, but only on the condition that the Maastricht agreement is systematically and thoroughly implemented, thus creating a strong and lasting dynamic towards political union. Both are partly right and partly wrong, for although the Maastricht agreement does not correspond to the federalist dream and mostly remains within the intergovernmental framework, it may well create a strong and lasting dynamic towards political union, a prospect which is pleasant for the pro-Europeans and dreadful for the nationalists.

A word of caution is in order before going further. The future-oriented considerations which follow are based on the assumption that the Maastricht Treaty will be ratified and implemented. The negative outcome of the Danish referendum on the ratification of the Treaty, the crisis on the currency market which weakened the European Monetary System and forced Italy and the United Kingdom to withdraw from it, as well as the perennial British temptation to slow down European integration and turn it into a free trade zone, are strong indications that the success of Maastricht is far from being a foregone conclusion. Still, it is worth thinking about the future European political organization and the fate of the nation state. If the movement towards integration fails, this essay will remain speculation. In the opposite case it may, with some luck, provide a few useful indications on future political directions in Europe.

2. THE STATE AND THE NATION AS HISTORICAL ARTEFACTS

General de Gaulle's *credo* was that in world politics the only permanent realities are the nation and the state, which is its political expression. At first sight, present developments seem to confirm this view. Major political and social ideologies have declined, while the nation – and nationalism, its hideous facet – has the world scene all to itself. The nation state is still the major actor in international relations and, at the same time, the world's most powerful organization. A considerable number of stateless national and ethnic groups are claiming, or fighting to create, a sovereign territorial state of their own. The evidence of its vitality and effectiveness as the dominant form of political organization can be seen in the fact that the membership of the United Nations increased to 179 states in 1991–1992 and may soon reach a size of 200 members. The UN Secretary-General Boutros Boutros-Ghali expressed his concern that the current ethnic conflicts and claims to statehood might lead, in the not too distant future, to an unmanageable UN membership of some 300 states, unless these conflicts can be settled through negotiations and some associative arrangements are made between the micro-states.[2] Charles Tilly is more pessimistic – or perhaps lucid – when he refers to the prospect of 'thousands of state-like entities, most of them tiny and economically unviable'.[3]

The world-wide diffusion of the modern Western state has accelerated since the Second World War.[4] However, the Gaullist postulate about its permanence has to be considered in the light of historical evidence. In this way it is possible to show that the nation state is a construct that is historically, geographically and culturally determined.[5] The nation state is also subject to transformation. It has been a dominant form of political organization since the early nineteenth century, but it may cease to be so in the future.

The transformative trend is linked to the way the capitalist world economy operates, to the globalization of production, trade and finances. These, as well as world-wide networks of illegal trades like the arms and drug traffics, challenge the nation state and escape its control. This trend is also related to the constitution of rival actors on the world scene, e.g., intergovernmental organizations, non-governmental organization, economic communities, free trade areas and transnational corporations. All of these global and international structures, regimes, actors and flows threaten the status of the nation state as the dominant political actor and impose legal or practical limitations to its sovereignty. European integration may be interpreted as a response to such global challenges on the part of a group of medium and small nation states.

The nation state still has powerful symbolic dimensions. Any development which appears to interfere with its sovereignty is perceived by people as a threat to their identity. This is hardly surprising, since in Europe the states powerfully shaped national identities and played a civilizing role in both public and private spheres.[6] Hence, the public image of the nation and the state takes on certain immemorial, sacred overtones, a perception which is not consonant with the relatively recent origin of these artefacts. Research in historical sociology has shown the specific historical circumstances through which in Western Europe the feudal system was followed – through a development lasting several centuries – by the emergence of the sovereign, territorial modern state.[7] Its emergence was by no means inevitable, nor is its future guaranteed in the *longue durée*.

The same point can be made about the nation, which dates from the late eighteenth century.[8] No doubt there are also continuities between the older ethnic identities and the modern nations, but they are not identical.[9] Ethnicity is a primary phenomenon, whereas the emergence of the nation is intimately linked to the modern sovereign territorial state. Ernest Gellner has convincingly argued that nation and nationalism are artefacts, and that historically it is the state which generated the nation rather than the other way round: 'Nations, like states, are a contingency, not a historical necessity... Nationalism holds that they were destined for each other... But their emergence was independent and contingent. The state certainly emerged without the help of the nation... It is debatable whether the normative idea of the nation, in its modern sense, did not presuppose the prior existence of the state.'[10] By definition, therefore, these two very closely linked artefacts are and will continue to be subject to change.

In Central and Eastern Europe, the post-communist era is marked by the consolidation or rebirth of the nation states in Poland, Hungary, Romania, Bulgaria and the Baltic countries. New nation states have also emerged or are in the process of emerging, such as Slovenia, Croatia, Bosnia-Herzegovina, Macedonia, Ukraine and Belorussia at the expense of former entities like Yugoslavia and the Soviet Union.

In Western Europe, the cradle of the nation state, we observe a different picture, however. The twelve member states of the EC are gradually moving beyond economic integration and towards political union. The European Free Trade Association members Austria, Finland, Sweden and Switzerland are candidates to enter the Community, which may soon be a sixteen-member organization.

The process in the two parts of Europe may be less contradictory than it appears, since the majority of the Central and Eastern European countries have declared their intention to join the EC as soon as their economic development will allow them to do so. The same applies to Southern Europe, where Turkey, Cyprus and Malta are also eager to enter the Community. The perception of the consequences of the European economic and political union for the future of the nation state and national identity varies a great deal. For some of those who are already within the EC (for example, about half of the Danes and French) integration is a threat to the nation state. Apparently, the same process is not a problem for many Central, Eastern and Southern European countries which would enter the EC without any hesitation.

As noted earlier, during the ratification process of the Maastricht Treaty a highly symbolic cultural issue – the nation, national identity – became the major line of demarcation between the supporters and adversaries of the European Union. It is worth noting that the creation of a symbolic entity in the form of the nation/nationalism at the end of the eighteenth century continues to remain very powerful in Western Europe after two centuries of service – including countless wars and massacres. The purpose was to compensate for the destruction, caused by the economic modernization, of people's collective memory filled with religious and traditional notions that had prevailed in the agrarian societies.[11] A reason for this is that the idea of the nation is associated with a more fundamental, primordial requirement, which is the need felt by individuals to have a root, an identity, to belong to a community. The nation state, which is often perceived as a threat to sub-national cultures and identities within its boundaries, appeared in the summer of 1992 in its guise as a defensive device against the bigger and more distant European Community.

3. FUTURE SCENARIOS

In the forthcoming decades, the European nation state will realize one of three possible scenarios. The first scenario is the complete success of the movement towards political union, leading to the formation of the 'United States of Europe'. Given the resilience of the nation and its perception as the defender of national identities, this scenario looks very unlikely. The fact that large regional groups with strong cultural identities, such as the Basques and Catalans in Spain or Bretons in France, feel politically and culturally oppressed and resent the domination exercised by the nation state, does not fundamentally modify this situation.

According to the second scenario, the nation state may keep most of its present characteristics, especially in the event that the efforts towards a European Political Union, along the patterns set by the Maastricht Treaty, are not successful. In this configuration, which is not altogether unlikely, given the reactions observed in public opinion against the rather prudent move towards the European unification outlined in the Maastricht Treaty, European integration would continue to be restricted to intergovernmental cooperation in agricultural, economic, commercial and monetary domains. The Community would keep its intergovernmental character with limited supra-national dimensions.

In this case the pressure towards evolving common economic and monetary policies would fade away, while the determination to arrive at negotiated compromises in order to accommodate conflicting economic and political interests would weaken. The EC would soon be transformed into a free trade zone. Geopolitical considerations would dominate the scene, with Germany, France and Great Britain resuming their traditional alliances and balance-of-power games. Individual

European countries – with the exception of Germany – would be unable to compete with the Japanese and US economies. Germany would confirm its status as the dominant regional power, while the rest of Western Europe would decline. It would be unable to cope properly with the globalized economic and monetary, as well as illegal, flows. It would be easier for the Eastern and Southern European countries to enter a European free trade area. However, a disunited and declining Western Europe would not be in a position to provide the investments and financial and technological support that these countries badly need. To sum up, the nation-state-as-usual type of scenario may well prevail in Europe, but the price to be paid for it would be quite penalizing for all concerned.

4. TOWARD A POST-HOBBESIAN POLITICAL ORGANIZATION

The third scenario is the emergence of a new European political arrangement, partially replacing the nation state and partially coexisting with it. The nation states in Europe would be transformed, but they would not disappear altogether. This is the scenario that is most likely to prevail on the condition, however, that the momentum towards European integration is not interrupted. But it is particularly difficult, for two reasons, to anticipate with any degree of detail. It has no historical precedence, and it emerges through a rather unpredictable process of negotiations, alternating advances and set-backs.

So far, states have come into being either through expansion and military conquest by a single power, or through an agreement among several existing states.[12] The most recent example was the formation of an independent Namibia in 1990. A future Palestinian state may also fall into this category. In the nineteenth and early twentieth centuries Europe witnessed such cases of state-building for instance in Belgium and Serbia. The process of European integration is different, however. It first of all involves sovereign states which do not claim independence, nationhood or statehood. Now there is no nineteenth century-type concert of great powers, imposing the establishment of a new state, nor a UN participation as in the case of the post-World War state-building in the territories which belonged to European colonial empires. What we see is a process whereby these sovereign nation states – initially six, then twelve, and in the not too distant future possibly sixteen – voluntarily and gradually transfer elements of their sovereignty to common European institutions.

Historically new states have always started their build-up with political institutions – the bureaucracy, the army and the police – and then have continued with economic and social matters. European integration has progressed in precisely the contrary way: it started in 1950 with a typical functionalist strategy.[13] When the early incursion into the political arena, through the establishment of the European Defence Community, failed in 1954, it continued on the economic track up to the Maastricht Treaty.

In the meantime, all other political initiatives of federalist or confederalist orientations put forward in the 1960s, 1970s and 1980s proved unsuccessful. The integration through this functionalist approach mainly concerned the industrial, agricultural, commercial and monetary fields and activities related to production, exchange and consumption. It was also removing obstacles to the free circulation of capital, labour, goods and services and evolving common policies in such areas. What constitute the *Hobbesian core* of a sovereign state, i.e., the instruments of political domination and rule such as an army, a police force and a unified bureaucratic apparatus directly administering a given territory, were not at all parts of the integrative process.

Would the momentum created at Maastricht take the European political organization further? Although the Treaty foresees the building-up of common policies that belong to the core of a sovereign state, there is currently no question of working towards a European state in the Weberian sense. A political organization which exclusively controls the legitimate means of coercion within a territory is formally centralized and differentiated from the society, and claims the right to resort to violence if needed in order to obtain obedience, settle conflicts and allocate resources.

In the long run, however, where would the Hobbesian core of the European construction lie? Would it mostly remain within the nation state or would it substantially be transferred to the European level? An important criterion in deciding where the Hobbesian core lies is the location of the civil and military apparatuses. If, for instance, the national armies and police forces are superseded by a European army and internal security force (in the same way as in the federal US model, where the Federal Bureau of Investigation [FBI] supersedes the state police forces), then the European political organization would acquire more power. After that the nation states could be characterized as *post-Hobbesian* or *post-Leviathan.* Since a number of the problems of the next few decades (such as ethnic conflicts, environmental crisis, mass migration, illegal arms and narcotics trade, etc.) are global phenomena, policies and means to cope with them might well be transferred to the European entity, if not completely, then at least to a large extent. Such transfers would take place in a gradual fashion, over one or two decades. At the end of this process most military, policy, justice and administrative functions and apparatuses would become European by nature while more restricted parts would remain national, with an appropriate division of labour established between these two levels.

In certain areas the functions and powers of the nation state would be weakened not only upwards to Europe but also downwards to the regions, provinces and *Länder*. These sub-national units already act as European actors, concluding inter-regional agreements and establishing direct links with the EC institutions.

The new political organization which is emerging in Europe would most probably be a form of co-sovereignty. The European Union and the pre-existing nation states would end up by sharing the Hobbesian core, each side combining the features of a Hobbesian and a post-Hobbesian political entity in varying proportions which are quite difficult to discern at the present.

This picture is complicated by another major factor, the nation. Democracy and its representative institutions are very intimately linked to the nation state, the framework within which they developed. It will be very difficult for the national parliaments to accept the transfer of their legislative power and democratic legitimacy to European institutions. They are already unhappy that directives of the European Commission and rulings of the European Court of Justice prevail over the national legislation in member countries. The EC institutions will, no doubt, become more democratic in the future along with the strengthening of European citizenship. But would this go as far as fundamentally transferring democratic legitimacy from the national to the European level, so that the European Parliament would replace the national ones? If important parts of the Hobbesian core are likely to be transferred to Europe, these components need to be placed under democratic control. Here we are in a very complex area, all the more so because national traditions of democracy and citizenship are quite different. In any case, ways of linking European-level democracy and citizenship are yet to be discovered.

The emergence of a European nation, incorporating and superseding the pre-existing nations, does not appear to be likely, in the foreseeable future at least. Sometimes the future Europe is referred to as 'post-national',[14] to describe the articulations between the national identity/citizenship and the European identity/citizenship. In the context of this essay, I would prefer the expression 'post-nationalist', because the European identity would not so much suppress the national identities as broaden them, with the consequence that the hostility between identities existing within Europe would weaken. The weakening of nationalisn in intra-European relations would, of course, not eradicate nationalism and xenophobia *vis-à-vis* non-Europeans. That is another story, however.

While the European Union is likely to have a sobering effect on nationalistic feelings, the nation itself appears to be keeping all its symbolic and mobilizing vigour as the main component of people's identity. This is the case even if it is increasingly challenged by other layers – the local, the regional, and ultimately the European – that contribute to the identity of the European individual. One lesson to be learned from the passionate debates on the ratification of the Maastricht Treaty is that nowhere in Europe is the nation near extinction. The possible transformation of the sovereign state into a post-

Hobbesian state would, therefore, not basically change the age-old association between the state and the nation in Europe.

The nation will most certainly continue to have a function that cannot be handled at the European level, namely to act as an instance of intermediation between the global economic, financial and technological processes, on one hand, and the sub-national levels which constitute the life contexts of individuals and communities, on the other. Functions relating to participation, like social integration and cohesion, peaceful co-habitation of various social and ethnic groups, education and schooling, coping with sprawling conurbations and urban violence, can only be taken care of within the national framework. The public space for coping with such issues developed within the nation state; should a specifically European public space be ultimately created, it will accommodate different types of functions, but not the ones listed above.

It is important that the future post-Hobbesian state should keep its capacity to handle such functions and maintain its major artefact, i.e., the symbolic unity and common identity we call the nation. This is especially important if such undesirable developments plaguing modern societies as anomia, loss of direction, xenophobia and violence are to be kept under control. The gradual emergence of a European citizenship and identity would be of limited help in this respect. It would be, however, a strong antidote to nationalism, the pathological dark side of the nation. One can here see the advantages of a proper articulation between the sub-national, national and European identities.

The best configuration for European co-sovereignty would be one in which the post-Hobbesian nation state preserves strong cultural functions, while the political power, necessary to cope with global problems such as the economic processes, environmental protection, arms and narcotics trades, are transferred to the European Union. This would mean a welcome dissociation between the political power and cultural, symbolic, ritual functions. Maximum power to Europe and maximum symbolism and ritual to the nation would present many advantages, not the least of which is the secularization of politics.

NOTES

1. The term 'nation state' mirrors the nineteenth-century European idea, later diffused throughout the world, that each nation should have its own territorial sovereign state. (Y. K. Ferguson and R. W. Mansbach, *The State, Conceptual Chaos, and the Future of International Relations Theory*. Boulder and London: Lynne Rienner Publishers, 1989.) Today, nation state is widely used as the equivalent of the sovereign territorial state. Thus, I shall follow the popular usage, even if in many cases it is a misnomer and raises conceptual and terminological problems: for example, the sovereign territorial states of the United Kingdom or Belgium are often called nation states, which they are not. (On this, see K. Aun, A Critique of the Nation-State; in N. A. Nyiri and T. Milijan (eds), *Unity and Diversity*. Waterloo: Wilfred Laurier University Press, 1980; F. Riggs, Ethnicity, Nationalism, Race, Minority: A Semantic/Onomantic Exercise (Part Two). *International Sociology*, vol. 6, no. 4/1991, pp. 443–63.)
2. *Le Monde*, 21 March 1992.
3. Charles Tilly, *Coercion, Capital and European States, AD 990–1990* (Oxford: Basil Blackwell, 1990), p. 3.
4. On this, see Ali Kazancigil, Paradigms of Modern State Formation in the Periphery; in Ali Kazancigil (ed.), *The State in Global Perspective* (Aldershot: Gower/UNESCO, 1986).
5. See, e.g., B. Badie and P. Birnbaum, *The Sociology of the State* (Chicago: University of Chicago Press, 1983) and Y. K. Ferguson and R. W. Mansbach, *The State, Conceptual Chaos, and the Future of International Relations Theory* (Boulder and London: Lynne Rienner Publishers, 1989).
6. See Norbert Elias, *The Civilizing Process. Volume 2: State Formation and Civilization* (Oxford: Basil Blackwell, 1982).
7. On this, see Badie and Birnbaum, op. cit.; Tilly, op. cit. and Paul Anderson, *Lineages of the Absolutist State* (London: New Left Books, 1974).
8. E. J. Hobsbawm, *Nations and Nationalism since 1780* (Cambridge: Cambridge University Press, 1990).
9. Anthony D. Smith, *The Ethnic Origins of Nations* (Oxford: Basil Blackwell, 1986).
10. Ernest Gellner, *Nations and Nationalism* (Oxford: Basil Blackwell, 1983), p. 6.
11. Ibid.
12. See, e.g., Charles Tilly, War and the Power of Warmakers in Western Europe and Elsewhere; in Peter Wallensteen, Johan Galtung and C. Portales (eds), *Global Militarization* (Boulder: Westview Press, 1985).
13. On the basis of functionalism, see David Mitrany, *A Working Peace System: An Argument for the Functional Development of International Organization* (London: Oxford University Press, 1943).
14. On post-national Europe, see J. Lenoble and N. Dewandre (eds), *L'Europe au soir du siècle: identité et démocratie* (Paris: Ed. Esprit, 1992).

9. THE DECLINE OF SOVEREIGNTY: LEGAL PERSPECTIVES

Allan Rosas

This article is based on the assumption that we are gradually moving away from the 'Westphalian era'. By that we mean the period of the markedly horizontal system of independent and sovereign states the roots of which are often linked to the symbolic year of the Peace of Westphalia in 1648. We shall argue that we are heading towards a more 'pluralist' world system, where state sovereignty in the traditional (post-1648) sense is on the decline and may even be approaching its demise. We shall try to show how this shift is gradually being reflected in legal regulation and thinking. It is assumed that legal developments are, by and large, relevant indicators of societal change.

International law and to some extent constitutional law provide our main frame of reference. While 'sovereignty' is not an easy concept,[1] a lawyer may find that concept easier to tackle than the concept of 'nation state'. Our main task will be to look at the development of state sovereignty rather than notions of sovereignty of nation or of the people.[2]

1. THE CONCEPT OF SOVEREIGNTY

Sovereignty indicates supreme and, in principle, absolute power. According to a characterization of a well-known law dictionary, 'sovereignty' is 'the supreme, absolute, and uncontrollable power by which any independent state is governed'.[3] This description already links the concept of sovereignty to that of the 'independent state'.

This state, of course, is not any state. While the term 'sovereign' has been used since ancient times,[4] the focus of this chapter will be on the 'modern' state that emerged sometime during the sixteenth and seventeenth centuries. This was also the birth of 'modern' international law, based on a horizontal system of sovereign and equal states. Writers like Niccolo Machiavelli (1469–1528), Jean Bodin (1530–1596) and especially Thomas Hobbes (1588–1679) reflected the shift from a universal and Christian order to state sovereignty,[5] although it was left to the 'fathers of international law', such as Hugo Grotius (1583–1645) and especially Emerich de Vattel (1714–1767), to explain the existence of rules between independent states.[6] This inter-state system could be visualized in the following way.

Figure 9.1. The post-1648 inter-state system

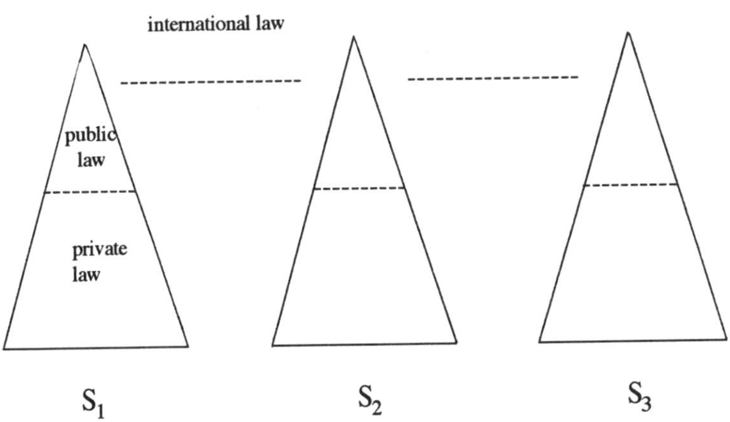

Within each state, there was a legal order with unilateral law-making. The distinction between the public and the private gained ground. In the private sector and inside civil society, property rights and civil freedoms such as freedom of movement and of contract gradually became key concepts.

The modern state was a markedly territorial unit, with more or less established and defined frontiers.[7] Within this state territory, 'internal' sovereignty implied exclusive jurisdiction. Laws could be enacted and enforced (although constitutional limits were established with the '*Rechtsstaat*'). It was, to quote Gianfranco Poggi, a feature of the nineteenth-century state that each operated 'in its own territory as the sole, exclusive fount of all powers and prerogatives of rule'.[8]

In its relations to other states (the international as distinct from the domestic), the state was 'externally sovereign' (independent). The often acknowledged right to resort to war in order to solve inter-state disputes made external sovereignty ultimately a question of power ('might makes right').[9] If one state was conquered and subjugated by another state, the former's sovereignty ceased. As it was not possible/feasible for one state to conquer all the rest of the world, the inter-state system was preserved, however.

Another attribute of statehood was population. Citizenship was established and defined in relation to each sovereign state. 'Aliens' could be denied entry to this national territorial space. The citizens formed the 'nation', which with the American and French Revolutions obtained a kind of internal political sovereignty. And there came a gradual perception of the nation also as the 'people', comprising the whole population and with political rights for all its adult members.[10]

But sovereignty in the legal sense was rather attached to the state (nation state) as a supreme order with respect to a given territorial space.[11] What has been sometimes called the 'Law of Nations' was, in fact, a law between states. There was no positive rule of public international law that required states to respect popular sovereignty in their internal constitutional order. Occasional efforts by the United States and some other countries to make recognition of new governments depend on democratic legitimacy did not mature into a norm of general international law.[12] From the point of view of international law, states could be monarchies, aristocracies or even totalitarian dictatorships. As late as 1948, an effort to include a separate clause in the Universal Declaration of Human Rights on the right of people to resist tyranny and oppression failed;[13] only a few national constitutions expressly provide for a right of resistance.[14]

According to the textbooks of international law, states should not have only territory and population but also a 'government', including a capacity to deal with other states in an orderly fashion. One could, in fact, speak about the requirement for an effective legal order and administrative system.[15] This requires some kind of a constitution, or basic rules about powers to enact and enforce legal rules and to enter into relations with other states.

Especially during the present century, the centralized nation state has delegated some of these powers to local and regional communities (municipalities, autonomous regions, etc.) and has, in some instances, constituted itself as a federal state. After the Second World War in particular, it has also entered into a number of legally binding international commitments and has transferred certain powers to international (inter-governmental) organizations. Given the inherent vagueness in the concept of sovereignty, these tendencies have been described by some as a limitation of sovereignty, while others on the contrary have said that it is a question of exercising sovereignty, that is, the capacity to enter into relations with other states.[16] The latter view has been the prevailing one, with the possible exception of the transfer of powers to supranational organizations such as the European Community.

As a general rule, there has still been a qualitative difference between the independent state on one hand, and local or regional government or an international organization on the other: the sovereign state has had the capacity to enact and amend its constitution, including the constitutions of these other entities. Sovereignty in international relations 'signifies constitutional independence of other states'.[17] The European Community cannot by itself amend its constitution; this requires a joint decision by the member states (Article 236 of the Treaty of Rome of 1957), a fact which has taken on a particular significance with the Danish referendum of 2 June 1992, rejecting the Maastricht Treaty on European Union. The Charter of the United Nations can be amended by a qualified majority of its member states (Articles 108–109), but the sovereignty of recalcitrant members is preserved by the interpretation that they may in this case withdraw from membership.[18]

This may be contrasted with the principle normally applied in a federal state: the constitution can be amended by a qualified majority, but recalcitrant member states of the federation cannot, under the national constitutional order, leave the federation. Member states are subjected to the sovereign will of the federal state, whose constitution is above the members. The Southern States were forced back into the United States in the 1860s; secession from the Soviet Union led to the dissolution of the Soviet Union itself.[19] The situation of a confederation may be different, and be like the constitution of intergovernmental organizations: the member states, in principle, retain their sovereignty and cannot – under the treaty establishing the confederation – be forced into a closer union against their will.[20]

As the examples above illustrate, these structures may be threatened by secessionist and revolutionary movements. To prevent such refractoriness (and to uphold its sovereignty against other sovereigns), the sovereign state monopolized the use of force, in particular by maintaining a permanent army. The army, not only formed by the state but also forming the state, has been the central institution of the territorial state.[21] It has been needed to uphold the effectiveness of the constitution and the legal order in general (or in more sociological terms, the power of the elite). The United Nations, the European Community or the German *Länder*, have not possessed armies of their own. Nor have they had a currency of their own, which is an important national symbol and a marker for an economic area.

Armies, currencies or other national power structures have not prevented secession from taking place. The Hague Peace Conference of 1899 was attended by 26 states. Today, in

Europe alone, there are more than 50 so-called independent states (at the time of writing, there are 52 CSCE member states), and close to 200 in the entire world. The globe has become more or less completely divided among these states. Their 'sovereign equality' is still held to be the benchmark of the international system. The UN is according to its Charter 'based on the principle of the sovereign equality of all its members' (Article 2, Paragraph 1). The first of the ten principles formulated in the CSCE Helsinki Final Act of 1975 concerns 'sovereign equality' and 'respect for the rights inherent in sovereignty'.

The dissolution of unions such as the Soviet Union and Yugoslavia has led some to speak about a renaissance of the nation state. As far as the concept of sovereignty is concerned, quantity should not be mixed with quality, however. An increase in the number of states does not necessarily imply that state sovereignty is thriving. Rather, the proliferation of states may contribute to the decline of sovereignty. This is because the solving of economic, environmental and other problems arguably requires large geographical areas of integration and cooperation. An increase in the number of states, on the contrary, means smaller territorial spaces. Such a development would underscore the need to go beyond the national territories of nation states.

2. MILITARY FORCE

In the universal (monist) legal order of feudalism, legitimate collective violence was supposed to be 'just', that is, to have a just cause. With the centralized modern state and the alliance between its ruling circles and a standing army, such considerations were brushed aside. Wars were just simply if undertaken by the lawful prince (= the government in power of an independent state). The development of sovereignty is inextricably linked to developments in the legal and political regulation of collective violence.

During the present century, we have witnessed a general trend to limit collective violence. We should ask what consequences this may have for sovereignty. It is useful to distinguish between four different areas of international regulation.

Table 9.1. International regulation of collective violence

	Rights in using force	Right to use force
Inter-state conflicts	1	2
Intra-state conflicts	3	4

During the era of sovereign and independent nation states, the first area of international regulation concerned the conduct of inter-state wars (*ius in bello*), that is, category 1. Especially since war became a relation between states,[22] wars had to be restrained, so as to minimize unnecessary violence and destruction.[23] Rules on methods and means of warfare and respect for prisoners of war and civilians were based on common interests and did not threaten sovereignty.

With the increasing economic and social costs of modern warfare, efforts were made to regulate the very decision to resort to war (*ius ad bellum*), that is, to enter category 2 above.[24] An armed attack on another state should not take place save under certain conditions, a principle included in the Covenant of the League of Nations. The next step was to outlaw resort to war altogether, which was accomplished by the Kellogg–Briand Pact of 1928 and the UN Charter of 1945. The only clear cases of the legitimate use of force at the international level recognized in the UN Charter are individual and collective self-defence (Article 51) and military sanctions approved by the Security Council (Chapter VII).

While this '*ius contra bellum*' has its advantages for the system of sovereign equality (stability and security for all states), it also poses a threat to the sovereign. First of all, many sovereign states (or rather, their governing elites) have sought expansion by military means, and a prohibition on the use of force has been seen as a threat to such aspirations. As territorial conquest, mainly for technological reasons, has become less feasible than economic and ideological conquest, it has become easier to accept the requirement of inter-state peace.

But the absence of a superstate has made many states reluctant to accept the prohibition on the use of force fully. What if other states resort to unbearable measures short of armed attack which cannot be effectively countered in other ways than by military force? These measures might even include collective measures to impose, through an international organization, a new constitution on a state; the army might then be needed to preserve the essence of sovereignty.

Moreover, a more powerful state may wish to impose its will or political system on another state. This explains various political or quasi-political doctrines allowing for military intervention in certain circumstances, such as the now outdated Brezhnev doctrine and the current efforts in the United States to legitimize its unilateral 'interventions for democracy'.[25]

Outright military conquest has become clearly illegitimate, however, as demonstrated by the international response to the Iraqi attack on Kuwait.[26] Although one should not jump to far-reaching conclusions solely on the basis of the Gulf War, it is possible to detect a growing tendency to pursue collective determinations as to when the use of inter-state force is lawful and when it is not.

All in all, the legitimacy of aggressive inter-state violence seems to have decreased. There is also a hypothesis – inspired by old Kantian visions – which seems to be gaining ground that 'liberal' democracies do not wage wars against each other.[27] These developments could be one explanation behind the present quest for disarmament.[28] In one particular instance (Iraq), a global organization (the UN) has recently prohibited a state from possessing certain types of weapons, namely weapons of mass destruction and long-range missiles, and asked the country in question to allow UN on-site verification of these obligations.[29] In most cases, however, arms control and disarmament still come about through agreement or parallel unilateral action (informal agreement), that is, by preserving formally the requirement of state consent. But rules establishing a duty to negotiate, the existence of some kind of 'soft law' legislation in this area (for instance, UN General Assembly resolutions), and in general the role of international organizations may point towards a more limited scope for 'sovereign' decision-making. And with respect to verification and control, current disarmament law contains interesting innovations of relevance for sovereignty (see below).

While the above developments mainly apply to the inter-state level, the use of force within states has survived longer as a national prerogative. The constitutional state and the rule of law brought domestic restraints on the rights of governments to use force against their citizens, but there was no international rule requiring an independent state to uphold the rule of law. Also in constitutional states, concepts such as national security and law and order served as ideological tools to quash, if necesary by force, serious threats to the constitutional order and the governing elite. Even at the beginning of this century, there were no expressed international rules for the conduct of civil wars.[30]

Only since the Second World War has non-international armed conflict become expressly regulated, which means that international law has entered the area of category 3 in the figure above.[31] At the same time, international human rights law has brought international legal restraints on the use of violence by the state against its citizens. The concept of crimes against humanity, appearing in the London Agreement for the Prosecution and Punishment of the Major War Criminals of the European Axis of 1945, the prohibition of genocide affirmed by the Convention on the Prevention and Punishment of the Crime of Genocide of 1948, and the prohibition of torture and inhuman or degrading treatment, affirmed by several universal and regional conventions, attest to these developments.[32]

These basic prohibitions have been supplemented by an abundance of more specific limitations on state action. There is no need here to go into details of the massive treaty-law that has emerged since the 1940s on the protection of human rights and fundamental freedoms, such as liberty and security of the person and the right to a fair trial. Suffice it to note that international human rights law today includes certain minimum guarantees applicable also during public emergency, including war.[33] Not even by invoking the concept of national security can a government any longer free itself of these legal restraints.

Human rights and humanitarian law basically regulate the use of violence without necessarily questioning the actual right of the government to resort to force against its own citizens. Surely force cannot always be avoided as a last resort against criminal violence. But what about the right of the government in power to maintain its power (the efficacy of its constitution) by force, without obtaining popular consent? Or the right of a revolutionary movement to use force to overthrow a constitutional and democratic government? We are now entering category 4 in the figure above.

Modern human rights law seems to provide for the right of peoples to 'internal' self-determination, that is, to have the final say in the government of their country. It is possible to interpret common Article 1 (right of self-determination) of the two International Covenants of 1966 in this way.[34] According to the Universal Declaration of Human Rights (Article 21), 'the will of the people shall be the basis of the authority of government'. The CSCE Helsinki Summit Declaration of 10 July 1992 refers to the 'responsibilities ... of governments towards their people' to uphold the CSCE guiding principles and common values (which include respect for democracy and human rights) and to the 'democratic rights of citizens to demand from their government respect for these values and standards' (para. 7). International human rights law also provides for individual political rights, such as the right to participate in public affairs, notably through regular, free and fair elections.[35]

But as was already noted above, international law and diplomacy have generally not drawn the conclusion that governing elites that violate the above principles, that in other words do not base their legitimacy on a democratic order and popular consent, lose their right to represent the state internationally. Fernando Téson puts it this way: 'While political theory and constitutional doctrine may support the idea that governments should be Lockean, or Kantian, to be internally legitimate, international law teaches that they need only be Hobbesian to become honorable members of the international community.'[36] If this is so, internal might would make right on the international scene. The question of the system of government would still be essentially an ingredient of the doctrines of sovereign equality and internal affairs.

This is not the case in the relation between a state and its regional and local governments. A bunch of hoodlums who take over a local government by force will not be recognized by the government of the state or by other states (unless they manage to take over central government as well, or to establish a political community which manages to secede from the state). Nor would gangsters who occupy the premises of an intergovernmental organization be 'recognized' as the lawful directorate of that organization.

There are signs that international law and diplomacy, too, may start to pay more attention to the international legitimacy of governments.[37] Suffice it to mention a few examples here. In the mid-1960s, the UN Security Council defined the situation in Southern Rhodesia, where a racist minority regime had made a unilateral declaration of independence, as a 'threat to the peace', branded the regime an 'illegal authority', to be isolated from all international contacts, instigated mandatory sanctions under Article 41 of the Charter and called upon the United Kingdom to quell the rebellion.[38] Since 1974, the credentials of the South African apartheid regime have been rejected by the UN General Assembly, despite the fact that there has been no competing regime claiming to constitute the lawful government. In 1991, the Ministers for Foreign Affairs of the Organization of American States adopted a resolution calling for the convocation of meetings of the relevant OAS organs 'in the event of any occurrences giving rise to the sudden or irregular interruption of the democratic political institutional process or of the legitimate exercise of power by the democratically elected government in any of the Organization's member states'.[39] Finally, the Document of the Moscow Meeting of the Conference on the Human Dimension of the CSCE, adopted on 3 October 1991, contains an interesting passage clearly inspired by the Moscow putsch of 19 August of the same year: '[The participating States] will support vigorously, in accordance with the Charter of the United Nations, in case of overthrow or attempted overthrow of a legitimately elected government of a participating State by undemocratic means, the legitimate organs of that State upholding human rights, democracy and the rule of law, recognizing their common commitment to countering any attempt to curb these basic values' (para. 17.2).

Without going into all the legal and political problems that this text certainly invites (and leaving aside here the precise legal nature of 'political commitments' contained in the CSCE documents), it is interesting to note its reference to the UN Charter. The proponents of the traditional inter-state order will no doubt find solace in the Charter's references to sovereign equality, non-use of inter-state force and non-interference in internal affairs, and the absence in Article 4 of the Charter of any express reference to democracy and respect for human rights as a condition of membership. But the proponents of change might point to the Charter's references elsewhere to human rights and fundamental freedoms, the principle of self-determination of peoples (assuming, as was argued above, that this principle may contain an 'internal' element) and the possibility of sanctions approved by the Security Council in cases not only of breaches of the peace and acts of aggression but also 'any threat to the peace' (Article 39).

These perspectives invite us to consider the question of collective intervention. For instance, if a government starts slaughtering its own population, other states may invoke a right to intervene on overwhelming humanitarian grounds. While individual states, in situations of great humanitarian urgency, may have a right to intervene, as it were, on behalf of the international community, we may see in the future an increasing direct involvement of international organizations such as the UN and the CSCE. There are many, including the present writer, who would argue that, at least in extreme situations, humanitarian intervention may be legitimate under existing international law.[40]

In resolution 688 (1991) of 5 April 1991, the UN Security Council stated that the 'repression' of the Iraqi civilian population, including the Kurdish minority, had consequences which 'threaten international peace and security in the region', and insisted that Iraq allow immediate access by international humanitarian organizations to all those in need of assistance and requested the Secretary-General 'to use all the resources at his disposal' to address urgently the critical needs of the refugees and displaced persons. While this resolution did not authorize UN military intervention but only a 'humanitarian' presence, it gave indirect legitimacy to the presence of US and other coalition forces in Kurdistan and also led to the dispatch of limited UN 'guard units' to Iraq.[41]

Later resolutions have endorsed a humanitarian assistance programme for Somalia, backed up by an arms embargo, and a peacekeeping and humanitarian assistance programme for the former Yugoslavia, backed up by comprehensive non-military sanctions.[42] In the CSCE Helsinki Summit Declaration of 10 July 1992, backed up by more concrete decisions, it is stated (para. 20) that 'CSCE peace-keeping activities may be undertaken in cases of conflict *within* or among participating States to help maintain peace and stability in support of an ongoing effort at a political solution' (emphasis added). Although these measures or statements have been clothed in the notion of 'peacekeeping' and humanitarian 'assistance', they seem to have strengthened the case for humanitarian intervention, especially as endorsed, directly or indirectly, by the UN Security Council.

It would be a further step to assert a right to intervene in order to establish a democratic order. Such a right might be based on an assumed collective right of popular resistance against tyranny and oppression (the intervening forces would 'assist' the people in its exercise of this right). But as was noted above, a right of resistance was not included as a separate right in the Universal Declaration of Human Rights. The legality of armed interventions for the sake of democracy alone, and in the absence of pressing humanitarian concerns, is doubtful, to say the least. It should be noted that in the Gulf War neither the UN nor the UN-endorsed coalition made any express and determined effort to change Iraq's political regime.[43] In any case, unilateral 'intervention for democracy' seems unlawful *per se*.[44]

Collective non-recognition of undemocratic regimes may offer a more feasible avenue. As was noted above, this avenue has been pursued in the cases of Southern Rhodesia and South Africa, and the OAS has made some statements calling for measures against undemocratic regimes. The possibility of non-recognition is hinted at but not spelled out in the CSCE Moscow Document quoted above. It is also noteworthy that the European Community in December 1991 made the recognition of new states in Eastern Europe conditional on their respect for 'the rule of law, democracy and human rights'.[45]

Continuing diplomatic and other relations with clearly undemocratic regimes (such as the Chinese government in power) are a reminder that there is still a long way to go, and many questions certainly remain. This is not the right place to answer all these questions. What is important to note is that current politico-legal discourse is starting to address issues of democratic legitimacy. The principle 'might makes right' is increasingly called into question, even with respect to situations prevailing within a given country. The monopoly of the state and its army to decide on the use of force seems to be threatened. If this is so, sovereignty is exposed as well.

3. INTERNATIONAL STANDARD-SETTING

Let us now look at the processes of international standard-setting and law-making. In the traditional inter-state system, the latter term especially seemed misplaced. International law was based on consent (although the concepts of customary law and general principles of law have posed some intricate questions in this regard[46]). With the emergence of international organizations, international law-making came up for consideration.[47] At the outset, some words should be said about the international standard-setting which is not unilateral law-making in the true sense.

One cannot avoid underlining, first of all, the profound change that has taken place during the last decades with respect to the contents of international norms. While international legal rules traditionally concerned questions of a more or less inter-state relevance only (inter-state war, the status of diplomats, merchants and other aliens, inter-state trade relations, etc.), the main focus of contemporary multilateral treaty law seems to be on issues which are at least partly of an intra-state relevance (human rights, environmental law, choice-of-law rules and harmonization with respect to various parts of 'private' law, etc.). This means that, from an international law point of view, the state is no longer free to legislate on these issues.

International human rights law may even curtail a state's freedom to amend its own constitution, a prerogative which we saw above as the core of 'sovereignty'. For instance, abolition of the equal political rights of adult citizens would be in contravention of international law at least for those states that are parties to the International Covenant on Civil and Political Rights, the European Convention on Human Rights, the American Convention on Human Rights or the African Charter of Human and People's Rights. A European state party to Protocol no. 1 of the European Convention on Human Rights may not abolish the system of private property.[48] A European state party to the European Charter of Local Self-Government of 1985 may not abolish the system of local self-government.

True, international human rights law, or international law in general, does not yet prescribe the primacy of international law, in cases where an open conflict between international and domestic law arises in the domestic legal order.[49] European Community law, however, must be given precedence also domestically. This is why some national jurisdictions (Germany and Italy in particular) have tried to make the national constitution a sanctuary against Community law. But in this field, too, there is a trend towards the primacy of Community law.[50] Outside Community law, there is a tendency of states to move from dualism (which means that international norms are not automatically part of the domestic legal order) towards monism, that is, a system where international norms and domestic norms are considered parts of the same legal order There also seems to be a tendency to recognize international norms as directly applicable ('self-executing') before domestic courts and authorities.[51]

Insofar as international norms are created by agreement (treaty), there is normally a right for the State Party to withdraw from the treaty, including membership of an international organization, upon the lapse of a defined time-period. This right may be seen as preserving sovereignty. But is it in the real world becoming close to a fiction? Joseph Camilleri and Jim Falk observe the following: 'Though not legislated by a central authority, and at times lacking precision or the support of force, international law, through customs, conventions, agreements, the decisions of tribunals and the development of contemporary ethical values, has come to prescribe rules of conduct impinging on almost every facet of human organization. As a consequence, international law – and the various types of international organizations which accompany it – feeds on itself and becomes so closely interwoven with domestic law as to make the dividing line increasingly blurred. In these circumstances it has become progressively more difficult to demonstrate the primacy of domestic law, which is arguably one of the cardinal premises of state sovereignty.'[52]

This statement rests on the premise that international norms are created mainly by agreements (treaties) between states or through practice. In addition, international law-making seems to be making progress. For instance, texts adopted by international organizations have a tendency to develop into 'soft law' or even into binding customary international law, even when the formal decision adopted is a recommendation *per se.* The Universal Declaration of Human Rights of 1948 offers an example. There are also today many special devices employed by international organizations to increase the persuasiveness of recommendations, such as the obligation for the government to submit recommended International Labour Organization conventions to national parliaments and to report to the ILO on the implementation of non-ratified conventions and recommendations. Some organizations also have an opting-out procedure, making decisions binding on states unless they have 'opted out' before a given time-limit.[53]

International law-making in the strict sense is still rare. The most important instances are provided by the regulations adopted by the competent European Community organs. These automatically become part also of the national legal orders; in fact, member states are prohibited from adopting domestic acts of implementation. In the EC case-law, directives, too, have under certain conditions been accorded direct applicability in the domestic law.[54] Insofar as this 'secondary' EC law will be given primacy even in relation to national constitutions (see above), sovereignty as characterized above (competence to enact and amend the national constitution) would be severely crippled. At the very end of the day, sovereignty could be saved by allowing the affected state to withdraw from the European Community (European Union). But there are those who claim that withdrawal from the EC, an issue on which the Treaty of Rome is silent, is legally foreclosed.[55]

At the global level, the powers of the UN or its specialized agencies to adopt binding decisions are much more limited. But the competence to adopt binding non-military sanctions has been used in situations short of inter-state armed attack, namely Southern Rhodesia (1966; these sanctions were subsequently abolished when Southern Rhodesia became Zimbabwe), South Africa (1977), Yugoslavia (1991–1992), Somalia (1991) and Libya (1992). As was noted above, the Security Council may base its binding measures under Chapter VII of the Charter on the existence of a 'threat to the peace', a phrase which seems to provide the Council with a wide margin of appreciation.[56]

In the case of Iraq, again, the Security Council not only adopted binding economic sanctions, but also prohibited Iraq from possessing certain types of weapons and asked her to allow UN verification of these obligations (see above). On 31 March 1992, the Security Council adopted a programme of sanctions against Libya, to force this country to comply with a request to extradite two of its nationals to specified foreign countries.[57] It should be noted that the Security Council in the latter case gave concrete orders as a response to an alleged violation of international law (an allegedly Libyan-sponsored terrorist attack on civil aircraft) which falls short of large-scale military force (Iraq, Yugoslavia, Somalia) or the basic issues of legitimacy which arose in the Southern Rhodesian and South African cases. While these measures are primarily conceived as sanctions, they also contain a 'legislative' element.

There are increasingly vocal demands to broaden the scope for international law-making. The need to combat environmental threats may become a cataclysm. Geoffrey

Palmes writes: 'International law has never been confronted with a set of problems of the nature and quality of the global environmental problems. To meet the challenge, a new approach is needed, one that builds on the international law and institutions we have. The thesis advanced is that in those ways that international law seems different from municipal law, there will have to be changes. To deal effectively with the global problems, a form of legislative capacity is essential. Rules that are binding on nations will have to be made by means other than unanimous consent.'[58] One only wonders whether in due course such awareness will come to fruition in political decisions, or whether this will require alarms in the form of outright environmental catastrophes.

4. VERIFICATION AND DISPUTE-SETTLEMENT

It is a well-known fact that international organizations generally lack the powers of adjudication and enforcement that abound in domestic jurisdictions. Internal sovereignty implies jurisdiction not only to legislate but also to execute and enforce on the state territory. There has been a strong presumption of the exclusive jurisdiction of the territorial state, although general international law of long standing has known some deviations (for instance, the right of foreign ships to innocent passage in the territorial sea). States have also resisted being drawn into disputes before foreign national courts (often invoking immunity) and have been reluctant to accept generally the compulsory jurisdiction of international courts. As to enforcement and sanctions, states have been unwilling to accept the idea of collective sanctions decided by majority voting; the international sanction system has been markedly horizontal and 'decentralized', with reprisals and other countermeasures resorted to by states against other states, often in circumstances when it has been virtually impossible to distinguish law and politics from sanction and revenge.

In the post-1945 period, this picture has become more diverse. First of all, the state's exclusive competence to verify what goes on in its own territory has been somewhat modified by the fairly recent institution of on-site inspections (*in loco*). Arms control and disarmament law have show the way.[59] Without going into details, one can note that some international conventions on the non-proliferation of nuclear weapons[60] extend certain on-site verification powers to an international organization. An even more far-reaching international verification regime will be established when the new (1992) Convention on the Prohibition of the Development, Production, Stockpiling and Use of Chemical Weapons and on Their Destruction enters into force. Some European instruments relating to conventional forces and the so-called confidence- and security-building measures grant other states participating in the regime a right to conduct on-site inspections.[61] Also some bilateral treaties between the Russian Federation and the United States contain on-site verification regimes.[62]

Similar arrangements have recently been established in the humanitarian and human rights field.[63] For instance, a Committee functioning in accordance with the 1987 European Torture Convention has the right to visit all places of detention in State Parties to the Convention. The so-called mechanism of the human dimension of the CSCE, as developed at the Moscow meeting in September–October 1991, contains some (politically) mandatory elements, including a commitment under certain conditions to allow a CSCE mission of rapporteurs to enter the territory of the state. On a more voluntary basis, the UN has an elaborate system of rapporteurs, special representatives and working groups, and even permanent missions (for instance, Cambodia and El Salvador), which carry out fact-finding missions and investigations in various Member States.

As to the settlement of international disputes and claims, there is a trend towards an increasing role for international (third-party) judicial settlement. The International Court of Justice, a UN organ, which had hardly any cases on its list during the 1970s, is now facing a crammed docket and is 'busier than it has ever been in its entire history'.[64] The European Court of Human Rights and especially the Court of Justice of the European Communities play an important role in settling concrete issues and developing European law. The CSCE Follow-up Meeting in Helsinki in July 1992 gave new impetus to the creation of compulsory mechanisms for the settlement of disputes between the CSCE states, including the idea of a court of conciliation and arbitration.[65] The general political climate is today much more conducive than before to third-party settlement and international adjudication.

5. CONCLUSIONS

Let us begin with a note of caution. While the developments outlined here seem indicative and interesting, they generally do not abolish what was seen above as the core of state sovereignty, that is, constitutional independence. In most cases, states have specifically agreed to certain specific international norms or granted certain limited powers to international organizations, while they have retained the right to veto additional norms and amendments to existing ones, as well as the right to renounce treaties they are parties to. Formally, international law is still largely based on consent. In the rare cases of true international law-making, a right to withdraw from the organization may exist. And most importantly, the nation states retain a near-monopoly over the ultimate enforcement mechanism, the standing army.

Commenting upon the quest for a 'New World Order', articulated in the aftermath of the Gulf War, Stanley Hoffmann argues that the principles of state sovereignty and (external) self-determination are still given precedence over popular self-government (internal self-determination) and the protection of human rights: 'In other words, world order still remains tied to the distinction between domestic affairs and relations among states. International and domestic legitimacy remain distinct, in conformity with the doctrines of realism based on traditional balance of power, which prescribe that states attempt to affect each other's external behaviour but not the domestic conduct and institutions of political regimes.'[66]

There are many policy-makers and commentators who would agree with this thesis, or would at least continue to emphasize the importance of sovereign statehood.[67] Still, our own tentative conclusion, based on the observations made in the foregoing, would be that the very foundations of the traditional inter-state system are shaking. Seen in a wider historical context, the international legal system has undergone almost revolutionary changes especially since 1945, and this within an astoundingly short period of time.

The increasing interspersion of the 'international' and the 'domestic' implies that states are losing some of their former constitutional independence. It is the firm conviction of the present author that these normative developments reflect realities as well. No state will be able to 'opt out' completely from the web of security, human rights and environmental commitments accomplished during the last fifty years or so. If such a daredevil were to emerge on the international scene and start to renounce its main treaty commitments, the common interests of the international community would cause other states and international organizations to take countermeasures. The concepts of *jus cogens* (peremptory international law),[68] general customary international law and general principles of law would offer the legal tools to crush such unilateral acts of insubordination.

It is impossible within the confines of this article to explain more fully the reasons behind these developments. Suffice it to underline the importance not only of regional economic and social integration (such as the European Community) but also of the 'overall trend towards economic integration and interpenetration ... at the global level'.[69] At the bottom are technological developments, which make space as territory less important. Markets and human interaction are moving beyond national territories. The urgent need for joint environmental action needs no further explanation.

As the territorial nation state is unable to solve these and other global problems, its and its rulers' legitimacy as 'sovereign' is increasingly called into question at the level of paradigms and perceptions. Some would even speak of 'war making and state making as organized crime'.[70] Global communication and information networks make it possible to expose criminal or negligent government. Economic and political interdependence between states makes it easier for the international community to bring such governments back in line, by denying access to joint cooperation arrangements.

The decline of state sovereignty is not only explained by the 'internationalization' of affairs that used to be domestic. It is not only a question of states delegating powers 'upwards', to international organization, but also of a more general fragmentation of the centralized state and central government.[71] Seen from the perspective of central government, the situation could be described as follows (figure 9.3).

Figure 9.2. Fragmentation of government

The size of each arrow reflects the probability, rather than the degree, of transfer of powers. Each arrow reflects a bilateral relation; all in all, the 'people' may not obtain a greater say in decision-making, as the other benificiaries (such as integration organizations) may be tainted by a 'democratic deficit'.

Figure 9.3. Layers of public decision-making

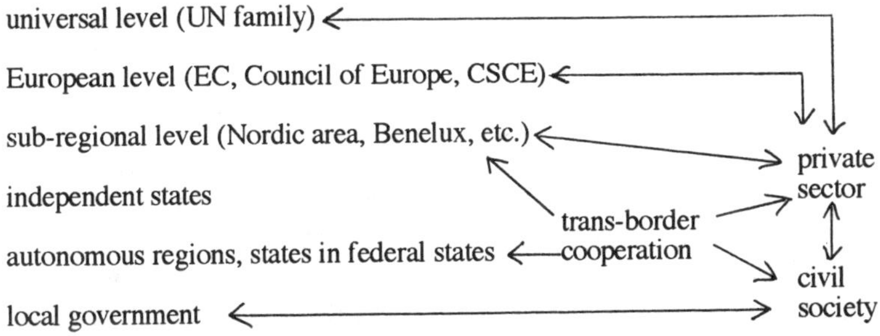

It goes without saying that the interpretation expressed in the figure above applies above all to Western Europe. It is our belief, however, that the general trend will spread to other parts of the world as well. With such developments it may also be time to start looking at the world in terms of several layers of public decision-making rather than a dichotomy between the international and the domestic.

Needless to say, these 'layers' of decision-making are not clearly defined as to their geographical area, powers or functions. In fact, the picture should be multifaceted. The concept of state we are approaching could be termed the civic state. Let us compare this state with the feudal and capitalist states.

Table 9.2. Different concepts of state

	Feudal	Capitalist	Civic state
Mode of production	agrarian	industrial	information technologies
Legal structure	monism	dualism	pluralism
Legal sources	natural law contract	written laws private contract	plurality, incl. reason and justice
Ideology	authority religion	liberty nationalism	equality human rights
Administration of violence	private armies	standing state armies	police

Without explaining this scheme in greater detail, the importance of its last component, the 'administration of violence', should be stressed. State sovereignty in the traditional sense seems to be linked to military force. While armed forces will continue to exist in the foreseeable future, it seems likely that their functions will move from 'might' towards 'right', that is, towards law-enforcement and protection. The shift from an 'army' to 'police' at the same time implies a dispersion of competences: in addition to the national police (including national armed forces), there will be not only local police but also international police forces (peacekeeping forces, European police forces, environmental police, etc.). The monopoly of the nation state over collective violence is in jeopardy.

We seem to be entering a more 'pluralist' world, with a patchwork of authorities. The state will remain, but the concept of 'sovereignty' seems less and less suited to describe its essence. Rather than facing the 'end of history', we seem to be approaching the 'end of sovereignty'.[72]

NOTES

1. The Permanent Court of International Justice noted in an advisory opinion of 1923 that sovereignty is an 'essentially relative question'. (Nationality Decrees in Tunis and Morocco, *Permanent Court of International Justice*, Ser. B., no. 4(1923), p. 24. See also Martti Koskenniemi, The Future of Statehood. *Harvard International Law Journal,* vol. 32, no. 2/1991, p. 408.
2. Markku Suksi makes a distinction between three forms of sovereignty: sovereignty of the state, sovereignty of the nation and sovereignty of the people. Suksi's typology focuses on the 'internal' sovereignty (on the distinction between 'external' and 'internal' sovereignty, see note 34). (M. Suksi, *Referendum and National Decision-making: A Study of Constitutional Form and Practice* (unpublished dissertation, University of Michigan Law School, 1992), pp. 51, 54–68)
3. *Black's Law Dictionary: Definitions of the Terms and Phrases of American and English Jurisprudence, Ancient and Modern,* 5th edition. (StPaul: West Publishing Company, 1979), p. 1252.
4. H. Steinberger, Sovereignty; in R. Bernhardt (ed.), *Encyclopedia of Public International Law,* Instalment 10 (1987), p. 399.
5. See Juha Tolonen, Stat och rätt. En studie över lagbegreppet. *Meddelanden från Stiftelsen för Åbo Akademi forskningsinstitut,* no. 111/1986, pp. 8–37.
6. Martti Koskenniemi, *From Apology to Utopia: The Structure of International Legal Argument* (Helsinki: Finnish Lawyers' Publishing Company, 1989), pp. 73–98.
7. Joseph A. Camilleri and Jim Falk, *The End of Sovereignty? The Politics of a Shrinking and Fragmenting World* (Aldershot: Edward Elgar, 1992), p. 142.
8. G. Poggi, *The Development of the Modern State: A Sociological Introduction* (London: Hutchinson, 1978), p. 92.
9. According to Jean Bodin, the making of war and peace is 'one of the most important rights of sovereignty, since it brings in its train either the ruin or the salvation of the state' (Jean Bodin, *Six Books of the Commonwealth.* Oxford: Basil Blackwell, 1967, p. 44).

10. On the distinction between 'nation' and 'people' in the expressions of popular sovereignty in the French revolutionary acts, see Allan Rosas, Democracy and Human Rights; in A. Rosas and J. Helgesen (eds), *Human Rights in a Changing East–West Perspective* (London: Pinter Publishers, 1990), p. 19.
11. W. R. Bisschop has observed that 'the loss of territory is more serious than the loss of citizens, who can follow their own will, and be replaced by others' and, with respect to international cessions of territory, that 'the fate of the population has usually been taken as a matter of secondary importance, if it carried any weight at all'. (W. R. Bisschop, *Sovereignty*. The British Yearbook of International Law, vol. 2 (1921–1922), p. 132.)
12. Allan Rosas, International Legitimacy of Governments; in G. Alfredsson and P. Macalister-Smith (eds), *The Living Law of Nations. Essays in Memory of Atle Grahl-Madsen* (Kehl am Rhein: N. P. Engel, forthcoming) and C. Tomuschat, Democratic Pluralism: The Right to Political Opposition; in A. Rosas and J. Helgesen (eds), *The Strength of Diversity: Human Rights and Pluralist Democracy* (Dordrecht: Martinus Nijhoff, 1992), pp. 40–1.
13. Rosas, 1990, pp. 23–4.
14. H. van Maarseveen and G. van der Tang, *Written Constitutions: A Computerized Comparative Study* (Dobbs Ferry and Alphen aan den Rijn: Oceana Publications/Sijthoff & Nordhoff, 1978), p. 113.
15. Hans Kelsen and Robert Tucker speak of the state as a 'centralized legal order' and stress in this context the importance of the 'centralization of the use of force' or the 'centralization of the execution of sanctions'. (Hans Kelsen and Robert W. Tucker, *Principles of International Law*, 2nd edition. New York: Holt, Rinehart and Winston, 1967, pp. 182-4)
16. Koskenniemi, 1989, pp. 209–10.
17. R. H. Jackson, *Quasi-states: Sovereignty, International Relations, and the Third World* (Cambridge: Cambridge University Press, 1990), p. 32.
18. This interpretation was advanced at the San Francisco Conference of 1945 (Bengt Broms, *The United Nations*. Helsinki: Suomalainen Tiedeakatemia, 1990, pp. 145–8). Compare Hans Kelsen, *The Law of the United Nations: A Critical Analysis of Its Fundamental Problems* (New York: Praeger Publishers, 1951), pp. 122–35, who dissociates himself from this interpretation.
19. According to the Soviet Constitution of 1977, Union Republics retained 'the right to secede freely from the USSR' (article 72), which could be seen in the light of their 'sovereign rights', safeguarded by the Union (Article 81). However, the territory of the USSR was declared to be 'a single entity' and the 'sovereignty of the USSR' was said to extend throughout its territory (Article 75). Moreover, there was no constitutional clause on procedure in case of secession. When faced with aspirations for independence especially in the Baltic Republics, central government tried to assert its powers to regulate this matter by enacting a law on procedures for secession on 3 April 1990. This law would have made secession virtually impossible without consent from Moscow. (A.

P. Blaustein and G. H. Flanz, *Constitutions of the Countries of the World*. Dobbs Ferry: Oceana Publications, 1990, p. xvii.) In analyzing the rights of the Union Republics under the 1977 Constitution, one also has to take into account the centralized powers of the Soviet Communist Party, which according to Article 6 of the Constitution was 'the leading and guiding force of Soviet society and the nucleus of its political system, of all state and public organizations'.

20. This is not to deny that there have been differing views on the concept of confederation (*Staatenbund*) and the distinction between con-federations and federations (*Bundesstaat*). For an overview of the classical discussion, see e.g. P. Laband, *Das Staatsrecht des deutschen Reiches*. Vierte neubearbeitete Auflage. (Tübingen und Leipzig: J. C. B. Mohr, 1901, vol. I, pp. 51ff.)
21. E. Krippendorff, *Staat und Krieg. Die historische Logik politischer Unvernunft* (Frankfurt am Main: Suhrkamp, 1985), p. 301.
22. Jean-Jacques Rousseau, *Contrat social ou principes du droit politique, précédé de discours, lettre à d'Alembert sur les spectacles, etc., etc.* (Paris: Garnier Frères, Libraires-Éditeurs, no year), pp. 244–5.
23. Allan Rosas, in collaboration with P. Stenbäck, The Frontiers of International Humanitarian Law. *Journal of Peace Research*, vol. 24, no. 3/1987, pp. 219ff.
24. On this, see, generally, Ian Brownlie, *International Law and the Use of Force by States* (Oxford: Clarendon Press, 1963) and Yoram Dinstein, *War, Aggression and Self-Defence* (Cambridge: Grotius Publications, 1988).
25. For an overview, see Louis Henkin, Stanley Hoffman, Jeane J. Kirkpatrick, Allan Gerson, William D. Rogers and David J. Schefer, *Right vs. Might: International Law and the Use of Force* (New York: Council of Foreign Relations Press, 1989); see also Agora, a discussion on the US intervention in Panama; in *American Journal of International Law*, vol. 84, no. 3/1990, pp. 494–524.
26. See, in particular, UN Security Council resolutions 660 (1990), 661 (1990), 665 (1990), 670 (1990) and 678 (1990) and O. Schachter, United Nations Law in the Gulf Conflict. *American Journal of International Law*, vol. 85, no. 3/1991, pp. 452ff.
27. See, in particular, M. W. Doyle, Kant, Liberal Legacies, and Foreign Affairs. *Philosophy & Public Affairs*, vol. 12, no. 3/1983, pp. 205–35 and no. 4/ 1983, pp. 322–53. For recent comments, see, e.g., Francis Fukuyama, *The End of History and the Last Man* (London: Hamish Hamilton, 1992), pp. 262–4 and T. Franck, The Emerging Right to Democratic Governance. *American Journal of International Law*, vol. 86, no. 1/1992, p. 88.
28. For an overview of relevant treaties and arrangements, see, e.g., G. Lysén, *The International Regulation of Armaments: The Law of Disarmament* (Uppsala: Iustus Förlag, 1990) and J. Dahlitz and D. Dicke (eds), *The International Law of Arms Control and Disarmament*. Proceedings of the Symposium in Geneva, 28 February–2 March 1991 (New York: United Nations, 1991).
29. UN Security Council Resolution 687 (1991).

30. L. Hannikainen, R. Hanski and A. Rosas, *Implementing Humanitarian Law Applicable in Armed Conflicts: The Case of Finland* (Dordrecht: Martinus Nijhoff, 1992), pp. 27–31.
31. Common Article 3 of the four Geneva Conventions for the protection of war victims of 1949 and the Additional Protocol II of 1977. See also Rosas and Stenbäck, op. cit., p. 224.
32. See the UN Convention against Torture and Other Cruel, Inhuman or Degrading Treatment or Punishment of 1984, the Inter-American Convention to Prevent and Punish Torture of 1985 and the European Convention for the Prevention of Torture and Inhuman or Degrading Treatment or Punishment of 1987. In addition, the prohibition of torture is included in the general human rights conventions, such as the International Covenant on Civil and Political Rights of 1966 and the European Convention on Human Rights of 1950.
33. Allan Rosas, Human Rights at Risk in Situations of Internal Violence and Public Emergency: Towards Common Minimum Standards; in A. Eide and J. Helgesen (eds), *The Future of Human Rights Protection in a Changing World: Fifty Years since the Four Freedoms Address. Essays in Honour of Torkel Opsahl* (Oslo: Norwegian University Press, 1991), pp. 165–81.
34. Rosas, 1990, pp. 23–33, with references. See also Franck, op. cit., pp. 52–60. Compare Tomuschat, op. cit., who is sceptical about the existence of a right to 'internal' self-determination.
35. See Article 25 of the International Covenant on Civil and Political Rights, Article 3 of Protocol no. 1 of the European Convention on Human Rights, Article 23 of the American Convention on Human Rights of 1969 and Article 13 of the African Charter on Human and Peoples' Rights of 1981; Rosas, 1990 and Allan Rosas, Article 21; in A. Eide *et al.* (eds), *The Universal Declaration of Human Rights: A Commentary* (Oslo: Scandinavian University Press, 1992), pp. 299–317.
36. F. R. Teson, *Humanitarian Intervention: An Inquiry into Law and Morality* (Dobbs Ferry: Transnational Publishers, 1988), p. 79.
37. Franck, op. cit., pp. 46–9, 63–9; Rosas, International Legitimacy of Governments; in Tomuschat, op. cit., pp. 40–4.
38. Security Council Resolutions 216 (1965), 217 (1965), 221 (1966), 232 (1966) and 253 (1968). See also V. Gowlland-Debbas, *Collective Responses to Illegal Acts in International Law: United Nations Action in the Question of Southern Rhodesia* (Dordrecht: Martinus Nijhoff, 1990), pp. 365–486.
39. Quoted from Franck, op. cit., pp. 65–6.
40. See also Teson, op. cit., p. 156.
41. See Memorandum of Understanding between Iraq and the UN, signed on 18 April 1991, with an Annex of 18 May, 30 International Legal Materials 860 (1991). See also Schachter, op. cit., pp. 468–9.
42. Resolutions 713 (1991), 721 (1991), 724 (1991), 727 (1992), 740 (1992), 743 (1992), 747 (1992), 752 (1992), 757 (1992), 758 (1992), 760 (1992), 761 (1992), 762 (1992), 764 (1992), 769 (1992), 770 (1992), 771 (1992), 779 (1992) and 780 (1992) concerning Yugoslavia

and resolutions 733 (1992) and 746 (1992) concerning Somalia.

43. Schachter, op. cit., p. 468. In the case of Southern Rhodesia, on the other hand, the UN Security Council, in resolution 253 (1968), called upon the United Kingdom 'to take urgently all effective measures to bring to an end the rebellion' (cf. note 38).
44. Rosas, 1990, p. 35.
45. Guidelines on the recognition of new states in Eastern Europe and in the Soviet Union, adopted on 16 December 1991, UN doc. S/23293, Annex II, p. 4. See also Tomuschat, op. cit., p. 41.
46. Koskenniemi, 1989, pp. 342–421.
47. I. Detter, *Law Making by International Organizations* (Stockholm: P. A. Norstedt & Söners Förlag, 1965).
48. L. Condorelli, *Commentaire de l'art. 1 du Protocole additionel; manuscript for Commentaire de la Convention européenne des droits de l'homme* (forthcoming).
49. This means that general international law does not require states to adopt a system of monism, with primacy being given to international law (on monism, with primacy either of national or of international law, see, e.g., Kelsen and Tucker, op. cit., pp. 578ff).
50. R. Hofmann, Germany and an All-European System of Human Rights Protection; in Z. Kedzia, A. Korula and M. Nowak (eds), *Perspectives of an All-European System of Human Rights Protection. All-European Human Rights Yearbook* (Kehl am Rhein: N. P. Engel, 1991), vol. I, pp. 136–7.
51. For a recent and comprehensive discussion on the relationship between international law and domestic law, see Martin Scheinin, *Ihmisoikeudet Suomen oikeudessa* (Helsinki: Suomalaisen Lakimiesyhdistyksen julkaisuja, A-sarja, no. 189, 1991).
52. Camilleri and Falk, op. cit., p. 33.
53. Detter, op. cit., pp. 228–58 and H. Schermers, *International Institutional Law* (Alphen aan den Rijn: Sijthoff & Nordhoff, 1980), pp. 632–4.
54. P. J. G. Kapteyn and P. Verloren van Themaat, *Introduction to the Law of the European Communities,* 2nd edition (Deventer: Kluwer Law and Taxation Publishers, 1990), pp. 340–5.
55. Ibid., p. 40.
56. Kelsen, op. cit., pp. 727–31. Kelsen notes that 'it is completely within the discretion of the Security Council to decide what constitutes a threat to peace' (p. 727).
57. UN Security Council resolution 748 (1992). See also resolution 731 (1992).
58. Geoffrey Palmer, New Ways to Make International Environmental Law. *American Journal of International Law*, vol. 86, no. 2/1992, p. 282.
59. R. Hanski, A. Rosas and K. Stendahl, *Verification of Arms Control Agreements, with Special Reference to On-site Inspections* (Helsinki: ARNEK, no. A/10, 1991).
60. The Treaty on the Non-proliferation of Nuclear Weapons (NPT) of 1968, the Treaty on the Prohibition of Nuclear Weapons in Latin America (Treaty of Tratelolco) of 1967 and the South Pacific Nuclear

Free Zone Treaty (Treaty of Rarotonga) of 1985.
61. The CSCE Document of the Stockholm Conference on Confidence- and Security-Building Measures and Disarmament in Europe of 1986, the CSCE Document of the Negotiations on Confidence- and Security-Building Measures Convened in Accordance with the Relevant Provisions of the Concluding Document of the Vienna CSCE Meeting of 1990, the Treaty on Conventional Forces in Europe of 1990 and the Treaty on Open Skies of 1992.
62. They are listed in Hanski, Rosas and Stendahl, op. cit., Annex 1.3.
63. Allan Rosas, Human Rights Obligations: A Finnish Perspective; in Kezdia, Korula and Nowak (eds), op. cit., pp. 245–7.
64. K. Highet, The Peace Palace Heats Up: The World Court in Business Again? *American Journal of International Law*, vol. 85, no. 4/1991, p. 646.
65. See Chapter III, paras 57–72, of the Helsinki Decisions, adopted on 10 July 1992.
66. Stanley Hoffmann, Delusions of World Order. *The New York Review of Books*, vol. 34, no. 7 (April 9, 1992), p. 38.
67. See, e.g., Koskenniemi, 1991.
68. Lauri Hannikainen, *Peremptory Norms* (Jus Cogens) *in International Law: Historical Development, Criteria, Present Status* (Helsinki, Finnish Lawyers' Publishing Company, 1988).
69. Camilleri and Falk, op. cit., p. 5.
70. C. Tilly, War Making and State Making as Organized Crime; in P. B. Evans, D. Rueschenmeyer and T. Stocpol (eds), *Bringing the State Back In* (Cambridge: Cambridge University Press, 1985), p. 169.
71. Allan Rosas, Stat, statsmakt, statsförvaltning: några konstitutionella iaktagelser; in *Juhlajulkaisu Jaakko Pajula*. Osa 1: Ihminen ja yhteiskunta (Helsinki: Kansaneläkelaitos, 1989).
72. Fukuyama, op. cit.; Camilleri and Falk, op. cit.

10. TERRITORY, NATION STATE AND NATIONALISM

Raimo Väyrynen

1. INTRODUCTION

The connections between nationalism and territory cannot be meaningfully grasped without the concept of state. Nationalism has often been defined as being coextensive with the state. Thus, Elie Kedourie merges nationalism and state together and considers the doctrine of self-determination to be their common denominator. Together nationalism and self-determination define the national will which gives rise to a territorially defined state. Furthermore, Kedourie suggests that 'humanity is naturally divided into nations, that nations are known by certain characteristics which can be ascertained, and that the only legitimate type of government is national self-government'.[1]

This line of reasoning underlines the diversity of international relations. It is somewhat deceptive, however, as it accepts a rather simple idea of a nation. The fusion of the territorial state and the nation acknowledges only one special type of nationalism and forgets about other varieties. This is particularly the case with ethnic consciousness which is not necessarily grounded on shared territory.

In this connection, Hugh Seton-Watson speaks of the so-called *diaspora* nations, of which Jews, overseas Indians and overseas Chinese are the best-known examples.[2] Obviously, shared territory consolidates ethnic unity, but it is not a necessary precondition for its emergence.[3] In fact, a minority group can survive better if it is able to develop effectively other bonds and institutions than merely sharing a common territory.[4]

Among the overseas Chinese the dialect associations, formed on the basis of common geographical origin of immigrants, developed such institutional bonds. They were further divided into clan associations on the basis of a common surname. The immigrant Chinese penchant for institution building is epitomized by the *kongsi,* which could be, for example, a cooperative mining venture or a secret society. Such societies often developed into syndicates which controlled the life of immigrants. They were used, in turn, by the colonial authorities as a means of social control.[5]

Thus, national identities cannot be defined solely in the context of the nation state. It borders on triviality to point out that the state may embody more than one nation, while nations can exist without their own state. To define nation and state as coterminous imposes an unnecessarily static straitjacket on the dynamic diversity and complexity of real life. The nation states have been formed in a variety of ways. Smaller units have been aggregated by the process of nation-building into more encompassing entities, or multinational empires have been dissolved into nation states. In a way, one may speak, especially in the nineteenth and twentieth centuries, of a certain process of historical converge towards the nation state pattern.

A critical difference is whether the nation created the state or vice versa, or whether the nation and the state emerged in tandem. Anthony D. Smith has suggested that in the Western pattern state and nation emerged together and were consolidated around an ethnic core to which other groups and communities were attached. The two other possibilities are, respectively, the ethnic and the immigrant pattern.

In the former pattern, the fullyfledged ethnic nation upgrades itself into statehood. Norwegian independence in 1905 and Finnish independence in 1917 are examples of this pattern. In the immigrant pattern, the existing nation with a state absorbs various immigrant cultures into a territorial nation state. The Swedish experience after the Second World War provides an example of this pattern.[6]

There seems to be also a fourth pattern, in which various language and religious groups, none of them being a fully-fledged core group, grow together into one nation without destroying the individual culture of any of them. The Swiss case provides an example of such an equitable fusion into a nation state.[7] This development may have been possible only because of the decentralized character of the Swiss state which assures the autonomy of all the key groups.

The nation states may be demarcated either by ethnic or historical boundaries. In the former case, the effort focuses on the inclusion of the members of a given ethnic group within the boundaries, and the exclusion of others. In the latter case, the boundaries are drawn on the basis of historical criteria without giving any priority to the ethnic factor.[8] The demarcation of ethnic boundaries can happen peacefully, for example by elections. As the recent experiences in Yugoslavia suggest, however, the demarcation of ethnic boundaries may lead to ethnic 'cleansing' and to efforts to establish a 'canton system' for the minorities, to preserve purity.

The implementation of historic boundary principles can also lead to violence. It may dismember some traditional ethnic groups and thus foster confrontation, and it may catalyze old territorial disputes between different national groups. In fact, there is a constant tension between ethnic and historic boundary principles. The case of Ulster shows vividly how destructive the continuing conflict between these two sets of principles can be.[9]

A pertinent issue in the formation of territorial nation states is the relationship between the core and periphery areas. The material core areas are those which have communication networks. If they overlap with the ethnic cores, the resulting political structure is centralized, but probably solid. The nature and potential of resistance against this structure depends on whether the periphery is inhabited by the same or a different ethnic group. In the former case, the resulting conflict is more social in nature, while in the latter the ethnic divide may dominate and the territorial factor apparently gains a greater relative weight.

In Finland the state contributed decisively to the emergence of the nation and its nationalism. In the latter half of the nineteenth century the Fennoman upper class strove to strengthen the state and to integrate other social classes into the national culture and the collectivist political agreement. In Eastern Europe, nationalist groups came more often than in Finland from among the peasants and the middle class.[10]

The Norwegian case has similarities with the Finnish one, although the role of the state has been less pivotal. In Norway the nationalist cultural and political programme, opposing both the Danish and Swedish influences, gave rise to the nation rather than vice versa. Nationalism was carried by the liberal urban upper class which consolidated both the state institutions and the economic infrastructure of the country.[11] The lesser role of the state in Norway may explain, in part, why the territorial divisions have been stronger there than in Finland, where the overarching collectivism has weakened geographical cleavages.

The Finnish and Norwegian examples provide yet more evidence of the fact that the 'patriotic nation state card is held most firmly by dominant-class parties', while the non-state national movements derive their support from a broader class basis.[12] Initially, the nationalist programmes are fuelled by the elite groups, which then start disseminating their ideas to the common people in order to mobilize them to support the upper-class politics.

2. TERRITORY AND NATIONALISM

The preceding analysis shows that nationalism is often discussed in its ethnic, linguistic or historical context. This does not exhaust the theme, however. On the contrary, there is hardly any common approach to the study of nationalism. Instead, 'nation and nationalism are cognitive artefacts we invent to mark off an intellectual universe'. In that sense nationalism is a form of political rationalization which is used for a variety of political purposes.[13]

Debates on nationalism appear to be divided into two branches. In one of them, nationalism is linked with the ascribed characteristics and sentiments of individual people. In other words, territoriality and nationalism are not necessarily associated with each other. There are scholarly exercises in which nationalism and national integration are discussed without any explicit reference to their territorial dimension.[14]

This seems also to be the line followed by Ernest B. Haas, who defines nationalism as 'a belief held by a group of people that they ought to constitute a nation, or that they already are one'. Such a group is a nation if it wants to practice self-determination.[15] In his own definitions Haas scarcely mentions the state, and even less the territory. In so doing Haas seems to opt for, to use his own terms, the revolutionary national ideology which seeks to get rid of the traditional values and accepts the present territory held by the national body. On the other hand, syncretist national ideologies seek to retain the traditional values or, at most, to modify them. Such ideologies consider, as a rule, the territory held by the present state to belong properly to the nation.[16]

On this basis one can make a distinction between two types of nationalism and nationalistic ideologies. One of them bases its rationalization on ethnic homogeneity or class solidarity, and the other on the link between the nation and the state. The latter approach pays more attention to territory and is, partly for this reason, often considered more regressive. Historically, the consolidation of the nation state has, indeed, often been interpreted as winning control by a national group over a delineated geographical area.

Later on, territoriality has been conceptualized in broader terms, but its intimate relationship with the national political organization and nationalism has been accepted. The territorial aspect is, to use Peter J. Taylor's terms, most pronounced in state nationalism, unification nationalism and separation nationalism, while it is relatively less visible in liberation nationalism and renewal nationalism.[17]

The state-oriented tradition has governed political geography, as can be seen in the thesis about the close connection between state sovereignty, nationalism and territory. Recently, political geography has started, however, to move 'beyond the state'.[18] It has increasingly emphasized the relevance of both local, regional and global factors and their interlinkages. The state is just one of the many institutions which operate in subnational, international and transnational relations. In fact, the territorial state is buttressed between local and global demands, and the territorial dimension of the world system is losing its relative significance.

Originally, the territorial dimension of nation- and state-building were interpreted in a concrete manner as the physical basis of their existence. Common territory provides the land which the members of the state or the nation inhabit and from which they derive their living. In this conception, held for instance by Friedrich Ratzel, there was an organic link between the land, the people and the state. The state has two aspects, the human and the physical; it is *ein Stück Menschheit und ein menschlisches Werk und zugleich ein Stück Erdoben.*[19] The human activity causes the territory to become differentiated and form a basis for territorial politics as well.

The organistic conception of the triad of territory, state and nation was gradually replaced by the nationalistic conception. Territory was regarded as a space to which ethnic groups or nations attached identity. The nation state is, of course, only one type of territorial unit to which identities can be attached, although it has emerged as the dominant form of politico-territorial entity.[20] A key issue in the nationalistic conception of territory is thus whether all the groups inhabiting it accept it as legitimate or whether they want to challenge it by secessionist policies.

Secessionist movements are usually organized from below by the people themselves and constitute a genuine counter-national challenge to the indivisibility of the nation state. Irredentism is another challenge to the nation state as it means a territorial claim made by one sovereign state to lands within another. Occasionally, the borderline between secession and irredentism can become blurred; the external power may fuel secessionist sentiments or the secessionist group may enlist outside support for its policies. Obviously secession is a major challenge to an international order based on the sovereign state as it can be supported by the doctrines of minority rights and national self-determination itself.[21]

The American experience is illustrative in this context.

The Republican coalition that captured the federal government in 1860 aimed at strengthening the central state and risked, for this reason, a confrontation with Southern separatism. The civil war followed and the North, having won it, extended the state-centred solution through the Reconstruction to the South. Territorial expansion, concentration of power and Northern nationalism advanced hand in hand.

In the Civil War, the dissociationist strategy of the North defeated the association of the South with '*King Cotton*' and the British textile industry. The ensuing American state formation was built on the mercantilist industrial programme of the North, the establishment of national markets and the consolidation of corporate power.[22] In fact, Northern mercantilism did not start from the Civil War, but its roots can be traced back to the early 1820s, when advocacy for the 'American System' started. This System was based on the balance of industrial and agricultural development and the internal improvement of communications behind a protective barrier. The Northern objective was the establishment of a national self-reliant power of political and economic consequence in North America.[23]

The American example is useful in hinting at the connection between national territorial expansion, state formation and capitalist development. Capitalism territorializes space as a precondition to modernity, to use Cooke's expression. First, the territory becomes national by the establishment of boundaries, and subsequently it is divided in segments and parcelled out internally as property. In this sense territory has both a political and an economic element, although the political one dominates. 'Territory is national; space is reformed as a *series* of territories, it is cut up into *segments* of different sizes and *parcelled* out internally as property according not to an economic but a political logic. Territory not only is, in the sense of belonging to, the national, it constitutes it.'[24]

The doctrine of sovereignty and the ideology of nationalism are intended to enhance the coherence of nation states. Muir has defined the nation as a 'form of human group whose members usually share a range of objective cultural characteristics, values and aspirations, and a close political association with a particular piece of territory'.[25] In his terminology, state refers to a particular form of organization of people and territory. On that basis, Muir suggests that 'a political-geographical approach to the state will involve the investigation of the spatial causes and effects of the relationship between people, territory and sovereign government'.[26]

Nationalism is a particular way of classifying people and associating them with a given piece of territory. The territorial state is a 'power container' used to govern people residing in that territory. As observed earlier, the relationship between territory and nation is complicated. A homogeneous nation may, for instance, be divided between several states, or political unity may be imposed on national and cultural heterogeneity.[27] In the former case, political leaders try to dilute supernationalism, if it has existed, and create a political association between the people and the territory inhabited by them. In the latter case, there will presumably be an effort to expand the scale of nationalism to capture the new territorial unit.

In both cases nationalism has a common feature; it is 'a mode of constructing and interpreting social space'. Such a process aims at the 'transformation of territory into an enduring political space'.[28] This presupposes a lasting relationship between the emotions and interests of the citizenry and the political territorial foundations of the state. A territory is obviously transformed into a political space when people feel loyalty to it and define and communicate to others their identity in terms of a given national territory.

Williams and Smith suggest that there are three secular trends that pertain to the reinterpretation of territory. The abstraction of land confers new philosophical, linguistic and political meanings to it and makes it compatible with cultural nationalism. The hardening of space can be seen in its increasingly intensive utilization for commercial and political power purposes. Politically, it may mean the centralization and bureaucratization of power and the elimination of power vacuums. The third trend is the physical or symbolic activation of the environment, the mobilization of land.[29] These trends are dynamic forces that occur on subnational, national and transnational scales and are associated with nationalism, which may encourage both territorial integration and fragmentation.

3. SPACE AND POLITICS

Territory and exchange are the principal constitutive elements of (inter)national relations. Implicit in the concept of territory is the recognition of the fact that the natural unity of space has been partitioned by political and cultural criteria. Territory is thus a compartment of space defined by social interests and intentions.[30] Territory can thus be conceptualized either in physical or social terms.

The physical definition emphasizes such natural features as seas, rivers, mountains and steppes as borders of a given country. The physical conceptualization of territory has often given rise to the political doctrine of natural frontiers. Thus, in France its historical expansion has been every now and then interpreted as a relentless advance to its *limites naturelles* located at the Channel, the Atlantic, the Rhine, the Alps and the Pyrenees. The doctrine of natural frontiers was associated with that of natural law; the defence of territory within such frontiers was legitimate, while expansion beyond them was an offence against natural law.

Natural frontiers were seldom used, however, as the justification of French expansionism during the monarchy. Only during the revolutionary period did the doctrine of natural frontiers assume political significance. Thus, it is misleading to regard it as the guiding principle of French foreign policy. Rather it was one of the justifications, in addition to language and historical associations, advanced to defend territorial annexations and consolidation.[31]

The physical definition includes both stable and dynamic factors. Stability is provided by 'iconography' that distinguishes a territorial unit physically and symbolically from its environment. Iconographs dissociate political-territorial units from each other and provide both psychological and material security. Yet the physical divisions of space should not be so impermeable that they disallow 'circulation', i.e., economic and social exchanges between political-territorial units.[32]

Economic and other functional exchanges are fundamental to the social definition of territory. The circulation process may be considered either as an exchange of values between territorially defined political entities or as a global system of exchanges in which territorial compartments are embedded. In the latter interpretation, the political compartments may shape the economic and social flows, but cannot steer them effectively. Instead, the economic forces create a system which has a dynamic of its own. This distinction is related to the well-known association between nationalism and mercantilism on the one hand and the struggle between liberal internationalism and nationalist aims on the other.[33]

In a more theoretical vein one may say that the same difference is reflected in the distinction Sack makes between territoriality and action by contact.[34] Action by contact is a non-territorial form of interaction, while territoriality is based on the idea of control exerted by a political organization over a given compartment of space. Both the state and the nation need a territorial basis to exist, but the criteria, ethnicity vs. sovereignty, by which they delineate the territory, differ. This difference imposes a tension on international relations which is manifested in secessionism, boundary conflicts and ethnic confrontations.[35]

The dynamics of exchange can be regulated only imperfectly by territorially based state structures. The tension between exchange and territorial control constitutes an important and, one may add, a creative element of international relations. The creativity is due to its capacity to foster change and to maintain a certain balance between capitalist expansion and political control. Ivo Duchacek describes the same relationship as occuring 'between the complex interdependence and the territorial fragmentation of humanity'.[36]

It has been suggested that human life can be described as an interaction between two opposite tendencies, those of opening and closing.[37] The process of opening refers to the integration of a social community with its environment such that new values are gained for the growth of the community. The process of closing aims at enhancing the internal coherence and collective identity by separating the community from its environment. It should be borne in mind that both opening, or association, and closing, or dissociation, are relational processes between a political-cultural unit and its spatial environment. Even closing does not take place in isolation; rather, the identities and characteristics of a territorial community are even then defined in relation to the environment.

This observation undergirds the key distinction between classification and communication as the main strategies of territorial control. Sack has defined territoriality as the 'attempt to affect, influence or control actions and interactions ... by asserting and attempting to control over a specific geographical area'.[38] Later on, he has refined the definition and suggested that territoriality is a 'strategy to establish differential access to people, things and relationships'.[39]

Thus, the regulation of access to different kinds of resources becomes a central feature of territoriality, especially when it is considered a strategy of political control. Regulation is based on the ability to define and to enforce the rules of entry which confer both rights and obligations and define the payments expected. In order to be effective, regulation requires political authority and material capabilities. Authority and resources can be derived either from the formal territorial organization or from the functional organization of social and economic exchanges.

An important task of formal territorial organizations has been to stabilize, for the sake of control, the dynamic functional organization of space 'into a system of rigid and clearly delineated areal units which in themselves would define the boundaries of society and polity'.[40] With the globalization of business operations such a delineation is becoming, however, increasingly difficult and even counterproductive. Instead, states are supposed to develop such competitive advantage that the 'national' companies can venture into successful international operations, and that international business can be tempted to establish itself in the country to strengthen its economic base.[41]

The formal control of social and economic action never yields static outcomes because of the 'destabilizing' impact of the functional organization. This hints at the primacy of non-territorial economic and social exchanges which are subsequently moulded, but not effectively controlled, by territorial political strategies. Ultimately, the duality of territorial control and functional exchange boils down to the distinction between political organization and the economic market, of which the market appears to gain in importance.

The economic interests and their carriers have a tendency to lose their sense of place and view the world market primarily from the vantage point of economic restructuring. In this process production is relocated on the basis of the expected financial returns and the optimal mix of production factors obtainable in each location. Indeed, the location decisions of transnational companies appear to depend more on the size and the growth potential of the market than on the political and economic risks involved.[42]

The global economic restructuring thus changes, as a part of the process of unequal development, the relative value of places in relation to each other. Such changes foster, in turn, local socio-political mobilization 'according to a local, place-oriented logic'.[43] Global capitalist dynamics and local place-specific politics are enmeshed with each other. As a consequence, the impact of global and national forces can be mediated by local actors and factors.[44]

This perspective suggests that although the nation state is usually viewed in a mercantilist light, it can also be integrated with the global and regional dynamics of capitalist development. Neil Smith sees the contradiction between equalization and differentiation as the fundamental factor in global development. The expansion of capital creates and reproduces spatial integration in which capital and wage labour become universal. Such a universalization of capitalist economic processes brings about the equalization of space as well as integration. Equalization of space under the impact of capitalism is, however, counteracted by the process of differentiation.[45]

Differentiation is promoted by political and cultural forces which seek their own identities and shares of power. In a sense, the capitalist state grows out of the process of capital expansion by 'nationalizing' and 'expropriating' a part, but only a part of it. In fact, both capitalism and nationalism are geared to mobilize and assimilate people and resources and to integrate peripheries with the centres.[46] In that sense, capitalism and nationalism are not antidotes to each other. This argument can even be taken as far as to claim that interstate relations, founded on competitive nationalisms, and the capitalist world economy, based on a global division of labour, are parts of the same interactive logic.[47]

The territorial strategy of control is a practical manifestation of the tendency towards the differentiation of space. The politics of cultural identity and specificity would be an equivalent strategy of action. The territorial strategy of control rests upon the twin operations of classification and communication.[48] Classification by territoriality relies on areas rather than on types. Such classification is based on enclosure in the sense that the limits of a given territory usually define also the right of social control and property rights. Territorial classification does not deal, in other words, with geographical properties *per se*, but rather with socio-spatial relationships that reflect the synthesis of political power and functional exchange.

The relevance of the classification process is due to its role in establishing physical or symbolic markers between the external and internal spheres of territorial action. These markers, usually called boundaries, have at least two functions. First, they are devices to regulate exchange between the units they separate. Second, the markers are signs communicated to other political-territorial units regarding the spheres of control.

Communication and classification are, in essence, practices of discriminating in-groups from out-groups and regulating access to resources and other valuables. Communication of markers to the out-groups can have both positive and negative consequences; positive when classification helps the unit to draw upon its own memory and resources, negative when it leads to the loss of pertinent information.[49] Economic, political and cultural isolation is thus a double-edged sword; over the short term it can have benefits, but over the long term it tends to lead to domestic rigidity and collusion of interests.

The territorial aspect of political control rests on the view that spatiality has a place-character. John A. Agnew has forcefully argued that most of modern social science has intellectually devalued the place, without sufficient justification.[50]

This contradicts the often held view that historically the territorial conception of the nation state has replaced an ethnically based view of it. The relevance of territory, this time in the geographic sense, has made an unbridled annexation of another state's area a move which is hard to justify, except perhaps by historical arguments about the traditional rights of property and access.[51]

Agnew suggests, however, that the nationalization thesis is an inadequate way of discovering place and that it has become both theoretically and empirically unwarranted.[52] Instead, place as a more comprehensive notion has continued relevance in the study of society and its transformation. Although physical characteristics of place matter, any spatial explanation is insufficient without the notions of social control and intentionality.

Both Sack's theory of territoriality and Giddens' theory of structuration consider the place-character of society. In Giddens' theory, locales refer to settings of interaction which are defined jointly by territorial and socio-economic criteria. Locales are situated, in turn, in the broader contexts of social institutions and processes which tend to regionalize the locales. Locales are differentiated from their environment either by the boundaries, i.e., by physical or symbolic markers, or by the hierarchical nature of the social environment. In spatial terms, locales may be situated either in the front regions or in the back regions. This distinction leads, in fact, to the conception of a centre–periphery structure. The regionalization of locales means that they are differently exposed to the processes of enclosure and disclosure.[53]

The distinction between spatial and social criteria is at the focus of Rokkan's and Urwin's conception of the centre–periphery structure. Its horizontal dimension refers to the geographical distinction between the centre and the outlying periphery. In the vertical dimension, space is defined as the 'totality of a system of interaction, within which the center consists of a set of key decision makers, while the periphery is composed of those sets of participants who have the least influence upon the central group and upon the making of decisions'. The centre–periphery relationship is characterized both by geographical and social distance and differences as well as the penetration of the periphery by the centre. In this context one can make a distinction between 'boundary-opening' and 'boundary-strengthening' groups that are active in the centre–periphery structure.[54]

4. POLITICAL SPACE AND ECONOMIC INTEGRATION

The territorial notions reviewed and synthesized above can be put to the test of practice if we explore their ability to describe the process of economic integration between the EC and EFTA countries, in particular Norway and Finland. The development of these two countries can be primarily accounted for by the nationalization thesis; they were converted in the beginning of the twentieth century from politically subordinated positions into fullyfledged national states. After having gained independence in 1905 and 1917, respectively, they were classified as sovereign states. This characteristic was communicated by a variety of ways to other independent political units.

The internal centre–periphery structure has been quite visible in both Finland and Norway. The consolidation of the national state calls for both social and spatial equalization by means of resource transfers. These strategies of equalization have been antidotes to the process of economic differentiation. Equalization has been forced on these countries by the European-wide centre–periphery structure and the process of economic integration occuring within it. Within nations, the back regions have been distanced from the front regions, but the resources of the latter have been used to compensate for the losses of the periphery in an effort to preserve spatial and national unity. Thus, the so-called regional policy has served national objectives as well.

The national development of Finland and Norway has presupposed a measure of economic and political-cultural closure by which the process of differentiation has been alleviated. Dieter Senghaas portrays both Finland and Norway as examples of countries which have followed an associative–dissociative path of development. They have relied initially on the export of unprocessed staple goods, but have been gradually able to enhance the degree of processing and to diversify their economy and exports. In that way, Finland and Norway have developed rather coherent and advanced economies and have avoided the status of a dependent periphery.[55]

The associative–dissociative strategy has, as its name suggests, combined the processes of opening and closure. On the one hand, access has been granted to transnational capital, but on the other hand, it has been regulated as well. Otherwise the international market forces would have hardened and mobilized the land against the national and local preferences. They have rather favoured the abstraction of land into a homeland as a central ingredient of the local and national identity. Nationalism has obviously been an important factor both in Finland and in Norway in keeping the elongated territories as coherent political entities.

The economic size of Finland and Norway is too small to permit economic closure and protectionist arrangements over the long term. That is why the opening of their economies was started in the 1950s, though more slowly and partially in Finland than in Norway. It occurred initially by means of free trade which was first promoted through EFTA and subsequently expanded, in the early 1970s, to the EC region. The probable ratification of the agreement on the European Economic Space (EES) between EFTA and the EC in 1993 will make the intensity of integration much deeper, as it will lead to the free flow of capital, services and people in addition to commodities.

The implementation of these 'four freedoms' means that the ability of nation states to apply territorial control over the access of foreign interests will be significantly limited. In free-trade integration only tariffs and quotas have been forbidden, while other methods to control entry have been possible. This has permitted the preservation of a relatively large closed economic sector, primarily in agriculture, fishing and in industries processing their products. In effect, the closed sector in the Finnish and Norwegian economies is a carry-over from the earlier period in which they were based on the exports of staple goods to the world market.

With the EES arrangement the strategy of controlling

entry quite strictly becomes impossible to continue. The nation's economy will be gradually restructured and integrated into West European centres of power. This tendency becomes even more pronounced if Finland and Norway become full members of the EC, possibly during the second half of the 1990s. The EES agreement still permits the closure of the agricultural sector, while within the EC membership it is integrated with the Community's Common Agricultural Policy. The EES agreement already covers fisheries. This explains the tortuous negotiations between Norway and the EC on the rights of access to the fishing areas and to the markets for fish products.

A basic objective in the present phase of EC–EFTA integration is to standardize the rules of entry: all individuals and companies should have the same rights of operation in the entire EES. The rules of reciprocity and non-discrimination mean that, if seriously taken and unequivocally implemented, the entire EES market will be a homogeneous and uniform commercial space. Agriculture will be the only significant exception. The agreement on and the implementation of new rules and procedures in the EES means that it is evolving into a regime in which the actor's freedom of choice is significantly curtailed. This concerns in particular the members of EFTA.[56]

As a consequence, the weight of national issues and interests in the economic and political decision-making will decline. This has created a counter-reaction, not so much against the EES arrangement as against EC membership. The anti-EC attitude has been much stronger in Norway than in Finland. In an opinion survey carried out in August 1992 precisely one half of the Finns were in favour of their country's membership in the Community, while 31 per cent objected. In Norway, the corresponding figures were 38 and 42 per cent, respectively.

This difference can be explained by at least two factors. First, the Norwegians have a history of taking a critical stand towards EC membership, as they rejected the application for it in the 1972 referendum. Another explanation is associated with the different territorial character of Finland and Norway. The centre–periphery differences foster anti-EC opposition in both countries; it is stronger in the rural areas and in the central and northern parts. Yet the centre–periphery structure is more pronounced, at least mentally, in Norway.

This structure seems to account for the stronger opposition to the EC in Norway. It is genuinely feared that the Community will tear down the barriers of entry to the traditional Norwegian territory, and mobilize and harden it for alien purposes. Such a reaction exists also in Finland, but there the territorial counter-reaction is not deep-rooted.

NOTES

1. Elie Kedourie, *Nationalism* (New York: Praeger, 1961), p. 9.
2. Hugh Seton-Watson, *Nations and States. An Enquiry into the Origins of Nations and the Politics of Nationalism* (Boulder: Westview, 1977), pp. 383–415; cf. Ernest Gellner, *Nations and Nationalism* (Ithaca: Cornell University Press, 1983), pp. 101–9.
3. Peter M. Slowe, *Geography and Political Power. The Geography of Nations and States* (London: Routledge, 1990), pp. 88–91.
4. C. H. Williams, Minority Groups in Modern State; in Michael Pacione (ed.), *Progress in Political Geography* (London: Croom Helm, 1985), pp. 130–4.
5. Lynn Pan, *Sons of the Yellow Emperor. The Story of the Overseas Chinese* (London: Mandarin, 1991), pp. 37–8, 112–17.
6. See Anthony D. Smith, State-Making and Nation-Building; in John A. Hall (ed.), *States in History* (Oxford: Basil Blackwell, 1986), pp. 240–3.
7. Seton-Watson, op. cit., pp. 75–7.
8. John Coakley, National Territories and Cultural Frontiers: Conflicts of Principle in the Formation of States in Europe; in Malcolm Anderson (ed.), *Frontier Regions in Western Europe* (London: Frank Cass, 1983), pp. 36–43.
9. Ibid., pp. 43–6.
10. Risto Alapuro ja Henrik Stenius, Kansanliikkeet loivat kansakunnan; in Risto Alapuro et al. (ed.), *Kansa liikkeessä* (Helsinki: Kirjayhtymä, 1987), pp. 12–17.
11. Öyvind Österud, *Det moderne statssystem og andere politisk-historiske studier* (Oslo: Gyldendal Norsk Forlag, 1987), pp. 50–8.
12. Philip Cooke, Nation, Space and Modernity; in Richard Peet and Nigel Thrift (eds), *New Models in Geography. The Political-Economy Perspective* (Boston: Unwin Hyman, 1991), p. 278.
13. Ernst B. Haas, What Is Nationalism and Why Should We Study It? *International Organization*, vol. 40, no. 3, pp. 708–11.
14. See e.g. Anthony H. Birch, *Nationalism and National Integration* (London: Unwin Hyman, 1989).
15. Haas, op. cit., pp. 726–7.
16. Ibid., pp. 727–34.

17. Peter J. Taylor, *Political Geography. World-Economy, Nation-State and Locality* (London: Longman, 1985), pp. 128–32.
18. Peter J. Taylor, Political Geography within World-System Analysis. *Review*, vol. 14, no. 3, Summer 1991, pp. 397-400.
19. 'The state is a piece of mankind and a human product and at the same time a piece of the surface of the Earth.' (Friedrich Ratzel, *Der Staat und sein Boden geographisch betrachtet*. Leipzig: S. Hirzel, 1896, p. 18.)
20. See David B. Knight, Identity and Territory: Geographical Perspectives on Nationalism and Regionalism. *Annals of the American Association of Geographers*, vol. 72, no. 4.
21. James Mayall, *Nationalism and International Society* (Cambridge: Cambridge University Press, 1990), pp. 57–63.
22. See Robert O. Keohane, Associative American Development, 1776–1860: Economic Growth and Political Disintegration; in John Gerard Ruggie (ed.), *The Antinomies of Interdependence. National Welfare and the International Division of Labor* (New York: Columbia University Press, 1983), pp. 43–90 and Richard Franklin Bensel, *Yankee Leviathan. The Origins of Central State Authority in America, 1859–1877* (Cambridge: Cambridge University Press, 1990).
23. J. Ann Tickner, *Self-Reliance versus Power Politics. The American and Indian Experiences in Building Nation States* (New York: Columbia University Press, 1987), pp. 123–32.
24. Cooke, op. cit., pp. 275–6 (italics in the original).
25. Richard Muir, *Modern Political Geography* (London: Macmillan, 1981), p. 84.
26. Ibid., p. 81.
27. Ivo Duchacek, *The Territorial Dimension of Politics: Within, Among and Across Nations* (Boulder: Westview Press, 1986), pp. 9–13.
28. C. H. Williams and A. D. Smith, The National Construction of Social Space. *Progress in Human Geography*, vol. 7, no. 42/1983, pp. 502–3.
29. Williams and Smith, op. cit., pp. 512–4; Anthony D. Smith, States and Homelands: the Social and Geopolitical Implications of National Territory. *Millennium*, vol. 10, no. 3/1981, pp. 198–200.
30. Claude Raffestin, *Pour une geographie du pouvoir* (Paris: Librairies Techniques, 1980), pp. 129–31, 143–7.
31. See Norman J. G. Pounds, France and 'les limites naturelles' from the Seventeenth to the Twentieth Centuries. *Annals of the Association of American Geographers*, vol. 44, no. 1/1954, pp. 52–62; Fernand Braudel, *L'Identité de la France. Escape et histoire* (Paris: Arthaud-Flammarion, 1986), pp. 287–92.
32. On the concepts, see Jean Gottman, *La Politique des états et leur geographie* (Paris: Librairie Armand Collin, 1952).
33. Mayall, op. cit., pp. 70–87.
34. Robert D. Sack, Territorial Bases of Power; in Alan D. Burnett and Peter J. Taylor (eds), *Political Studies from Spatial Perspectives* (New York: John Wiley, 1981), pp. 53–71.
35. Smith, 1981, pp. 187–8.

36. Duchacek, op. cit., p. xiii.
37. Orrin Edgar Klapp, *Opening and Closing. Strategies of Information Adaptation in Society.* (Cambridge: Cambridge University Press, 1978).
38. Sack, 1981, p. 5.
39. Robert D. Sack, Human Territoriality. A Theory. *Annals of the Association of the American Geographers*, vol. 73, no. 1/1983, p. 56; see also Taylor, 1985, pp. 106–11.
40. Edward W. Soja, A Paradigm for the Geographical Analysis of Political Systems; in Kewin R. Cox, David R. Reynolds and Stein Rokkan (eds), *Locational Approaches to Power and Conflict* (New York: John Wiley, 1974), pp. 61–4.
41. See Michael E. Porter, *The Competitive Advantage of Nations* (New York: The Free Press, 1990).
42. John Stopford and Susan Strange, *Rival States, Rival Firms. Competition for World Market Shares* (Cambridge: Cambridge University Press, 1991), pp. 142–4.
43. Manuel Castells and Jeffrey Henderson, Techno-Economic Restructuring, Socio-Political Processes and Spatial Transformation: A Global Perspective; in Jeffrey Henderson and Manuel Castells (eds), *Global Restructuring and Territorial Development* (London: Sage, 1988), pp. 7–8.
44. John A. Agnew, *Place and Politics. The Geographical Mediation of State and Society* (Boston: Allen & Unwin, 1987), pp. 32–3.
45. See Neil Smith, *Uneven Development: Nature, Capital and the Production of Space* (Oxford: Basil Blackwell, 1984).
46. Karl W. Deutsch, *Nationalism and Social Communication. An Inquiry into the Foundations of Nationality* (Cambridge Mass.: The MIT Press, 1966).
47. Christopher Chase-Dunn, *Global Formation. Structures of the World-Economy* (Oxford: Basil Blackwell, 1991), pp. 131–50.
48. Sack, 1981, pp. 63–9; Sack, 1983, pp. 58–60.
49. Klapp, op. cit., pp. 156–8.
50. Agnew, op. cit.
51. Alexander B. Murphy, Territorial Ideology and International Conflict: The Legacy of Prior Political Formations; in Nurit Kliot and Stanley Waterman (eds), *The Political Geography of Conflict and Peace* (London: Belhaven Press, 1991), pp. 126–41.
52. Agnew, op. cit.
53. Anthony Giddens, *The Constitution of Society. Outline of a Theory of Structuration* (Berkeley: University of California Press, 1984), pp. 110–44.
54. Stein Rokkan and Derek Urwin, *Economy, Territory, Identity. Politics of West European Peripheries* (London: Sage, 1983), pp. 2–5.
55. Dieter Senghaas, *Von Europa lernen. Entwicklungsgeschichtliche Betrachtungen* (Frankfurt am Main: Suhrkamp, 1982), pp. 48–50, 114–26.
56. Finn Laursen, The Community's Policy Towards EFTA: A Regime Formation in the European Economic Space (EES). *The Journal of Common Market Studies*, vol. 28, no. 4/1990, pp. 303–25.

Part IV

REGIONAL PROCESSES

11. GERMAN NATIONAL CONSCIOUSNESS AND THE NATION STATE

Thomas R. Henschel

1. THE GERMAN QUESTION

'The German question will remain open as long as the Brandenburger Tor is closed.' This formula, created at the beginning of the 1980s, gave an accurate description of the divided German nation. One might have thought that with the opening of the Brandenburger Tor in Berlin the German question would have come to an end. But as it turns out, the German question seems to be like a never-ending story. It is a question that has always had two dimensions. 'How to unify Germany into one single state?' And: 'What will be the role of a united Germany in Europe and the world?' The first dimension has already been answered: Germany is now unified into one single state. But the second dimension is still unclear. It is not yet obvious how the united Germany will use her growing responsibility and importance in the world.

One single German state with a non-democratic system was twice in the twentieth century a powerful threat to her neighbours and the world. Fears about a united and powerful Germany still remained. Despite the rise of right-wing political parties across Europe, an electoral breakthrough by German extremists in regional elections since 1992 has sparked a particularly acute angst both in Germany and around the continent. Politicians argued that the high vote for right–wing extremists had been a protest against the inability of the main parties to tackle the important issues facing the country – particularly the problem of the ever-rising number of refugees.[1] However, it is questionable if this is the whole truth. According to studies on voting behaviour, the rise of the political right to become the third largest party in two state parliaments is no one-time phenomenon but part of a structural change in European politics, and a continuation of a trend already visible before the collapse of communism in 1989.

It is half a century since the Second World War. Post-war reconstruction of a Europe divided into East and West disappeared with the end of the Cold War, and world history has been set in motion with Europe as its driving force. The change has seized the whole continent. An historical epoch has ended and a new age of world politics has begun, with uncertain contours and structures, with new risks and conflicts, with hitherto unrealized demands on the political and intellectual abilities of Europeans.

2. RETURN TO EUROPE

The decline of the Occident has been postponed.[2] In all East and Central European countries the events of the year 1989/1990 are referred as a 'return to Europe'.[3] From a Western point of view, it is rather a 'reconstruction of Europe'.[4] The previous shape of Europe, a European diversity which thrives on differences, can now regain a European normality, long considered to be lost. In a remarkable speech in January 1990 at the EC Parliament, Jacques Delors, president of the EC Commission, emphasized that the events in Central and Eastern Europe force us to self-contemplation. He sketched a model for Europe, which was first mentioned by President François Mitterrand: a vision of a structure for East and Central Europe comparable to the way the German States were connected together in the *'Deutsche Bund'* in the nineteenth century.[5]

'A Return to Europe' – this term expresses the wish for

constitutions based on the idea of freedom and human rights and observing the principles of democracy. The collapse of the Eastern Bloc and the liberation from Soviet dominance in East and Central Europe has found one single goal: the nation.[6] The idea of the nation and of the nation state has become an instrument in the struggle against repression by the former Soviet superpower. For this reason, it must be concluded that the conflicts resembling civil war – for example in Yugoslavia and Nagorno-Karabagh (to mention only the most violent ones) – are caused by decades-long repression of national consciousness. What we are witnessing at the moment in East and Central Europe is the development of a new separate nationalism.

While East and Central Europe is experiencing a national renaissance, Western Europe faces a decisive step towards European Union. At the end of 1992, the European Common Market was completed and at the end of the decade the European Community as a whole will be determined by coexisting oppositions. The framework for explaining these complex changes in Europe is the concept of modernization.

The process of national renaissance taking place in East and Central Europe can be defined as 'simple modernization'. It means the rationalization of tradition by removing restrictions caused by the lack of independence. The idea of the nation thereby remains one which provides a sense of identity.[7] A self-confident national consciousness satisfies the wish for unity, identity and common self-determination.

The idea of the nation is also experiencing a new renaissance in the West. However, here the causes are completely different from those in East and Central Europe. In the West, it is a case of 'reflexive modernization' rather than that of simple modernization.[8] Industrial society, and with it internationalization in almost every aspect of life, has itself become a tradition already. The consequences of modernization – ecological risks, overpopulation, increasing lack of unity and loss of values – promote different concepts of modernization to those of simple industrial continuation. European integration, the end of East–West conflict, and the demands of a world which is acting on an increasingly international level all lead to a lack of orientation and, therefore, to uncertainty. Regional unity and national identification can again become a kind of reference point in a world which is becoming more and more diverse.

To make matters even more difficult, European integration is in a kind of success-trap. All hopes and expectations of the reforming states are focused on the EC. However, in the member states of the EC the benefits of integration, which certainly do have an historical value, are taken for granted. People in Europe only vaguely remember the logic of freedom which was intended to overcome national rivalry inside the EC. Instead, the reasons for European integration are again being questioned. Mistrust is increasing towards a Europe which has more and more influence on their daily life without representing democratic structures. This is also the reason why the ever-increasing costs are being considered more and more sceptically. Notions of a Europe not of the citizen but rather of economic interests, a Europe not of diversity but rather of monoculture are becoming more and more tempting. In addition, Europe is asking its citizens for a higher level of education. Knowledge of foreign languages and studies in foreign countries should be a standard part of education. Without these, it seems that one has no chance in a common European labour market. Some people feel that they will not be able to meet these new demands of European integration. For these people, the idea of the nation state can again become an alternative to integration.

3. DIVIDED LOYALTIES

The data for Germany show that people have divided loyalties.[9] Most Germans only feel 'emotionally and politically bound' to their local neighbourhood. Next they feel sympathetic towards their *Bundesland*, then to the *Bundesrepublik Deutschland* as a whole and last of all to the European Community.[10] The differences between various levels of loyalty are clearly marked. They run from the local to the universal with decreasing intensity. In their more immediate surroundings the satisfaction and the engagement of the German people is stronger than in the more abstract public field.

Germans in East and West have developed a more pragmatic national consciousness. During the process of unification, the national feeling, which is less marked in Germany compared to other countries, did not lead to national euphoria but remained at a normal level. Nothing was less expected than this. Indeed, there is no historical precedent for an amalgamation of two such contradictory political systems within such a short period of time. Mikhail Gorbachev's *perestroika* and the continued existence of the *Kulturnation* in Germany, combined with the desire of the East Germans for freedom, wealth and travel, led to the German unification. But as we know today, the creation of the unification proves to be more difficult than it seemed in the enthusiastic period of 1989.

In today's Germany, people actually live in one single state. But they still live in two different societies. Even if social and economic unification can be reached without too many social difficulties, Germany will still be a long way from political and cultural unity based on one single identity of West and East Germans. Experiences and living conditions in East and West Germany in the last forty years have been very different, and still remain so.[11] On one hand, there is the wealthy West, which finds it hard to accept that the situation also demands changes in its own system; and on the other hand, there is the poor and subsidized East which caused the revolutionary impulse that led to unification.

As long as the GDR existed, it was the society to be compared to the Federal Republic and vice versa. Each state saw itself as the democratic counter-identity to the other. Therefore, this way of looking over the iron curtain also had the function of legitimating the respective political and economic systems. It was part of West German identity to believe that one lived in the 'better Germany'. And now? Will the Federal Republic be able to find an identity without having this negative counterpart any longer? So far it seems that this is actually not necessary for the extended *Bundesrepublik*. The country can live quite well without a socialist counterpart. But in the long run the Germans will have to create a more positively based identity.

Unification did not fundamentally change the collective orientations of the West Germans.[12] The political link to the West did not loosen. After more than forty years it is part of the national consensus that to belong to the West means national security and wealth. So far it is the East that shifts towards the West and not the other way round. The former 'Eastern bloc' follows the suction of Western modernization. Concepts of neutrality or even a new *'German Sonderweg'* were hardly noticed even in the period of unification. The East Germans wish to become West Germans, but without losing their own identity. They do not want to establish something completely new but only to get what the West has always had. Their goal does not lead to a new Utopia but to something that is 'relatively better'.

This also shows that the subject of German unity only took precedence over questions of European integration for a short period in Germany. Integration into the West is very stable in view of the commitment to the Western defence alliance and to the EC. The Germans have diverse social relations: regionalism, national perspective and European orientation have an impact on each other. They remain guiding points although they are not of equal significance. At the moment, national interests in Germany take precedence over European ones. It is becoming obvious that Germans are participating much more in local affairs and are willing to be only spectators for dramatic events abroad. More than ever before in history, the foreign policy profile in Germany is caught in the tension between the rising expectations of other nations and the more sceptical attitude the Germans have about themselves. The chasm is growing between the role of the new and larger *Bundesrepublik* on the international arena and the German consciousness of this role.

Two basic developments determine the way in which the Germans perceive everything from national to European identification:

1. In the 1980s the return to local, regional and national levels of identification became stronger. The result has been regionalization.

2. In addition to this, universal and global perspectives also exist. The willingness to participate in international communication and exchange programmes is increasing. The focus now lies on the whole of Europe.

4. *MODELL DEUTSCHLAND*

Germany is witnessing history in a kind of time-lapse photography. The fall of the Berlin Wall, free elections in the GDR, the creation of the new *Bundesländer*, currency unification, state unification, first elections for the united Germany, achievement of full sovereignty – one event followed another with extraordinary speed.[13]

The process of unification between East and West meant an adaptation of one system to another. The new Bundesrepublik is in many respects almost the *Modell Deutschland:* the Constitution, D-Mark, social system, political institutions, and federalism are now also established on the territory of the former GDR. The Germans are saturated.[14]

The state consciousness of West Germans is marked by a positive identification with the political system of the *Bundesrepublik*, including its market economy and social elements. This attitude is a pragmatic and problem-oriented evaluation rather than an idealistic or Utopian one.

International comparisons show that there is a much higher level of acceptance of the political system in the *Bundesrepublik* than in other Western democracies. Democracy, republican attitudes, a parliament and a multi-party system have become self-evident parts of the political order.[15] The high level of and the stable satisfaction with the political system of the *Bundesrepublik* also depends on the level of individual concern and estimation. In fact, it depends on the estimation of the economic situation, on the preferences of the political parties and on their own political orientation towards values. Finally, for the development of the high-level acceptance of the political system of the *Bundesrepublik* by the citizens, economic power and growing wealth played a dominant role.[16]

The need for wider political participation has been

increasing, but this development is overlapped by an obviously more critical attitude towards politics. Criticism is expressed especially by the younger generation towards political parties, the government, politicians and public institutions. This criticism clearly shows fundamentally changed values. On one hand, attitudes belonging to an authoritarian state are dissolving. On the other hand, this criticism creates a more post-industrial mode of consciousness: both freedom of self-determination and a notion of the quality of life, which is no longer linked to the economic growth process, have increasingly become criteria for political processes.

Political interest grew, but the ways of participation diversified. A passive interest in politics was replaced by more active and direct ways of supporting political goals. More and more citizens of the *Bundesrepublik* are no longer willing to accept being only an object of governmental decisions. And the more they are concerned the more they want to participate. The growing number of action groups *('Bürgerinitiativen')*, the peace movement and environmental protection groups clearly prove this thesis.

It is questionable, however, whether the East Germans have already identified or will identify with the Western democratic political system. Above all this depends on whether German unification will succeed.

The institutional and economic system of the former GDR has dissolved. Despite the efforts during the 'velvet revolution' it is no surprise that the link to the West in the 'five new federal states' is not as strong as in the former West Germany. Instead, the five new federal states seem to represent a political-cultural continuity of the values of the lower middle class tradition in Germany.[17] Two years after unification it is still not obvious whether such common values of the lower middle class as etatism, political inwardness, formalism and a high potential for hostility towards foreigners will remain or decrease.[18]

To the citizens of the new federal states unification also means a kind of modernization shock. The social and cultural framework of their daily life has disappeared – in the political and economic sense. There is no time for self-reflection:

competition and risk in political and economic life, closing down or rehabilitation and privatization of thousands of enterprises represent the end of a static society. The mood of the people in the new federal states is therefore ambivalent: there is satisfaction with the newly gained freedom, but people are experiencing this new freedom as the uncertainty of an unpredictable future.[19]

5. UNITED GERMANY AND EUROPE

For the first time, Germany has found its unity not against but in agreement with its neighbours. Germany is still firmly integrated into the Western system of alliances. The German way has found one of its most important aims. Unity and freedom have become a reality for the German nation in a completely changed Europe, which now is able to provide for itself a new order.

In view of this political and cultural background the question of the relationship of Germans to Europe has to be put into its historical context. Where do the Germans belong? This standard question seems to have a lasting relevance. There have been many suggested answers: from relations with the West to the orientation to the East, from neutralism to the German '*Sonderweg*', and from the romantic dreams of the old German empire to the hopes of 'another Germany'. The old *Bundesrepublik* realized the relation to the West in the 1950s: military security, economic prosperity, inner stability and a limited national sovereignty at least for the Western part of the divided nation have since then characterized the attitude to the state and the consciousness of its people.

The terrible destruction and experiences of the two world wars of this century, which can be described as a 'European civil war', gave birth to the idea of the EC as a hope for freedom in Europe. 'The history of the German nation state has come to an end', said Karl Jaspers in 1960 and continued: 'Today the idea of the nation state is fatal to Europe and to all other continents.' However, the enthusiasm towards the idea of Europe had a very specific function in Germany in the 1950s.

The idea of the nation could be replaced by the idea of Europe. The confidence which resulted from the integration of Germany into the European Community brought sovereignty and the ability for political action back to the *Bundesrepublik*.

The German question had always been a European one, and the European question had always been a German one. Without cooperation with the West, there would have been no chance to solve the national question even if the Soviet Union had agreed. The *Bundesrepublik* therefore had a national interest in Europe.

The idea of the nation is experiencing a renaissance throughout Europe: in East and Central Europe as a process of simple modernization in the form of a liberation from the dominance of the former Soviet Union, in Western Europe in the form of an alternative identity in opposition to the consequences of advanced modernization. The global interdependencies which demand a higher level of integration than the nation state are too abstract to satisfy the social and psychological need for identity. So the nation remains a framework for identity.[20] The nation state is by no means unnecessary although its importance has diminished. The need for national identification and sovereignty is growing at the same rate as the political and economic process of levelling-out in Europe. The more diversity disappears in Europe, the greater the resistance towards further integration becomes. The concept of Western Europe as a single common and production market is already a reality. However, people are reacting against the levelling-out of cultural diversity. Europe's strength has always been this cultural diversity.[21] The multicultural society, as a concept which promises opportunities for participation, independent of ethnic origins, will remain only an intellectual one as long as nation states such as the *Bundesrepublik* define their idea of the people more in an ethnic than a republican way.[22]

Europe is the home of the multicultural society. But it will not be the national cultures which will become multicultural. Since this would constitute the feared levelling-out process, it will be a society of European nations. Here the chances lie in the diversity which protects against a levelling-out and at the same time describes the tasks of the nation state. The nation state is therefore a necessary supplement to European integration.

Until now Europe has only been able to unify against threats from outside and never in favour of a positive goal. With the disappearance of these external threats, the idea of unification faded and the danger of inner conflicts increased. The disappearance of East–West confrontation left a new disorder in its wake. That is why it is so important to give European integration new impulses, to make these clear to the people of Europe and to apply them to their daily lives. Should this fail, the danger of nationalism, which we all hoped had been overcome, will re-emerge in Europe.

To learn from history means to learn in contrast to history: one of the lessons of European history is that European unity cannot be achieved by working against nations. It can only be achieved by taking nations and their characteristics into account. Nations for their part must learn that they are made up of many regional, ethnic and linguistic components.

With the post-war era behind, Europe has the chance to rediscover itself.[23] The dualism of two political systems, which divided Europe into two parts, has been overcome. But a centralistic monostate with all the modern instruments of power is not the answer to a lasting unity in diversity. A European constitution can only be a lasting one if it takes into account the European nations, their long history, their languages and their states.

The European nations can only be put together into a whole if the Europe of the future is built in the spirit of subsidiarity. Joseph Rovan imagined Europe as a loose formation of nation states with several political levels, in which 'only that which cannot be solved by the lower level is passed to the next highest level'.[24] Considering this, Germany's European neighbours may learn from the experiences of a land which has been divided for centuries. The communal self-government and the principles of federalism, as they are installed in Germany, may provide model characteristics for European integration.[25]

Only if Europe succeeds in finding unity, not against but for positive goals – a Europe for the people and not only for economic interests – will there be a chance of overcoming its old conflicts. Germany needs Europe, but Europe also needs Germany. This was the early realization of the fact that Germans and their neighbours depend on each other and therefore need to cooperate. If this succeeds, it speaks well for Germany's peaceful integration into Europe.

NOTES

1. Ute Knight and Wolfgang Kowalsky, *Deutschland nur den Deutschen? Die Ausländerfrage in Deutschland, Frankreich und den USA* (Erlangen: Straube, 1991).
2. Hagen Schulze, *Die Wiederkehr Europas* (Berlin: W. J. Siedler, 1990), p. 5.
3. Timothy Garton Ash, *Ein Jahrhundert wird abgewählt. Aus den Zentren Mitteleuropas 1980–1990* (München: Hanser, 1990).
4. See also Hans-Georg Gadamer, *Das Erbe Europas* (Frankfurt: Suhrkamp, 1989).
5. Jacques Delors, Speech at the EC-Parliament in Strasbourg, 17 January 1990; in Renate Fritsch-Bournazel (ed.), *Europa und die deutsche Einheit* (Bonn: Aktuell, 1992), p. 37.
6. Ulrich Beck, Der Konflikt der zwei Modernen; in W. Zapf (ed.), *Die Modernisierung moderner Gesellschaften* (Frankfurt, New York: Campus, 1990), pp. 40–53.
7. Ibid.
8. Ibid.
9. Werner Weidenfeld und Karl-Rudolf Korte, *Die Deutschen. Profil einer Nation* (Stuttgart: Cleo Cotta, 1991).
10. Ibid.; See also Heinrich Schneider, Europäische Identität: Historische, kulturelle und politische Dimension. *Integration*, no. 4/1991, pp. 160–76. Schneider emphasizes that European identity in fact means the political identity of a European Union, which cannot be derived from tradition but has to be defined by European politics.
11. Felix Philipp Lutz, Vergangenheit als politischer Faktor: Zum Geschichtsbewusstsein in Deutschland. *BISS Public*, no. 8/1992, p. 25.
12. Werner Weidenfeld und Karl-Rudolf Korte, Die pragmatischen Deutschen. Zum Staats- und Nationalbewusstsein in Deutschland. *Aus Politik und Zeitgeschichte, Beilage zu Das Parlament*, no. B 32/1991, pp. 3–12.
13. Werner Weidenfeld, Die Perspektiven der weiteren Entwicklung Deutschlands; in Eckhard Jesse und Armin Mitter (eds), *Die Gestaltung der deutschen Einheit* (Bonn und Berlin, 1992), p. 388.
14. Weidenfeld and Korte, Die Deutschen.
15. See Dieter Fuchs, *Die Unterstützung des politischen Systems der Bundesrepublik Deutschlands* (Opladen: Westdeutscher Verlag, 1989) and Bettina Westle, *Politische Legitimität* (Baden-Baden: Nomos, 1989).
16. See Weidenfeld and Korte, Die pragmatischen Deutschen.

17. See Karl-Rudolf Korte, Die Folgen der Einheit. Zur politisch-kulturellen Lage der Nation. *Aus Politik und Zeitgeschichte, Beilage zu Das Parliament*, no. B 27/1990, pp. 29–38 and Helmut Klages, Es fehlt die Bereitschaft zum bedingungslosen 'Ärmelaufkrempeln'. *Frankfurter Allgemeine Zeitung*, 16 February 1991.
18. See Gerda Lederer *et al.*, Autoritarismus unter Jugendlichen der ehemaligen DDR. *Deutschland Archiv*, no. 40/1991, p. 587; Andreas Pietsch, Ist es schon wieder soweit? *Pfeil*, no. 1/1992, pp. 4–5; Bartholomäus Grill, Hasst du was, dann bist du was. *Die Zeit*, no. 23/1992, p. 5 and Eberhard Seidel-Pielen, Voll und ganz gegen Ausländer. *Der Tagesspiegel*, 12 July 1992.
19. Weidenfeld and Korte, Die pragmatischen Deutschen.
20. It is questionable if complex societies can create a reasonable identity. See Jürgen Habermas, Können komplexe Gesellschaften eine vernünftige Identität ausbilden?; in *Zur Rekonstruktion des historischen Materialismus* (Frankfurt: Suhrkamp, 1982), p. 144ff.
21. Schulze, op. cit.
22. See Thomas R. Henschel, Europa – eine multikulturelle Gesellschaft; in *Jugend 2000* (München: Deutsches Jugendinstitut, 1992). For further information, see Stefan Ulbricht (ed.), *Multikultopia. Gedanken zur multi-kulturellen Gesellschaft* (Vilsbiburg: Arun, 1991) and Claus Leggewie, *MultiKulti. Spielregeln für die Vielvölkerrepublik* (Berlin: Rotbuch, 1990).
23. Fritsch-Bournazel, op. cit., p. 119.
24. Joseph Rovan, Wo ist die vierte Etage? *Rheinischer Merkur/Christ und Welt*, no. 25/1989.
25. Schulze, op. cit.

12. CIVIL SOCIETY IN RUSSIA?

Risto Alapuro

1. INTRODUCTION

The notion of 'civil society' has become prominent in the recent debate on the prospects for democracy in Russia.[1] It is more useful than 'democracy' only, because it refers to the social conditions that must be fulfilled for a democracy to prevail, that is, for people to be able to act independently of or in opposition to the state authority in a sustained way. But how enlightening is it in the Russian context?

Originally the term implies a conception of the organizational differentiation of the state in the West from the eighteenth century onwards. Citizens' economic activity was increasingly assigned to the institutions of private property, contract and market – distinct from the state as an interested party. At the same time, there evolved a private sphere of personal freedom, as a contrast to the domination of collective social bonds. These processes provided a resource basis for laying claims to the state in the sense of an effective autonomous use of political rights, such as rights to organize, to speak publicly, to assemble and to demonstrate.[2]

What implications does this notion have, if used to describe prospects for democracy in a country very different from the West? The adoption of the term is not unproblematic. As Richard Pipes, for example, has pointed out, in Russia society has throughout history 'proven unable to impose on political authority any kind of effective restraints'.[3] The tradition of patient institution-building that marks modern Western civil society is absent in Russia. Also the separation of the political and economic realms, so central to the rise of civil society in the West, occurred very late and very partially in Russia.[4] The separation that occurred in this respect at the end of the old regime was certainly not strengthened during the Soviet period.[5]

This review first discusses a few, mainly Western applications of the notion of 'civil society' to today's Russia as well as some problems in its use. Second, it gives examples of Russian phenomena linked to the emergence of civil society, and finally suggests that they should be related to the specifically Russian variety of modernization more explicitly than is usually the case.

2. VIEWS OF 'CIVIL SOCIETY' IN RUSSIA

Among the first to introduce the notion in the Russian case was S. Frederick Starr, who in 1988 argued that a civil society is emerging in the Soviet Union. 'People...are taking on the mentality of citizens', and to the extent that the Communist party and the state will follow suit, the country 'will move toward becoming...a civil society'.[6] Starr referred to a number of social transformations that long before the mid-1980s strengthened 'dynamic elements' in society and made people more prone to 'assert their individual rights' *vis-à-vis* the party and the state. Most fundamental he found the rapid urbanization of the past decades, which has meant the waning of peasant Russia with its controversial national archetype. 'City air', spurred by rapid economic development, has emancipated rural migrants' offspring, and made them more independent than their forebears. Another crucial factor for Starr was the immense progress in education in the post-war decades.

When the decline of fear as an instrument of control in the post-Stalin period is added to these transformations, it becomes understandable that 'the process of individuation' has advanced. Today 'life decisions formerly made by the state –

such as the selection of a career, employer, and place of residence – are either subject to personal influence or left fully to individual choice.'[7] Furthermore, the privatized 'twilight second economy...has come of age...so that it now touches every segment of the population'. The processes of 'individuation, decentralization of initiative, and privatization', which were making progress during the Brezhnev regime, are increasingly imposing themselves.[8]

Improved communications have created among the citizens a degree of 'networking' completely unprecedented in the Soviet history: 'interest groups of like-minded people are formed with relative ease and they establish regular channels of communication among their devotees.' Starr has even seen signs of 'what Western political scientists call 'interest group articulation'.[9] As a related phenomenon, public opinion seemed to be gaining in strength and growing in diversity.

Today, with the advantage of hindsight, Starr's assessment appears over-optimistic. Still, his basic approach as well as many elements he takes up are shared by other observers. Insofar as the efforts to bring about a fundamental economic transformation have advanced, the economic dynamics of the market can be stressed more promptly than Starr did. David W. Lovell reminds us that separating the economy from the state is 'perhaps the most important step in the revival of civil society', and 'a prerequisite to the establishment of genuine political freedoms' among the Soviet people.[10] Besides, even those modest market impulses that existed in the previous period may seem significant.

T. H. Rigby sees 'vestigial elements' of the civil society in a limited market of labour, the retail marketing, and the family plots, all of which existed, at least to some extent, even during the Stalinist era. He likewise considers important "the shadow economy and clientelist groupings and networks" that 'superimpose an unofficial contractual dimension onto the system's official command-structure'.[11] All these trends are thought to have eroded the monopoly of the party-state to the benefit of individual room for manoeuvering.

Starr's stress on urbanization is echoed in Moshe Lewin's view that the powerful urbanization of the last forty years created a new urban society which began to look for a new civil order, and there emerged a new 'civil society'. Finally, 'the new social realities forced the issue of a fundamental shake-up' in the form of *perestroika.*[12]

Some commentators argue that elements of civil society were built into the functioning of the Soviet system itself, either within the official sector or in practices symbiotic with it. Rigby refers, along with the existing market impulses, to such formally voluntary organizations as trade unions, the *Komsomol*, sporting associations, the unions of writers and composers, which appear to have included elements of civil society. He also refers to the potential implied in the democratic rules that various organizations and institutions had, even though in practice those rules were not followed: 'The daily travesty of democracy helped to nourish the soil for its eventual revival.'[13]

Vladimir Shlapentokh sees the civil society as having included practically the same sectors as the official one did. In addition to the shadow economy, which functioned partly in symbiosis with legal economic activities, he lists various educational services (largely existing inside state medicine), the bard movement, the *samizdat*, the dissemination of foreign literature, and the vacation industry. Moreover, in a way reminiscent of Rigby, Shlapentokh cites the use of legal organizations for semilegal or illegal purposes. Finally, he mentions the open challenges to the state.[14]

3. CIVIL SOCIETY, DEMOCRACY, AND COLLECTIVE ACTION

All these conceptions imply the relevance of civil society for the establishment of democracy. They also posit the emergence of at least some of its elements in today's Russia. Many of them do not clearly specify, however, just which aspects are most significant for democracy. This is understandable, because observers may be interested not only in politics but in other spheres of life as well.[15] Still, the problem is there. Arguably, a specification is particularly important in analyzing a case which definitely differs from the one in the West.

Crucial for democratic politics is, as stated above, people's capacity to act jointly and in a sustained and regulated way to influence the government. In the West it was precisely the gradual institutionalization of this challenge that came to be known as 'civil society'. In the first phase, there was a liberal-bourgeois challenge to the state, relying on the economic dynamics of the market in the frame of egalitarian legal guarantees and liberties. Then, in the nineteenth century, the challenge was pursued further, mainly by the social-democratic labour movement that demanded social justice and economic security from the state.[16] Political rights were gradually won through hard and often protracted struggles against state machineries, first in strikes and then, after gaining some rights, in elections fought with political parties.

For the present purposes, the question may be reformulated as one of the preconditions for collective action that establishes for the contenders membership in the polity.[17] The crucial element is – along with interests, mobilization, and opportunity – the organization, which 'most directly' affects a group's capacity to act, that is, organization understood as a combination of categories (e.g., industrial workers, intellectuals, Orthodox believers) and networks of people linked to each other by an interpersonal bond. 'The more extensive its common identity and internal networks, the more organized the group.'[18]

In this view the problem is, first, what kind of a potential is there in Russia for the formation of sets of individuals comprising both a category and a unifying structure that apply 'pooled resources to influence the government'?[19] And second, what are the prospects for the contenders thus defined to enter the polity, or to participate in the institutionalized competition for resources controlled by the same government?

4. PROBLEMS AND OBJECTIONS

Soviet rule disintegrated from above rather than through a sustained challenge from below. This makes a marked difference to the Western development, in which popular groups or, to put it more precisely, organizations representing them, fought a protracted struggle to enter the polity – possibly, it is true, in a coalition with certain dominant groups. In the present Russian case, no party or movement was tested in a hard political struggle for a longer period and had time to work out a political and economic programme.

Boris Yeltsin and his allies had power thrust upon them by the coup attempt in 1991 before they actually knew what they wanted to do with it.[20] That is, the so-called Democrats entered the polity easily, without a long and powerful popular push forcing their entry into the polity against the will of fiercely resistant power-holders. This was so, even if we take into the account the Democrats' success in the national and local elections of 1989 and 1990, and Yeltsin's victory in the Russian presidential elections in 1991.

What does this easy takeover imply about the character of the group that entered the polity? In effect, which group entered it? One view relevant for the problem of civil society holds that the abrupt takeover by Yeltsin did not really dismantle the former power structures. A number of old arrangements may still be viable, in a way stifling the emergence of civil society. They may have been seriously undermined but not necessarily destroyed in the process. An extreme view even maintains that the takeover was in essence only a rearrangement within the confines of the old polity.[21]

Another related conclusion is that those elements of civil society identified above asserted themselves only passively in the years preceding August 1991 (as they have done after it). To argue that it takes time to (re)activate civil society would tell no more than a part of the story: many of the analyses cited above do point to a growing separation between the state and the society, but they do not necessarily point to an increasing capacity to challenge the state.

Both conclusions warrant attention. Old institutional arrangements seem to persist at least in the economic sphere. The present transition period may lead to a 'corruption economy', as suggested by André Grjebine, comparable to the economies of the Latin American countries. In this kind of an economy, the exchange is based rather on social-political power than on economic relations. Property remains a form of organization dependent, above all, on holding an office.[22] This view echoes not only Pipes' but a number of other commentators' opinions.[23] It is probable that 'this mixture of provision of services, contraction of debts, giving bribes, privileges exercised at the cost of multiple compromises, ancient complicities, [all these phenomena] that serve as a basis for a corruption economy will simply adapt themselves to the new rules of the game'.[24] Another variant of the same view suggests that the new economy will lean heavily on the 'shadow economy' or the *'mafia'*, consolidated in the last years of the Soviet period in a symbiotic relationship with state structures.[25]

Urbanization, in turn, may serve as an example of a field in which the increasing autonomy of the social sphere does not necessarily lead to a sustained popular effort to enter the polity. The overall character of urbanization may differ from the Western experience in a way that restrains the capacity to organize and act collectively. According to one ethnographic study, in middle-sized Russian cities 'town and country are [still] two variants of one and the same culture'. 'Peasant values, and consequently also Orthodox-peasant values...are not utopian for...the rank and file living in urban conditions.'[26] There may be strong networks in this culture, but it is not obvious that they lead to proactive claims directed against the state.

A related view is put forward by Alain Blum, who argues that the forced modernization in the Soviet Union led to a specific kind of separation between the political discourse and everyday life, 'a remarkable autonomy of the society *vis-à-vis* the sphere of politics'.[27] The impressive figures of growth of the industrial and urban population, reflecting the political determination of the party-state, were not matched by corresponding changes in social relations. Rather, the figures covered an increasing gap between the administrative efforts from above and the reaction of a restive society that adapted itself to changes only insofar as it was necessary. There arose an illusion of a profound change of society, which, however, existed independently of the political system, sticking to old habits. 'Urbanization...has long been presented as a sign of [social] upheavals, because the urban growth seemed more rapid than anywhere else. But even if it prevails in figures, one can probably speak rather of a ruralization of cities than of the urbanization of the country.'[28]

In this perspective, the social relations of large urban groups, the educated strata excluded, are still encased within the traditional design. Both views mentioned above may be linked to the often-cited importance of informal networks in the Soviet society. Consisting of interaction between members of the family, friends, and friends of friends, these networks functioned in a symbiosis with official structures or exploited them. They provided basic resources for survival in various spheres of everyday life, from financial support to the distribution of all kinds of goods and services and to job opportunities.[29] Vladimir Shlapentokh sees in these networks a basis for a future civil society: 'Family and friendship were the only social institutions to survive the destruction of Soviet civil society. These institutions now form a part of the foundation of a new civil society in Russia.'[30]

If this is so, the impression of the political passivity of the Russian civil society is reinforced. Additional support can be found in Ilya Srubar's analysis, which is complementary to Blum's and Shlapentokh's views. Srubar focuses on changes brought about by the Communist period, but like Blum, he argues that while in statistical terms the social structure in socialist countries resembled the Western one, at the level of social relations this was not true. In the socialist shortage economies 'social networks of distribution', such as family relations and relations of 'functional friendship', became crucial. The observable social inequalities were not legitimated on the basis of achievement or professional qualifications but were attributed to a membership in a politically privileged group or a distribution network. In other words, a high level of industrialization and urbanization did not imply modern social relations, if these presuppose, for example, money as a universal mechanism of mediation and the legitimation of inequalities on the basis of individual achievement.[31] And it was just this kind of modernity, one could add, that served as a foundation for the Western-type group solidarities and processes of organization.

In this perspective, the reintroduction of the market mechanism may actually reinforce the orientation to the existing networks, rather than eliminate them. Even though the legalization of the private economy may spur the private initiative that exists in the distribution networks, this initiative is not able to break free from the 'premodern' division between in-group and out-group morals, especially in conditions of economic misery. As a consequence, then, the 'remodernization' process may lead to completely different results from those we know from Western modernity.[32]

Srubar portrays a society in which individual and group-based survival strategies stifle active mobilization and organization, rather than create preconditions for them, at least among the not highly educated majority. Even with modifications brought about by the collapse of state socialism, the situation seems to suggest what Charles Tilly calls defensive mobilization. It often occurs simply as an 'extension of the group's everyday routines for doing its work', induced by a threat from outside.[33] Distribution networks and the like hardly function as frames for collective action in the sense of organized movements making new claims against the state authority. Other kinds of mass reactions, on the other hand, are not excluded.

But if doubts can be cast on the role of the dynamics of the market and urbanization, what about the third potential source for a civil society referred to above, namely, the organizational frames of Soviet society itself? Can they, or some of them, serve as a basis for a civil society, as in particular Rigby suggests? Perhaps urbanization and even economic reforms gain importance in their context? They merit attention for the simple reason that new organized challenges cannot possibly arise from a vacuum. Effective action must almost invariably be built on a strong organization, and if no organized opposition was consolidated in protracted struggles during the previous period, its construction (if there is any) is bound to be based, at least in part, on those elements that are available – with all the ambiguities that may arise from the connection with the old.

5. FORMS OF POLITICAL ORGANIZATION

What signs are there, then, of organized movements influencing the government? And in which ways are they linked to former institutions and forms of organization?

An example of a tendency favourable to civil society is provided by Marie-Hélène Mandrillon's study on the unfolding of three major ecological conflicts from the 1960s to the late 1980s. The conflicts were the *'Baikal affair'*, plans to turn the flow of big rivers from north to south, and the nuclear explosion in Chernobyl. The groups opposing the official line had their strongholds in scientific and other cultural institutions and organizations, notably in certain institutes of the Academy of Sciences of the Soviet Union. From one conflict to the next, the activists were increasingly able to gain autonomy *vis-à-vis* the top of the administrative hierarchy, and to establish horizontal ties and networks based on common intellectual affinities.

Furthermore, from the ecological opposition a line goes to the Gorbachev administration: a number of key figures arrived at important positions during the *perestroika*. And third, the challenges also found a larger audience in the population. In the opposition to the river project were united, with different arguments, two currents, reminiscent of the traditional division of the Russian intelligentsia into the Slavophiles and the Westernizers. The modernist opposition had supporters in educated urban strata, willing to enhance the prestige of their professional competence, and to gain access to information and a modern way of life.[34]

The process has been seen as a sign of the emergence of civil society.[35] And indeed, it combines themes familiar from Rigby's and Lewin's reflections. The movement was initiated within official institutions, but thanks to popular support mainly from urban groups it was able to turn some of them effectively against other parts of the administration. Also, the opposition began roughly at the same time as the Stalinist terror disappeared, and it gathered momentum with the advancing urbanization and finally with the political liberalization in the 1980s.

Oleg Yanitsky's observations on neighbourhood movements and initiatives in the 1980s in various cities, especially Moscow, reveal a related story. Many of the initiatives had roots in the previous decades. Attempts to organize and mobilize people to defend their environment against the projects of the planning authorities progressively gained, in the course of the 1980s, a character of grassroots organization that united local activists, a larger number of residents, and finally also representatives of new political structures. The main role among the activists was played by educated professionals.[36] Yanitsky's results refer to a change in the character of political activists during the 1980s. Local activists brought not only their expertise, as the former generation did, but also their personal experiences and political value preferences.[37] This type of public personality has gained influence in Russian politics in recent years.

How strong, however, is the democratic impulse, exemplified by Mandrillon's and Yanitsky's studies? Ernest Gellner is presumably right when he writes that one cannot doubt 'the existence of an ardent desire for the civil society, the pluralism, the absence of a political, ideological, and economic monopoly and, above all, a desire for the elimination of the catastrophic fusion of the three forms of centralism'.[38] The results of the national and many local elections between 1989 and 1991 bear this view out.[39] Still, the limits of the democratic impulse seem evident as well, and not only in the sense that socio-political confusion and material scarcity have dampened the Russians' democratic enthusiasm since 1990. In dealing mainly with educated urban strata, Mandrillon's and Yanitsky's studies reinforce the existing view that the intellectuals play the leading role in the new, especially the so-called democratic, politics. It is not clear, however, what potential there is for wider coalitions, uniting intellectuals with larger groups.

It may be true, as one estimation puts it, that the new political organizations are anchored not only in 'the scientific-technological part of the humanitarian and creative intelligentsia' but also in 'a few strata of the working class'.[40] Still they seem to be heavily marked by the former and their culture. These 'informal organizations', 'political parties' (or 'proto-parties'), 'social movements' (or 'quasi-movements'), 'citizen initiatives', 'party clubs', and so on,[41] as they are variously called, are mainly small ('generals without armies'), there are at least hundreds of them, and they are in a perpetual process of emergence, division and disintegration.[42] Their mode of organization recalls, in effect, that of the Russian intelligentsia in the nineteenth century, the 'circle' *(kruzhok)*.[43] As a matter of fact, even the notion of 'social movement' *(obshchestvennoe dvizhenie)*, one of the most popular terms for the current party groupings, originally refers to the activities of intellectuals.[44]

Two Russian historians, V. Berezkovsky and N. Krotov, actually draw a parallel between the turn-of-the-century organizations and the present movement, the social movements of the 'informal politicized groups'.[45] The repertoire of action consists notably of demonstrations, picketing, lectures, debates, collection of signatures for petitions, meetings, exhibitions, and the like.[46]

In stressing the 'informal' character of these party groups, Berezkovsky and Krotov link them with a wide variety of non-official organization forms in the 1980s, from youth gangs, rock music fans and Hare Krishnas to ecologists and many kinds of political groupings.[47] Up to the beginning of the 1990s, all of them were generally conceived as 'informal' *(neformaly)*. In other words, the politically active organizations were viewed as belonging to a sphere evolving outside the state but not necessarily making claims against it (it is another matter that until *perestroika* simply a striving for autonomy constituted a challenge to the prevailing system). Perhaps more importantly, Berezkovsky's and Krotov's conceptualization implies that the intellectuals' 'informal' political movement represents the personal sphere in contrast to the public one. The movement gives expression to 'informal phenomena of personality'; in it the personality can 'express what has hurt the soul, to bring the others his [own] truth'. On this view, 'informal' relations are always profoundly personal, establishing themselves, as a rule, in a narrow circle, for example in the family and among friends.[48]

A personal involvement is, of course, a part of any social movement. But in emphasizing the personal quality of the new political movement as a whole, Berezkovsky's and Krotov's conception may catch something especially typical in the Russian case. It appears no accident that they see the entire civil society from the same angle: it is 'the personality of the ordinary informal man [that activates] the civil society'.[49] In this analysis, it is the expressive, or perhaps verbal, character of the intelligentsia's political activity that is manifest. The new parties concentrate on 'self-realization', to cite Yuri Levada's nasty remark.[50] Therefore, the Democratic parties' inability to make inroads into the large masses does not seem surprising.

Parallels with the pre-Soviet period may be viewed from another perspective as well. E. Mareeva, among others, claims that the Russian communal tradition is still strong, modifying the relationship between the activists and the supporters of the new political movements. As a member of the community, an individual had no particular will or interest. There prevailed, instead, a common will, represented by the person of the leader. In today's politics, this mentality implies populism, as a contrast to an active organization from below. People do not see the leader as a representative of an interest group but as a force that controls the bureaucrats and maintains the ideal of equality, understood in the sense of pronounced egalitarianism. Such a relationship between the leaders and the followers legitimates political privileges as a mode of defending the large masses. The only way to resist this tendency, Mareeva argues, is through organized forms of self-administration for concrete issues, be they the needs of the labour collective, the reorganization of leisure, or the defence of the environment.[51]

Populist tendencies are well discernible in the practices of Democratic groupings.[52] Moreover, in the absence of an organized pressure from below, those Democrats who have established themselves in the present system through elections, or the failure of the 1991 coup attempt, tend to be easily co-opted to the existing power structures.[53] Or, to put it somewhat differently, because the movement did not emerge as an organized challenger to the party-state but as a result of its dissolution, it has been able to fill the vacuum rapidly, adapting itself to the political struggle in the upper echelons of the state and society and being ready to leave the organizational efforts to a secondary plane.[54] This is one answer to the question of which group entered the polity, presented above.

In these conditions it is no wonder that the most influential political trends are linked to the decayed apparatus. According to a recent estimation, they may be loosely divided into three groups. The 'post-communist' camp includes, among other organizations, Vice-President Alexander Rutskoi's People's Party of Free Russia (formerly Democratic Party of Communists of Russia) and Nikolai Travkin's Democratic Party of Russia. The other two tendencies are the 'National-Bolsheviks', gathering a number of groups (for example, the United Workers' Front, linked to elements of the dissolved Communist Party of the Soviet Union) making various chauvinist, imperial and egalitarian demands; and finally the 'Anti-Communists' who are close to Yeltsin and among whom central political and economic figures are well represented.[55] What is significant is not the division as such, but rather the fact that all effective trends are dominated by former Communists, and in every case their political message reveals clear populist overtones.[56]

All this said, there is one important instance of an organized grassroots challenge: the miners' and other workers' strike movements in 1989 and 1991. In many cases they led to more permanent forms of interest organization – to 'worker collectives', 'committees of enterprise', 'worker clubs', and other strike committees or new trade unions at a local level, as well as 'worker unions' and other organizations at a regional level.[57] Some students believe that the fate of democracy in Russia is primarily dependent on the working class and its organization process (e.g., Gordon and Kagarlitsky). To cite Leonid Gordon:

> The importance of the worker movement is due...to the fact that it apparently constitutes the most powerful force for democracy. For the time being the worker movement, or, more precisely, the movement of the labour collectives, constitutes in the central regions of our country practically the only form of inclusion of the masses into active political life.[58]

Gordon discerns a number of democratic demands in the declarations of the independent worker movement, but he admits that an alliance between it and the intellectuals' Democratic movement is difficult to establish, thanks to the 'psychological alienation of the worker milieu from the intelligentsia',[59] and that it is far from evident that the democratic tendencies will prevail.[60]

An example of the constraints of worker organization is provided by A. A. Shkreba's study of a strike in an industrial centre of the Ural region. He stresses the traditional character of the workers' challenge. The pervasive mutual distrust among the workers was apparently 'a phenomenon of a pre-class or a non-class pattern'. In the prevailing paternalistic conditions there was no clear consciousness of conflicting interests between the workers and the management. Discontent was not directed against the paternalistic control as such but against its excesses. Workers were not conscious of a common interest even in terms of the labour collective, the organizational nucleus of Soviet working life, and they tended to see conflicts in a local framework only. Shkreba thinks that his case is largely typical of the prevailing situation (or at least was in 1989).[61] The results illuminate Blum's view that the socialist industrialization may have transformed social relations much less than appears at first sight.

The problem is aggravated by the economic crisis, which may not exclude new movements but which apparently does not encourage further organization, if we are to trust Srubar. On this point, two different case studies seem to be in agreement. Shkreba argues that the economic misery can have adverse effects on the activities of strike committees. Michael Burawoy and Kathryn Hendley show, in their case study of a rubber product enterprise, how the council of the labour collective, stepping into the political vacuum that resulted from the downfall of the old monolithic regime, was not able to gather the support of the workers, but crumbled under the pressure of contradictory turns of legislation and of insoluble economic difficulties. Apparently the weight of the traditional political culture played a role as well.[62]

It is possible, however, that the short-term and long-term effects are different and that Gordon's optimism is not groundless in the long run. His stress on the democratic potential of the labour collectives is interesting, in taking up an existing organizational framework in an otherwise little-organized society. In conditions where civil society is lacking, he says, the labour collectives provide the only available basis to structure a challenge of the majority of the people. Moreover, he thinks that they could unite within the same organizations both educated groups and 'ordinary people':

> ... such as they [the latter] are today: most of them are not very literate, not used to assuming responsibility for themselves, sometimes passive, and not very reasonable *(trezvye)* either. [But] this is the only people we have now, and the country will avoid catastrophe only if this people, whose social life takes place in the labour collectives, engages itself in the democratic process. ... It is precisely the social role of the labour collectives that produces the special place of the worker movement in the socio-political life of the present Soviet society. What we call today the independent and democratic worker movement is primarily a movement of the labour collectives. It is not simply an association of individuals having common views, as in most other democratic organizations [in other countries], but an association of the rank-and-file working people *(rabotniki)*, who share not only common aspirations but also a common job in the same plants, factories, mines, building sites and institutes.[63]

Gordon's view merits attention because he asks what specifically Russian features there are that could affect the character of a large-scale organization process. In stressing the importance of the working place, the suggestion implies that the challenge in an eventual civil society may take a peculiar form. Economic, political, and cultural aspects may fuse in a way that makes Russian organizations 'multifunctional' and therefore different from political parties in the Western sense.[64] Another matter is that Gordon's sceptical (realist?) way of speaking of 'ordinary people' exemplifies a typical approach among the intellectuals. It is in itself an aspect of the problem of alliance between the educated strata and the large masses.

The above examples lead to no simple conclusion

concerning the prospects for an organized challenge in a Russian civil society. True, among the (educated) urban strata the process of organization has undoubtedly made progress both before the present crisis and especially in the course of it. But the limits of the democratic impulse appear clear as well. Graphically, both the prospects for democracy and their limits are shown by the results of the elections in various provincial centres in 1989–1991. In most provinces a definitely anti-establishment organization took place, possibly based on or supported by the miners' grassroots movement. The activists were intellectuals coming from healthcare professions and from environmental and ethnic groups, young officers, entrepreneurs and journalists.[65] But many of them were reformist Communists, which is perhaps somewhat ambiguous for the prospects of civil society. And more importantly, in most cases the 'establishment' was able to stay in power.[66]

Likewise, the studies cited above identify both the continuing predominance of the traditional design and the existence of organized 'Democratic' claims that nevertheless tend to be influenced by structures inherited from the Soviet and even the pre-Soviet past. It is not obvious which trend will prevail in the long run. Despite the doubts above, it may be argued that in the end a civil society will establish itself, thanks to the high overall level of education in Russia, the eventual consolidation of a new urban tradition, etc. Moshe Lewin, for example, holds that even though mental attitudes deriving from an agrarian society are still prevalent among city dwellers, their dominance will wane with time.[67] Perhaps the labour collectives, for example, can then be activated as organizational frames, as Gordon suggests. In this view the present economic problems will be a passing phenomenon, not seriously compromising the basic democratic tendency. Yet the view may underestimate the extent to which the present economic misery, combined with the legacy of the Russian and Soviet past, is able to perpetuate a non-democratic political pattern. Many reflections reviewed above bring forward arguments why this latter alternative could be more plausible than the former one.

6. THE RUSSIAN VARIETY OF MODERNIZATION

The above reflections raise a more general question. Should Russia be viewed as another country that will more or less follow the Western path? This seems to be an implicit idea in most analyses applying the notion of 'civil society' in the Russian circumstances. Will the present juncture bring Russia into the Western mainstream, with a 'normal society', 'normal historical process', or 'normal market democracy', and with the dominance of 'universal human values', as so many Democratic Russian commentators like to put it today? Or will Russia follow a different line of development, as it did in the past and up to our own time?

In the light of the above review, the Western path does not seem a very likely alternative. In effect, the present debate on Russia's future, especially the often rather unreflective references to 'civil society', is reminiscent of the controversy between the modernization theorists and their historically oriented critics in the 1960s and the 1970s. At that time what was at issue was the political development of the Third World countries. The critics paid attention to the ideological character of the 'modernization' as an attempt to 'universalize historically specific values and institutions deriving from Western societies'.[68]

A denial of all modernization tendencies conducive to a civil society in Russia would be absurd, of course. The industrialization, the character of urbanization, the relatively high level of education and the disappearance of the rural-peasant base for the politico-economic system separate Russia from the majority of the Third World countries, even with the reservations presented above. Rather, an approach is needed that takes seriously the country's specific route to modernity. Such an approach should systematically view Russia in relation to the West; that is, it should take into account the earlier efforts to learn from the West in order to defend Russia against the Western challenge, or even to supersede it, from the reforms of Peter the Great to Bolshevism as a Russian variant of Marxism.

Today we are witnessing a new round in the complex process of imitation, adoption and modification of Western influences. As many times before, the intelligentsia, itself born from an encounter with the West, is reacting to the challenge of the West by looking for inspiration there, an inspiration that would help to modernize their country. And as before, they face the majority of the population, which is culturally alien to the intelligentsia, and still attached to the ideal of simple reproduction, the historically evolved standards of needs and demands, and a strong egalitarianism.[69]

The Soviet period has certainly undermined the basis for the traditional division, but at the same time it may have contributed to a new type of atomization among the popular groups, as shown by Srubar and implied by Gordon.[70] An indication of the intellectuals' continuously difficult role between the West and the large masses is provided by the way the notion of 'civil society' *(grazhdanskoe obshchestvo)* itself is used in the Democratic discourse. It appeared in the discussion during the late 1980s, as a catchword to describe those conditions that were required to further *perestroika* and consequently democracy in the Soviet state.[71] Even the CPSU adopted it in 1990, declaring then as its objective the formation of 'civil society, in which the individual *(chelovek)* does not exist for the state but the state for the individual'.[72] Usually the term conveys the same aspects of economy and society as in the West. 'The proprietary right ... provides the basis for the civil society'; the emergence of civil society presupposes 'the self-organization of the population in terms of dwelling areas, reconciliation of different group interests, ... the creation of self-administrative councils and committees [and] of consumer cooperatives *(potrebitel'skie obshchestva)*'; the consolidation of the 'democratic structure of civil society' requires, among other things, 'development and expansion of socially significant middle classes' and 'social institutions guaranteeing the citizens' rights and freedoms'; and so on.[73]

However, the fact that here the Russians are adopting a ready-made model makes their project fundamentally different from the emergence of civil society in the West. There the people in the evolving popular organizations of the eighteenth and nineteenth centuries did not know that they were creating a 'civil society'; the present conception of it was established only retrospectively. That is, Western society developed without any idea of a 'Western orientation', whereas in Russia this orientation has meant a conscious, rapid and forced imposition of reforms copied from the West.[74]

A graphic illustration of the problem is V. Bibler's exceptionally detailed analysis of the 'civil society and the social contract'. On the one hand, he derives the necessity of civil society in Russia from the logic of the industrial society (it is needed in order that the industrial 'civilization' can function normally), but, on the other hand, he proposes that preconditions for it should be created 'in an accelerated tempo' and 'to a certain extent, artifically'.[75] This attitude implies a kind of Utopianism and elitism *vis-à-vis* the majority of population.

Utopianism among intellectuals seems inherent in the whole-sale adoption of a historical model from elsewhere, in giving an (abstract) idea of where the society is going.[76] Consequently, the notion of 'civil society' becomes an ingredient in the intellectuals' own self-definition and not only a part of their political programme. And insofar as 'civil society' constitutes an aspect of the intellectuals' adaptation to the present situation, the ideal may acquire a function very different from the original model, to some extent like the ideas of economic liberalism acquired a new meaning when adopted in Russia in the nineteenth century.[77]

* * *

The question of the emergence of civil society in Russia is of the utmost importance and urgency. As it was depicted above, civil society implies the denial of ideological monopoly, the acceptance of compromise on fundamental issues and the abandonment of messianism in its various forms. There is another available basis for political mobilization that can easily dispense with civil society, however. Nationalism, based on cultural identification, on the role of culture as the marker of collective boundaries, on a direct linkage between the leader(s) and the followers, and frequently on political messianism, does not require painstaking institution-building, but it can be activated quickly, not least in conditions of increasing economic misery and deepening feelings of national humiliation.[78]

NOTES

1. David W. Lovell, Civil Society and Soviet Studies: An Introductory Essay; in Chandran Kukathas, David W. Lovell and Wiliian Maley (eds), *The Transition from Socialism: State and Civil Society in the USSR* (Melbourne: Longman Cheshire, 1991), p. 6. Lovell speaks of the East Central European countries as well. Besides the volume above and other studies cited there, see various articles in Judith B. Sedaitis and Jim Butterfield (eds), *Perestroika from Below* (Boulder: Westview Press, 1991).
2. Jean L. Cohen, Strategy or Identity: New Theoretical Paradigms and Contemporary Social Movements. *Social Research,* vol. 52, no. 4, Winter 1985, p. 681; Gianfranco Poggi, *The State: Its Nature, Development and Prospects* (Stanford: Stanford University Press, 1990), p. 21, and Ilya Srubar, War der reale Sozialismus modern? Versuch einer strukturellen Bestimmung. *Kölner Zeitschrift für Soziologie und Sozialpsychologie*, vol. 43, no. 3/1991, pp. 416–18.
3. Richard Pipes, *Russia under the Old Regime* (London: Weidenfeld and Nicolson, 1974), p. xvii.
4. Ibid., p. xviii.
5. See, e.g., E. Mareeva, O krainostiakh neformalnogo politicheskogo myshleniya ili surrogatakh demokratizma; in V. I. Vyunitskii (ed.), *Neformaly: kto oni? kuda zovut?* (Moskva: Politizdat, 1990), pp. 71-5.
6. S. Frederick Starr, Soviet Union: A Civil Society. *Foreign Policy*, no. 70/1988, pp., 35.
7. Ibid., pp. 30.
8. Ibid., p. 31.
9. Ibid., p. 33-4.
10. Lovell, op. cit., p. 7.
11. T. H. Rigby, Mono-organisational Socialism and the Civil Society; in Chandran Kukathas, David W. Lovell and Willian Maley (eds), *The Transition from Socialism: State and Civil Society in the USSR* (Melbourne: Longman Cheshire, 1991), pp. 112–14.
12. Moshe Lewin, Russia/USSR in Historical Motion: An Essay in Interpretation. *The Russian Review*, vol. 50, no. 3, July 1991, pp. 265, 266.
13. Rigby, op. cit., p. 114.
14. Vladimir Shlapentokh, *Public and Private Life of the Soviet People: Changing Values in Post-Stalin Russia* (New York: Oxford University Press, 1989), pp. 190–202.
15. Shlapentokh, for example, defines civil society as 'the sphere of social life where people as private citizens interact with each other, creating their own organizations not controlled by the state' (ibid., p. 190). Rigby's definition is similar (Rigby, op. cit., p. 110).

16. Claus Offe, Reflections on the Institutional Self-Transformation of Movement Politics: A Tentative Stage Model; in Russell J. Dalton and Manfred Kuechler (eds), *Challenging the Political Order: New Social and Political Movements in Western Democracies* (Cambridge: Polity Press, 1990), p. 233.
17. Charles Tilly, *From Mobilization to Revolution* (Reading: Addison-Wesley, 1978), pp. 7–8.
18. Ibid., p. 63.
19. Ibid., p. 52.
20. On this, see Theodore Draper, Who Killed Soviet Communism? *The New York Review of Books*, vol. 39, no. 11/1992, p. 14.
21. See, e.g., Vladimir Pastukhov, God nesostoyavsheisya revolyutsii. *Megapolis-Express*, no. 31/1992 (5 August 1992).
22. André Grjebine, Ni plan ni marché: l'économie de corruption. *Le Debat*, no. 67/1991, p. 42.
23. See, e.g., Shlapentokh, 1989, esp. chapter 9; Vladimir Pastukhov, Novogodnie razmyshleniya o sudbe Rossii. *Obshchestvo*, 1 January 1992.
24. Grjebine, op. cit., p. 51.
25. See, e.g., I. A. Goldenberg, Klassovaya sushchnost 'simbioza'. *Sotsiologicheskie issledovaniya*, no. 1/1991, pp. 39–49.
26. S. R. Budina and M. N. Shmeleva, Gorod i narodnye traditsii russkikh (Moskva, 1989), as summarized in A. T. Shabanov, *V poiskakh opory dlya natsionalnogo samosoznaniya russkikh* (manuscript, 1991).
27. Alain Blum, *Systèmes démographiques soviétiques* (Thèse de doctorat, École des Hautes Études en Sciences Sociales, Paris, 1992), p. 15.
28. Ibid., pp. 14–15, cf. p. 442.
29. Shlapentokh, 1989, pp. 153–89.
30. Vladimir Shlapentokh, The Destruction of Civil Society in Russia (1917–1953); in Chandran Kukathas, David W. Lovell and Willian Maley (eds), *The Transition from Socialism: State and Civil Society in the USSR* (Melbourne: Longman Cheshire, 1991), p. 102.
31. See Srubar, op. cit., pp. 416–17, 420–5, 428.
32. Ibid., p. 428, 429; quotes in the original text.
33. Tilly, op. cit., pp. 73, 75.
34. Marie-Hélène Mandrillon, Les Voies du politique en URSS: l'exemple de l'écologie. *Annales E.S.C.*, no. 46, 1991, pp. 1376–85.
35. Jean-Marie Chauvier, *URSS: une société en mouvement* (Paris: Ed. de l'Aube, 1988); cited in Mandrillon, op. cit., p. 1376.
36. Oleg Yanitsky, Lefortovo, Moscow: Resolving the Conflict between Urban Planners and the Residents; in Tjeerd Deelstra and Oleg Yanitsky (eds), *Cities of Europe: The Public's Role in Shaping the Urban Environment* (Moskva: Mezhdunarodnye otnosheniya, 1991), pp. 367–71, and Oleg Yanitsky, *Sotsialnye dvizheniya. 100 intervyu s liderami* (Moskva: Moskovskii rabochii, 1991).
37. See especially various interviews in Yanitsky, Sotsialnye dvizheniya; cf. Mandrillon, op. cit., p. 1385.
38. Ernest Gellner, Nationalisme et politique en Europe de l'Est. *Le Débat*, no. 63/1990, p. 84.

39. Andrei Alekseev *et al.*, *Obshchestvennye dvizheniya i stanovlenie novoi vlasti v Leningrade (1986–1991)* (Institut sotsiologii Akademii Nauk SSSR, Leningradskij filial, Sektor sotsiologii obshchestvennykh dvizhenii, mimeo, 1991), is an illuminating case study of Leningrad.
40. A. P. Kochetkov, Politicheskie partii i grazhdanskoe obshchestvo; in *Mnogopartiinost i obshchestvennye dvizheniya. Tendentsii i prognoz*, vol. 1 (Moskva: Institut Sotsiologii AN SSSR. Tsentr po izucheniyu sotsialno-politicheskikh i ideologicheskikh protsessov, 1990), p. 44.
41. A. M. Davtyan, *Alternativnye politicheskie dvizheniya: realnost i perspektivy. Programma Otdeleniya filosofii i prava AN SSSR 'Sotsialnye protsessy v usloviyakh perestroiki'*. Informatsionnye materialy, vol. 4 (Moskva: Akademiya Nauk SSSR, Institut Sotsiologii, 1990), p. 62.
42. A good description of developments in Moscow is provided by Vyacheslav Igrunov, Öffentlichkeitsbewegungen in der UdSSR: Vom Protest zum politischen Selbstbewusstsein; in Klaus Segbers (ed.), *Perestrojka: Zwischenbilanz* (Frankfurt am Main: Suhrkamp, 1990), pp. 76–105. There are several reference works on new political organizations, for example A. Morozov (ed.), *Novye politicheskie partii i organizatsii 1988–1990* (Kishinev, 1990); Gleb Pavlovskii (ed.), *Slovar oppozitsii. Novye politicheskie partii i organizatsii Rossii* (Moskva: PostFactum, 1991); V. N. Berezovskij, N. I. Krotov and V. V. Chervyakov (eds), *Rossiya: Partii, assotsiatsii, soyuzy, kluby*, 2 vols (Moskva: Izdatelstvo "Rau-Press", 1991): B. I. Koval (ed.), *Rossiya segodnya. Politicheskii portret v dokumentakh 1985–1991* (Moskva: Mezhdunarodnye otnosheniya, 1991) and Vladimir Pribylovskii (ed.), *Dictionary of Political Parties and Organizations in Russia* (Moscow: PostFactum/Interlegal, 1992).
43. See Pipes, op. cit., p. 264.
44. Ibid., p. 256.
45. V. N. Berezkovsky and N. I. Krotov, 'Neformaly' - kto oni? in V. N. Berezkovsky and N. I. Krotov (eds), *Neformalnaya Rossiya* (Moskva: Molodaya gvardiya, 1990), p. 23 (quotation), 24–6.
46. Igor Sundiev, Nashestvie marsian...? in S. N. Yushenkov (ed.), *Neformaly. Sotsialnye initsiativy* (Moskva: Moskovskii rabochii, 1990), pp. 21, 23, 29, 33–6, 39.
47. Starr, op. cit., p. 33; and to take examples of two different but representative views, see Yuri Bluvshtein and Viktor Yustitskij, Neformalnaya gruppa: chto eto takoe? *Molodoi kommunist*, no. 6/1987, pp. 61–8 and V. F. Levicheva, *Molodezhnyj Vavilon. Razmyshleniya o neformalnom dvizhenii* (Moskva: Molodaya gvardiya, 1989).
48. Berezkovsky and Krotov, op. cit., pp. 14–15.
49. Ibid., p. 15.
50. Jurij Levada, Was sagt des Volkes Stimme? in Klaus Segbers (ed.), *Perestrojka: Zwischenbilanz* (Frankfurt am Main: Suhrkamp, 1990), p. 132.
51. Mareeva, op. cit., pp. 79–82, 85–7.
52. See, e.g., Levada, op. cit., pp. 132–4, 140–1.
53. There are illuminating remarks about such developments in Leningrad,

in Alekseev *et al.*, op. cit., pp. 32–4, 41–6; and in E. Zdravomyslova, *Mobilizatsiya resursov demokraticheskogo dvizheniya v Leningrade (1987–1990 gody)* (manuscript, 1991).

54. Vladimir Pastukhov, *Obshchestvennoe dvizhenie Rossii v epokhu perestroiki* (Moskva: Komitet VS RSFSR po delam molodezhi, 1991).
55. Vladimir Koulistikov, Droles de partis... *Belvédère*, no. 4/1992, pp. 23–4.
56. Koulistikov, op. cit., pp. 23–4; cf. Pastukhov, 1991, pp. 27–39.
57. Leonid Gordon and E. Klopov, Perestroika i novoe rabochee dvizhenie; in A. A. Protashchik (ed.), *Cherez ternii* (Moskva: Progress, 1990), pp. 754–70; Nicholas Werth, Renaissance et dilemmes du mouvement ouvrier en Union soviétique. *Le Débat*, no. 67/1991, esp. p. 59.
58. L. A. Gordon, Protiv gosudarstvennogo sotsializma: vozmozhnosti rabochego dvizheniya. *Politicheskie issledovaniya*, no. 1/1991, p. 75. See also Boris Kagarlitskij, Eshche odno zharkoe leto; in S. N. Yushenkov (ed.), *Neformaly. Sotsialnye initsiativy* (Moskva: Moskovskii rabochii, 1990), pp. 134–5.
59. Gordon, op. cit., p. 78.
60. L. A. Gordon, Rabochee dvizhenie v poslesotsialisticheskoi perspektive. *Sotsiologicheskie issledovaniya*, no. 11/1991, pp. 16–17.
61. A. A. Shkreba, Tsugtsvang ('Chernye' i 'belye' na polyakh zabastovki). *Politicheskie issledovaniya*, no. 1/1991, p. 116 (quotation), 117–21.
62. Ibid., pp. 120–1 and Michael Burawoy and Kathryn Hendley, Between *Perestroika* and Privatization: Divided Strategies and Political Crisis in a Soviet Enterprise. *Soviet Studies*, vol. 44, no. 3/1992, pp. 392–5. See also Temkina's informative case study of the limits of the workers' movement: Anna A. Temkina, The Workers' Movement in Leningrad, 1986–91. *Soviet Studies*, vol. 44, no. 2/1992, pp. 209–36.
63. Gordon, Protiv gosudarstvennogo sotsializma, p. 76.
64. Gordon, Rabochee dvizhenie, p. 11.
65. Joel C. Moses, Soviet Provincial Politics in an Era of Transition and Revolution, 1989–91. *Soviet Studies*, vol. 44, no. 3/1992, p. 484.
66. Ibid., p. 482. On the role of the workers' movement in local politics, see also Werth, op. cit., pp. 60, 70–1.
67. Lewin, op. cit., p. 251.
68. Dean C. Tipps, Modernization Theory and the Comparative Study of Societies: A Critical Perspective. *Comparative Studies in Society and History*, vol. 15, no. 2/1973, p. 206.
69. On this theme, see e.g. A. S. Akhiezer, Chto mozhet i chego ne mozhet reforma? *Politicheskie issledovaniya*, no. 1/1991, pp. 58–66.
70. See also Vladimir Kostyushev, Die 'postkatastrophale Gesellschaft' und ihre Bewegungen; in Klaus Segbers (ed.), *Perestrojka: Zwischenbilanz* (Frankfurt am Main: Suhrkamp, 1990), pp. 143–53.
71. Rigby, op. cit., p. 108.
72. Cited in B. I. Koval (ed.), *Rossiya segodnya. Politicheskii portret v dokumentakh 1985–1991*, p. 39; cf. Kochetkov, op. cit., p. 54.
73. The quotations come, repectively, from the programme of the Free Democratic Party of Russia (*Informatsionnyj Byulleten*, no. 1 [St. Petersburg: Dvizhenie 'Demokraticheskaya Rossiya, Sankt-

Peterburgskoe regionalnoe otdelenie, 1992], p. 7); from the programme proposal of the Social Democratic Party of the Russian Federation (*Politicheskie issledovaniya*, no. 1/1991, p. 208); and from the annual report of the Institute of Sociology of the Academy of Sciences of the USSR (*Otchet o rezultatakh vypolneniya nauchno-issledovatelskikh rabot i nauchno-organizatsionnoi deyatelnosti instituta za 1990 god* [Moskva: Akademiya Nauk SSSR, Institut Sotsiologii, 1990], p. 31–2); see also formulations in Rigby, op. cit., pp. 108–9.

74. See Boris Kagarlitski, *Hajonnut monoliitti* (Helsinki: Orient Express, 1992), pp. 74–7.
75. V. Bibler, O grazhdanskom obshchestve i obshchestvennom dogovore; in A. A. Protashchik (ed.), *Cherez ternii* (Moskva: Progress, 1990), pp. 335–61 (quotations come from pp. 350, 352, 358).
76. Cf. Yu. S. Pivovarov, Zametki o russkoi politicheskoi kulture, ee raskolakh, tselostnosti i ee mifakh; in *Novoe politicheskoe myshlenie i protsess demokratizatsii* (Sovetskaya Assotsiatsiya Politicheskikh Nauk, Ezhegodnik 1990 [Moskva: Nauka, 1990]), pp. 146–8.
77. See, e.g., Esther Kingston-Mann, In the Light and Shadow of the West: The Impact of Western Economics in Pre-emancipatory Russia. *Comparative Studies in Society and History*, vol. 33, no. 1, January 1991, pp. 87–105.
78. See Ernest Gellner, From the Ruins of the Great Contest... *The Times Literary Supplement*, 13 March 1992.

13. NATIONALISM, NATION STATE AND PROSPECTS OF DEMOCRATIZATION IN EASTERN EUROPE

Maté Szabo

1. INTRODUCTION

Recent political developments in East Central Europe[1] have produced contradictory and ambivalent tendencies towards the nation state in post-communist democracies. The emancipation from Soviet influence and the dissolution of the Soviet empire opened up political space for the reconstruction of national sovereignty in former Soviet-dominated states. The liberation from Soviet rule and the institutionalization of new constitutional structures was a 'national' issue. National unity, traditions, culture and interests are reaffirmed and resurrected in post-communist politics, as factors that were formerly neglected and marginalized. In this 'national renaissance' in Eastern Europe, there are different political traditions and tendencies that are being awakened and reconstructed. Their relationship to the values of pluralist democracy and human rights is sometimes overshadowed by anti-modernist and traditionalist orientations. Karl Deutsch has stated on nationalism in Eastern Europe: 'The psychology of total disregard for individual rights was cultivated in Eastern Europe by nationalism. Almost every nationalist move or movement by one nationality produced nationalist counter-movements by its neighbours, and both nationalism and counternationalism agreed in disregarding the rights of individuals.'[2]

Parallel to the tendency of stressing nation state and nation as ultimate values and actors in the political universe, the political élite of the new post-communist democracies wish to join the Western European and North Atlantic economic-political integration, the European Community and NATO. The same political forces, preaching national engagement and the rebuilding of the nation state and culture, argue for European integration (or reintegration) as a precondition of the stabilization of democracy and modernization. Paradoxically, there are at the same time nationalist and integrationist political forces in Eastern Europe.

During the system transformation, national consciousness has been reshaped in Eastern Europe. The construction of new elements of national identity has different levels. First, there is a selective reconstruction of the past. Traditions of the communist system are severely criticized or directly rejected as alien elements in the national history. Second and parallel to this, pre-communist and anti-communist traditions have undergone a rather undifferentiated and uncritical revival. Inter-war and even older traditions of nationalism and nation state may be integrated into the new patterns of political identification. The present condition of the nation and nation state is seen in the phase of starting, restarting or continuing the nation-building processes which the communist intervention interrupted. Conflicts with rivals and challengers, with neighbouring nation states or ethnic minorities, could re-emerge.

The future vision of the nation and nation state in East Central Europe is rather illogical from the point of view of the past and present situations. As Eric Hobsbawm has postulated, 'at the end of the twentieth century, diminishing economic and political competence of the nation state toward global challenges contradicts the idea of new nation states in Europe'.[3] In fact, the first thing most of these hypothetical new European states would do is, almost certainly, to apply for admission to the European

Community (EC), which would once again limit their sovereign rights, though in a different manner from their previous situation. The foreign policy strategies of the new European nations all aim at membership in the EC. But this membership, which thus involves the limitation of the sovereignty of its members, contradicts the traditions of nation states in Eastern Europe. The EC is a symbol of modernity, democracy and civic culture for East Europeans. But the past and present of these nations, resurrected by the post-communist national revival, involve counterproductive tendencies.

2. PRE-COMMUNIST TRADITIONS

Empires vs. National Cultures

According to the historical schema of Ernest Gellner, nation-building in Eastern Europe was confronted with the existence and predominance of religious and dynastic empires in the eighteenth and nineteenth centuries.[4] The development of national consciousness and nationalism originated from the ethnic and culture-based framework of Johan Herder and Friedrich Meinecke.[5] Eastern European nations have tended to build up their own nation states according to the logic of 'one nation – one state', and their objectives conflict with the existence of multinational empires and with the independence of other nations in the framework of these empires. The imperial past was not concerned with the idea of national autonomy, and gave birth to ethnic and cultural mixtures, hardly organized according to the logic of nation states.[6]

Under these circumstances, as Jenö Szücs has pointed out, very direct connections developed between national and historical consciousness.[7] Emerging culture-based nations, without the traditions of a nation state, tried to find their historical predecessors before the establishment of empires. The existence of the nation and national consciousness was traced back by national-minded individuals into ancient and medieval times. Competing and mutually exclusive historical constructions and arguments emerged in the development of nations in East Central Europe.

Nationhood in East Central Europe was overladen with functions of modernization, democratization and state-building. Popular expectations of the dissolution of the Austro-Hungarian monarchy united national, social and democratic issues in the popular mind, as Peter Hanak pointed out when analysing letters of soldiers and prisoners-of-war to their families.[8] Deutsch emphasized the strong affiliation of ethnic and social segregation in Eastern Europe, giving nationalism a social impetus, directed both to the elites and to the empires.[9] According to Gellner, the dissolution of empires has been retarted in this region recently, because the Soviet Union succeeded in re-establishing and even extending the traditional Russian Empire on the basis of a new, secular legitimation. Cultural nations striving for independence from the Russian-Soviet Empire, and their conflict with each other, dominate the political scene in Eastern Europe.

Despite the fact that the imperial framework was preserved in the Soviet Union, nation-building and state-building proved to be the mainstream tendency in East Central Europe. The dissolution of the Austro-Hungarian and Soviet empires were both followed by the establishment of nation states. The pre-communist political traditions of the new nation states were based on the experiences of the interwar period. This short period was overshadowed by the military-political threat of fascist Germany and communist Soviet Union. But it was not only the foreign threat and military conflict that contributed to the loss of sovereignty of these nation states.

Unstable Nation States

Hugh Seton-Watson concluded in his analysis of the interwar socio-political condition of this region that unsolved problems of modernization and democratization led to sharp national, social and political conflicts, creating a crisis of democracy and the establishment of authoritarian regimes.[10] With the exception of Czechoslovakia, a weak bourgeoisie, strong agrarian and feudal structures and traditional military-bureaucratic elites produced unfavourable internal conditions for democratization, hindered also by the fascist and communist threat and different national conflicts. Popular expectations of the establishment of nation states with higher social and democratic standards on the ruins of Austria-Hungary were widely disillusioned. According to Hobsbawm, the interwar conditions of nation states in East Central Europe reproduced the national conflicts and problems of the empire in another way: 'Most of the new states built on the ruins of the old empires were quite as multinational as the old prisons of nations they replaced.' He argues that the establishment of nation states in this region was even a step toward 'later fascist and communist violence against ethnic groups'.

The logical implication of trying to create a continent neatly divided into coherent territorial states, each inhabited by a separate ethnically and linguistically homogenous population, was 'mass expulsion or extermination of minorities'. Such was and is 'the murderous *reductio ab absurdum* of nationalism in its territorial version'.[11] The interwar period during which nation states flourished in East Central Europe is hardly to be estimated as a proper basis for progressive political orientations – with the exception of Czechoslovakia – towards the recent democratization period. This should be stressed against the conservative-nationalist stream of resurrecting all anti- and pre-communist traditions as a healthy basis for a political culture in new democracies.

In Eastern Europe, conflicts of democratization and nationalism occur when their common enemy, the imperial order, has been dissolved. There are some analogous elements between the situation during the interwar period and today's post-communist conditions, in the sense that democracy and nationalism could cooperate in the underground and within the opposition movements against the anti-democratic imperial order, while since the breakthrough and establishment of the new political system their conflict and differentiation seem to be inevitable.

Interwar traditions, too, are upheld in the most influential political parties of the following period, i.e., in the East European communist parties. One of the main targets of the critique of the communist parties in the interwar period was 'bourgeois nationalism'. The national critique made communist parties attractive for the Jewish population and for other minorities, and all this contributed to the image of communists as 'alien to the nation'. But, on the other hand, communists tried to establish political coalitions with the 'patriotic nationalist opposition' against fascists in the framework of 'people's fronts', which helped their acceptance by other political forces in the postwar period.[12]

To sum up relevant pre-communist traditions for the recent political development in Eastern Europe, there is an ambivalent relationship between democratization and nation-building in this region. The national consciousness and the idea of a nation state developed contrary to supranational entities, and this united nationalists and democrats in a common political camp against the empires and their elites. But after the dissolution of the empires, the new nation states were not able to establish stable democracies. Authoritarian regimes, suppression of minorities, national conflicts and their involvement in the fascist–communist confrontation dominated the political scene in East Central Europe until the end of the Second World War.

3. COMMUNIST RULE AND THE NATION STATE

Stalinist 'Internationalism' and Defensive Nationalism

Between the end of the Second World War and the communist takeover, coalition governments with the presence and sometimes with the predominance of Soviet-backed communists ruled in East Central Europe.[13] During the democratic interlude, communist parties played their political role as parts of the Soviet-directed network. They ended up in a confrontation with their former allies, with the national-democratic liberal and peasant parties that defended national independence against Soviet dependence, and tried to uphold Western connections. Former 'democratic' coalitions split and became communist-dominated. Communist politics in Eastern Europe were deeply involved in the Soviet imperial strategy set up by Stalin, and forces insisting on national and bourgeois values were forced underground by the supporters of the Stalinist Soviet models. The following and copying of the Soviet model was extremely exaggerated; for example, serious experiments to produce cotton in Hungary were propagated by the communists as a future-oriented innovation.

The suppression of all non-communist political orientations after the communist takeover produced a type of 'negative coalition'. Partisans of the previous authoritarian-nationalist regimes were persecuted in the same way as liberals, social democrats or reform communists. In the political emigration and in the underground opposition against Stalinism and communism, representatives of various political orientations were able to create a limited political solidarity, which sometimes reached the level of joint political action. A good example of the anti-Stalinist and anti-communist national upheaval and protest was the Hungarian revolution of 1956.[14]

From the reform communists to the supporters of the Horthy regime and the Catholic Church, national mobilization occurred against the Stalinist, pro-Soviet regime. Of course, splits and conflicts among different political orientations and traditions appeared in the dynamics of the revolution and the protest. But the national character of 1956 was upheld during the decades of communist rule. Paradoxically, suppression sometimes even strengthened nationalism. Nation states were not abolished by the new order. In terms of social mobilization and assimilation, the Stalinist modernization policy with its forced industrialization and urbanization and extreme centralization could even contribute to further processes of nation-building. Communication and economic relations were highly inward-oriented and excluded trends of the European and world economy, favouring thus some autharchic tendencies. As Karl Deutsch has summed up, 'communism has not abolished the nation state... If we judge it by an analysis of transactions leads, it may have even strengthened it.'[15]

Post-Stalinist Prospects

Post-Stalinist communist systems tried to integrate elements of national legitimation and to destroy the unity of nationalism and anticommunism.[16] During the post-1956 'restoration policy' of Janos Kadar, after the first waves of counter-revolutionary violence and suppression, leading representatives of the 'populist' intellectuals became reconciled with the new regime, which was ready to support the national culture and identity to a certain extent and to give up Stalinist patterns of 'internationalism'. Communism and nationalism had a certain limited playground where they could cooperate and work together in Eastern Europe: both pleaded for total social mobilization, emphasized social issues, and disregarded human rights and pluralism.[17]

The national autonomy and independence within the policy of individual communist coutries was limited by Soviet intervention and the cooperation of institutions of the socialist countries. Soviet-dominated Eastern bloc created integrative economic and security mechanisms such as the Warsaw Treaty and COMECON, functioning as 'transmission belts' of the Soviet centre.[18] There were more and more cooperative elements built into these integrative institutions, but their compulsory character was sanctioned by Soviet military forces in crisis situations, for example in 1956 in Hungary and in 1968 in Czechoslovakia. The effects of this integration in the socialist countries were overwhelmingly counterproductive and strengthened the desire for national autonomy and integration with the West. In the shadow of internationalist slogans, national foreign trade and policy patterns were put forward.

The crisis of the planned economy, centralized one-party rule and various international conflicts opened up more possibilities for autonomous 'national' policies within the Eastern bloc in the 1970s and 1980s. This political space was used in different ways in the domestic and foreign policy of individual Eastern European countries. As Charles Gati has shown in his analysis of the policy of Kadar's Hungary, the communist political élite stood between a double legitimation challenge: loyalty to the Soviet centre on one hand and the legitimation by the nation and civil society on the other. In the Hungarian case, limited foreign policy indepencence towards the Soviet Union was the price paid for domestic economic and social reforms based on popular social and national expectations. This produced a kind of national support for the Kadar regime.[19]

In the case of Romania, autonomous foreign policy became mixed with a strong Stalinist domestic policy and nationalist tendencies. The general trend in East Central Europe was the use of the political space by the communist elites to gain national support by formulating autonomous foreign and domestic policies. In these experiments, such as in Hungary and Romania, pre-communist patterns and traditions reappeared, together with problems of national minorities, national interests in foreign policy, national traditions in culture and history, discussions on the reinterpretation and 'messages' of national history, etc. Through this trend in the 1980s, nation and nation state re-emerged in the communist politics in East Central Europe, with reminiscences of the pre-communist past.

These developments in autonomous foreign and domestic policies and the emphasis on national development did not necessarily coincide with democratization and liberalization in the former socialist countries. Romania's well-known example from the 1980s showed that the emphasis on national elements and an anti-Soviet orientation could coexist with a post-Stalinist authoritarian orientation.[20] The same differentiation among nationalists and liberal democrats can be found in the political opposition. Political oppositions in the communist states have been divided by the national issue. As Herbert Kitschelt in his analysis on the re-emerging Eastern European party system has stated: 'Opposition to communists in East Central Europe was probably more strongly driven by national and religious fervour than the yearning for democratic liberties... Hence, opposition forces may combine a rejection of socialism and redistrubutive policies and a preference for free markets with authoritarian conceptions of political decision making and exclusive definitions of citizenship. In contrast, an intelligentsia that combines libertarian and redistributive prgrammes will constitute a distinct minority view.'[21]

According to the analysis of George Schöpflin, at the end of the 1970s there were already clear-cut differentiations among the Hungarian opposition between national-populist and liberal-democratic tendencies.[22] Of course, there is a variety of acceptance of the national issue both at the level of communist elites and at the level of alternative political groups, depending on different domestic and international factors in East Central European countries.

At the edge of the system transformation, the unity of the Eastern bloc and the solidarity of the socialist countries were highly endangered. There were more or less open tensions and conflicts between the Soviet Union and the East Central European states, appearing sometimes even as economic and political disputes among them, inside their joint organs. The opening up by Mikhail Gorbachev helped to speed up the formulation of independent national and international policies by the members of the Eastern bloc. This different development and the new political orientations resulted in a web of conflicts and tensions which paved the way for the decomposition of the integrative mechanisms.

The process of democratization in 1989–1990 in East Central Europe was the first sign of the dissolution of the Soviet Union. Nation-building and democratization processes there were again settled in the framework of the nation states, which proved to be the basis of political freedom and cultural identity against the Soviet empire and communist ideology. National protest movements and nation-wide alternative organizations emerged as leading forces of the breakthrough. But during the process of institutionalizing the new political system, differentiation at organizational and ideological levels occurred between the nationalist-populist and liberal-democratic forces. The communist party with its monopoly on political power disappeared as the common enemy. The first 'founding' elections and the discussions over the policies of the first freely elected governments produced different cleavages and differentiations among new political movements. The national issue played an important role in this process.

National Issues in the System Transformation

The system transformation and the democratization processes in East Central Europe had a twofold connection with nation and nationalism. First, national problems and grievances were mobilizing actors in the new political field. Secondly, in the 'umbrella organizations', within the all-embracing 'national fronts', in agreements on round-table talks by all 'national' political forces to constitute a new political community and in 'national institutions', national unity and national leaders represented the symbolic and integrative forces of the new field, claiming to represent the political community as a whole. The first aspect is rather a problem of policy input and output, that of agenda setting, while the second is a matter of policy, of institutional setting. The two levels are connected with each other. National issues could integrate the political community, but also divide it. National issues appear in the system transformation as unifying and mobilizing forces against the old system, but later they may become the cleavages of the new political differentiation. The organization and political leadership during the first period cannot sustain the restructuring of political conflicts. As long as the communist party maintains administrative-political control, the counter-movements are connected to a national front with national leaders. After the dissolution of the monopoly of power and after the establishment of new political opportunity structures, national leadership and unity have to fit into a pluralistic political field.

The processes of system transformation in East Central Europe had similar dynamics, but with considerable national differences.[23] Steps typical to these processes can be identified. The first step is the phase of crisis, with the destabilization of the old political institutions and elites and the emergence of new political forces. During this phase, different strategies of elite reactions interact with the dynamics of protest. The opening up of new political space, agreements on the framework of transition and the division of the old elite into conservatives and reformers are distinctive features in this phase. The elite reaction is constitutive for the differentiation or unity of the new political forces. Some elements of cooperation between new non-communist political directions can be found everywhere, but the organizational and strategic unity may be temporary or longer-lasting.

The next phase is that of the breakthrough, the

dissolution of the communist monopoly on political power and their political-administrative control. This phase occurred in East Central Europe in a non-violent way, through negotiation. But there were considerable differences as to whether mass mobilizations were necessary to push the communists to bargain and accept compromises with the new political forces. Round-table talks were typical of this phase, establishing contemporary institutions with the task of carrying out political change. Before the first free elections, the axis of political conflicts might emerge among the new political organizations. The former 'national unity' against communist rule dissolved 'national front' organizations faster or more slowly on the way towards a multi-party system.

Institutionalization of the new political system followed similar patterns: from constitutional change to free election and then to the differentiation of the new political forces along the separation between government and opposition. The distribution of power took place according to the recently established rules, based on constitutional democracy. The very end of the process, institutionalizing the new political system, is still far away: stabilization of new institutions, formulation of new policies and acceptance of the rules of the game of the new political culture are a long-lasting process. During this phase, differentiation of the original 'national' unity is necessary so that the interest articulation can occur along the lines of political cleavages, political ideologies and programmes, and the institutionalized political opportunity structures.

During the phase of system transformation, a structural change of social-political subjects is also taking place. Social movements, mobilized by crisis and protest, set up transitory coalitions with temporary organizational implications. The emergence of the party system is an important step in this institutionalization. With free elections, the distribution of power and the formulation of national policy led to the setting up of new institutional structures, representing 'national' interests within pluralistic, conflict-based modern societies. It is a long way from 'national unity' embodied in 'umbrella organizations' and 'round tables' to the establishing of public and constitutional institutions, but East Central European societies had to make this transition very rapidly. Fast and conflict-ridden political learning processes marked this development, which varied from country to country. But in East Central Europe there are also some common elements, based on a common historical and cultural heritage and on geographic, economic and social ties to Western Europe, especially compared to the post-communist development in the Balkan area and in the former Soviet Union.

One of the important distinctive features in East Central Europe is the absence of violent ethnic and territorial conflicts, such as those which followed the dissolution of multi-ethnic federal states such as the Soviet Union and Yugoslavia. Despite the fact that territorially based ethnic minorities exist, they do not provoke violent mobilization of majorities, nor do they serve as starting points for such mobilizations. Ethnic violence seems to be under control in this region, where new political institutions, constitutional arrangements and political parties are used as acceptable channels for the distribution of power. It will not be discussed here whether the political tradition of the coexistence of different ethnic groups, the understanding of and experience with ethnic minorities, and a feel for political compromises and the rule of law are distinct characteristics of political culture in Central Europe, as Zdenek Mlynar puts it; nor whether the recent political learning processes from social mobilization to political institutionalization have been successful.[24] In the following section, I will compare the democratization processes in East Central European countries in order to determine their common and distinct phenomena and features.

The democratization processes in East Central Europe thus stress the transitory character of national mobilization and leadership. The institutionalization of pluralist democracy and the dissolution of the communist power monopoly led to the differentiation of the political scene, with conflicts and tensions between national and democratic directions. Issues of nation- and state-building are especially invoked in the democratization processes of the former GDR and Czechoslovakia. A general problem seems to be the institutionalization of the political representation of ethnic minorities and the providing of political space for them in new democracies. The establishment of new constitutional structures have to meet demands of pluralization and democratization in a situation of economic and social crisis, which may result in an ethnic-based or nationalist social-political mobilization.

New democracies have to establish their relations with other nation states and respond to the challenge of European integration and the problems of nation building in Central Europe. How is the future of the nation state then to be reconsidered in post-communist societies? There are some intellectual and political debates going on about alternative futures of the nation state in the new Europe, which seek to answer the problems and experiences of the nation states in East Central Europe. New foreign policies are also being formulated. Intellectual and political discussions on the perspectives and alternatives of the nation state are confronted with the rather uncertain future of this region.

4. POST-COMMUNIST TENDENCIES

In various analyses of the democratic transformation in East Central Europe, the ambivalent character of nationalism in this process has been emphasized. Some postulate a type of polarization between nationalist-conservative and European-type democratic political forces. According to Adam Michnik, a well-known Polish politician, the most important political cleavage in post-totalitarian Europe is that between 'supporters and leaders of a democratic, pluralist and tolerant Europe' and 'the national centrist authoritarianism'.[25] After the defeat of communism, a comeback and restoration of elementary ethnic identity can be observed. The emerging nationalism is ambivalent; it involves elements of emancipation from the Soviet rule, but at the same time it produces old and new conflicts among nation states as well as among ethnic groups and their political organizations.

Jacques Rupnik has asked how far the communist suppression and persecution can steer learning processes in East European nationalism to be more tolerant and pluralist, or whether it will restore its fundamentalistic ethnic character as a 'freezing in a fridge?'[26] Jadwiga Staniszkis for her part sees nationalism as an important mobilizing and solidarizing force against the atomization and privatization of the communist past.[27] According to her, the dominance of nationalism is inevitable in societies with fragile and discontinuous traditions of civil society and civic culture. The development of civil society and the stabilization of its institutions in the economy, law, politics and culture could counterbalance the central and uncontrolled role of the national revival in Eastern Europe. Another argument is that East Central European countries should extend their political ties with each other, and reduce their potential and actual conflicts of the national past and present in the spirit of a democratic and European future. The idea of a Central European federation and even statehood, as a step in this direction, is present in the intellectual and political discourses of these countries.

Utopia and Reality of a Central European Community

There are traditions in the intellectual-political discourses of former opposition intellectuals concerning more extensive political frameworks beyond nationalism and nation states in East Central Europe. In the 1980s, the discussion started by Milan Kundera, György Konrad, Vaclav Havel, etc. resulted in a postulate of some common traits of East Central European cultural identity, seen as a possible origin for alternative political developments within the Soviet bloc, opening up to Western Europe and demanding more autonomy from the Soviet empire.[28] On the margins of these discussions, there also appeared some proposals for a loose confederation of some East Central European countries, with remnants from older federation plans in this region.[29] Although some leaders of the former civil rights opposition gained political influence and leading positions in post-communist politics, the realization of these ideas seems not to be on the agenda in the foreign policy of the new democracies.

The transformation of the political systems in East Central European countries were related to each other, but they included much fewer elements and phenomena of solidarity than their great predecessors, the revolutions of 1848–1849. After the breakthrough there were some kind of ‘negative coalitions’ in different countries, leading to the dissolution of COMECON and the Warsaw Treaty. But even during the negotiations with the Soviet Union on the withdrawal of their troops and on the new economic-political treaties, considerable differences on standpoints and strategies appeared among countries such as Poland, Czechoslovakia and Hungary. The developing regional cooperation among these three countries was based on their experiences of the rather reluctant reactions of the EC and NATO to their individual applications for membership, and on the dangers produced by the dissolution of the Soviet Union. Regional cooperation is seen in East Central Europe as directly connected to the prospective West European integration, as formulated in the slogan ‘come back to Europe’.[30] The existing relations of Poland, Hungary and Czechoslovakia are far away from the hopes entertained by intellectual supporters of the idea or Utopia of an integrated Central Europe. The existing cooperation is overshadowed by conflicts and competition, it is limited in scope, it is transitory by nature and a type of ‘compensation’ instead of being a part of Western integration, and highly dependent on Western support and aid.[31]

In the intellectual-political discussions of post-communist democracies, the idea or Utopia of Central Europe has further relevance, but the realization of a type of solidarity community in the region, through federal boundaries, is becoming more and more unlikely. Ferenc Miszlivetz, a Hungarian sociologist, concluded his analysis of the debate on Central Europe during and after the breakthrough as follows: ‘While Western European integration develops toward the twentyfirst century, the other half of the continent reaffirms the economic and philosophical myths of the eighteenth and nineteenth centuries, hoping to get their help in the comeback to Europe. The proposals for regional integration or confederation are marginalized by the individual, country-specific strategies... The empty space, due to the absence of the spirit of cooperation, is filled by ideological residues. The disillusions of hopes awakened the nationalisms from their long dreams.’[32]

Miszlivetz, analysing the causes of defeat of Central

European integration, makes a distinction between external and internal factors. External factors for him are the reluctance of the EC to initiate collective regional aid programmes and the exclusion of East Central Europe from the European integration process represented by the EC. On the other hand, the internal political conditions of regional integration seem to be lacking also. Beyond this actual political situation, structural reasons such as the weakness of civil society and civic culture are the main obstacles in building up new identities beyond national culture and ethnicity. The missing links are 'greater measures of cooperation, patterns of non-violent conflict resolution, tolerance toward minorities and the ability to live together with different people'. A new identity should be found, not by 'rejecting the traditions of the nineteenth century, but also not by taking them as sources of revival'.[33]

Alternative forms of relations between nation states and ethnic minorities for East Central Europe were proposed by the Hungarian novelist György Konrad in his speech held on the occasion of his accepting the Peace Prize of the German book trade in autumn 1991. These included the acceptance of multiple citizenship. He said that both culture and the nation state could help in building up ties among the new democracies of the region and in calming down minority conflicts. The collective should give up the demand for total control of the individual; pluralism and citizenship should become the institutionalizations of the existing multiplicity of identities. 'Citizenship' instead of 'ethnicity' as a solution for reconstruction in Central Europe was the proposal of the Hungarian sociologist Ivan Szelenyi.[34]

These proposals are quite opposite to the mainstream of nation-building patterns in this region. Instead of Eastern European patterns of ethnic-cultural roots underlying nation states, the 'spirit of constitution', 'the patriotism of the constitution' should be the integrative element in new democracies. In this way, we could escape the defunct patterns of nineteenth-century nationalism and support the 'comeback' to Europe.

An important cleavage in the new party systems connected with the problem of reorganizing the nation state and ethnicity is formulated by Herbert Kitschelt as follows:

'Questions of citizenship relate to cleavages concerning ethnicity, race, and territorial autonomy... At one end of the spectrum of the East Central European party systems are demands for the inclusive definition of citizenship, no longer identified with a dominant national ethnicity but building on a cosmopolitan and culturally pluralist notion of citizenship. At the other end is an exclusive definition of citizenship based on the natural cultural homogeneity.'[35] According to Kitschelt, the citizenship cleavage divides libertarian-cosmopolitan from authoritarian-localist groups. This conflict is embedded in the context of other cleavages such as the differentiation according to political preferences for market or non-market allocation of goods, egalitarian or meritocratic distribution principles, participatory or hierarchic organization of society and politics etc. The political universe of the post-communist democracies is a multipolar political space divided by a variety of political cleavages, which partly overlap each other.

There is a danger that the re-emergence of nation states in East Central Europe will give rise to problems similar to those of the inter-war period. Seton-Watson concluded his analysis of the minority problems in this region as follows: 'The problem can only be solved if it is possible to combine free use of the native language and the recognition of the personal nationality of the citizen with the loyalty to a state which stands above the ethnical principle and includes men of different nations.'

This solution based on cultural autonomy and supra-national states' is opposed by the same force that Seton-Watson described as prevailing during the Second World War, based on the experience with the nation states in Eastern Europe: 'It is doubtful, however, whether the nationalist intellectual class and its pupils in the army, bureaucracy and commerce ... could ever accept this principle. These people could not be satisfied with cultural autonomy. They require nothing less than a National State in which the whole military, bureaucratic and commercial apparatus of State Sovereignty is monopolized by them as rulers of the majority nation within the State. They require this partly because it affords them opportunities for personal enrichment and power which would be denied them under any other system, and partly because their ideological leaders ... are convinced and have implanted in their own heads the conviction that no nation can escape physical annihilation that does not possess a Sovereign State of its own, equipped with all the tools of modern Integral Nationalism.'[36]

Of course, there are different forms of nationalism in post-communist East Central Europe, determined by different factors such as political cultures etc., and they are not necessarily in conflict with democratization. In Eastern Europe, nationalism must not be ethnic-based, exclusive and intolerant or even violent, in spite of the fact that this image and experience dominates its history. Kaminski and Kurczewska have criticized Michnik's thesis of the dichotomy of nationalism and democracy in social movements in post-communist Eastern Europe: 'Whether one type of nationalism prevails over another will depend on many factors, namely on the character of new political elites, on the direction and rate of institutional transformations, especially on the effective institutionalization of the rule of law, of the competitive party-system and on the ability of the East Central European economies to enter the path of accelerated growth. Therefore, obstacles to the emergence of civil society and to the establishment of stable democratic regimes cannot be reduced to the nationalist factor alone.'[37] According to this argument, one could hardly reduce relevant political cleavages in post-communist democracies to the conflict between liberal democrats and conservative nationalists.

Criticism of the anti-democratic character of Eastern European nationalism easily leads to the idea of 'federation' between East Central European states as a solution to the problem of conflicting nationalisms. But this conclusion is a rather formal Utopian proposal. Seton-Watson points out that 'the word 'federation' enjoys at present a vague popularity', that 'there is even an inclination to regard it as a cure for all troubles,' that 'it should be understood that the creation of a federation is only a structural measure' and that 'everything depends on the content of the structure'.[38] The recent debate on the East Central European community has not produced any plausible proposals on the structural qualities of a new federation. In this sense, the idea of East Central Europe is a beautiful principle based on cooperation or even the existence of a community, but without such political and social content as is present in the re-emerging nationalism or in the challenge of a European community.

National Renaissance and European Integration

The discussion of alternative futures and forms of the nation state are marginal undercurrents compared to the mainstream, which is a resurrection of interwar nationalism, with a strong emphasis on the nation state in Hungary and in Central Europe in general. Nevertheless, there is an important difference compared to interwar nationalism and nation states; they are now confronted with the EC, an integration with supranational trends, and realizing democratization and modernization is something that they cannot avoid if they want closer relations with the EC. We have a national renaissance with a past-oriented character, but our future images are connected to the EC, a moderating factor in relation to nationalism and nation state policy in East Central Europe.

Of course, to build up a new historical and national consciousness and community, some way of resurrecting the past and reconciling the future is unavoidable in the process of post-communist transformation. I will demonstrate the problems of historical, national and European consciousness with respect to Hungarian political and intellectual discussions and developments. The national grievances and 'wounds' are important elements of the new political and national consciousness constructed by the populist-nationalist political directions and positions.[39] During the communist rule, important problems and conflicts of national history were made taboos, like Katyn in Poland, the 1956 uprising in Hungary and the 1968 intervention in Czechoslovakia. The reconciliation with the past involves breaking the taboo on former suppressed subjects, banned from the official discussion during the past decades. As Miklos Szabo, an analyst of Hungarian national consciousness and political culture, has put it, the problem is that the reconciliation with the past should not leave out the complexes and contradictions of the pre-communist national history.[40] For the mainstream of nationalist populism, the pre-communist and anti-communist traditions are glorified by political persecution, and that is why it is felt that there is no need for their critical analysis.

This 'resurrecting' attitude towards national history results in discussions about establishing a monument of the president of the 'independent' Slovak state Tiso, or about the official reinterment of Admiral Horthy, the leader of interwar Hungary. The glorification of the pre-communist past is connected to the condemnation of communists as 'enemies of the nation'. Meanwhile, legal responsibility for criminal acts that had formerly remained unpunished for political reasons may be an outcome of the reintroduction of the rule of law but the mechanisms for new types of political persecution, identification of scapegoats and condemnation of 'enemies of the people' produce patterns which are easily applied to other groups designated as 'enemies' by the majority, as in Hungary the liberal opposition or protesting taxi drivers, criticized by the government and its populist supporters.

As Schoepflin has argued, there is an especially strong preoccupation with the 'resurrection' of pre-communist traditions in Hungary, because Hungarian conservatives cannot refer to the traditions of anti-communist mobilizations after 1956, while the 1956 revolution itself was too radical and 'socialist' to be a source of tradition for them.[41] Hungarian political scientist Attila Agh criticized the policy of the Christian-Democratic government for its backward orientation in its European policy, its 'quest for historical legitimacy, its forcible preoccupation with the question of nationality and who is Hungarian'. In this way, the new government proved that the traditional political class, the middle-class gentry, and its political values had made a comeback. According to Agh, 'it seems that they have turned these negative traditions into a system which a considerable part of the press and the public interpreted as a reinstatement of a modernized Christian course', which is a blatant contradiction of the 'back to Europe' slogan and its related party-political and foreign policy ambitions.'[42]

In interwar Hungary, an important political

differentiation emerged within the intellectual-political elite, namely between 'urbanists' and 'populists'.[43] Both opposed the realm of the authoritarian-feudal Horthy regime. But 'urbanists' favoured Western models of modernization and democracy and emphasized Hungarian ties with European culture. 'Populists' stood for a 'third way' between East and West, between capitalism and communism, individualism and collectivism. Their main concern was to integrate the Hungarian rural population into the elite and to uphold 'Eastern' and 'popular' elements of Hungarian culture. To realize this social programme, some of them were ready to cooperate with the fascist collectivism, to neglect formal democracy and to suppress Jewish and German minorities. The tradition of this conflict and differentiation survived communist rule, and it is integrated in the cleavages of the new multi-party system of modern Hungary.

In the Hungarian party system, the division between 'urbanists' and 'populists' has re-emerged, connected to different ways of understanding the Hungarian nation state and national consciousness. The parties in the present Hungarian government coalition (Hungarian Democratic Forum, Independent Smallholders, Christian Democratic People's Party) have emphasized national, religious and rural values, while the liberal opposition (Alliance of Free Democrats and Alliance of Young Democrats) and the socialists (Hungarian Socialist Party) tend to appreciate international-cosmopolitan, secular and urban values in their programmes and ideologies.[44] But this division does not involve their basic economic and foreign policy goals; they are all united in their acceptance of the market economy and in the idea of 'coming back to Europe' in the form of joining the EC.[45]

The indifferent relationship of the values of political parties to some important elements in their programmes is explained by George Schöpflin in terms of the difference of levels in the socio-economic and socio-cultural dimensions in East European politics.[46] Unity among the new political parties in important material issues and conflict at the post- or non-material level are, according to him, based on the lack of a clear socio-economic basis underlying new party systems and on their dominance by intellectuals who overimposed their own issues on a rather inactive public. In the Hungarian case, Schöpflin argues, the parties of the government coalition picked up national, religious and etatist elements in their policy. They put on the political agenda questions such as problems of Hungarian minorities, the Jewish assimilation, representation of 'real' Christian and Hungarian values, etc.[47] This agenda provoked the liberal opposition to reactions and overreactions, while at the same time the main political camps, preoccupied with the understanding of nationhood and Europeanism, failed to formulate pragmatic solutions to the economic crisis, which reached its climax in October 1990. The material interests of civil society should be represented and met in the new policies, instead of intellectual discourses between liberals and nationalists. According to Schöpflin, Eastern societies are still unable to articulate their interests in a proper way.

In spite of the 'resurrection' of pre-communist nationalism, East Central European societies are directly confronted with the challenges of modernization and integration in the form of the EC. The socio-economic basis of the EC contributes to the realization of the main goal of East European transformations: functioning market economies, pluralist democracy and civic culture.[48] Because of this, to join the EC is the ultimate goal of all post-communist democracies, and all relevant political forces support this goal. Political parties and nation states in Eastern Europe measure and evaluate themselves and each other by 'European' standards set up by the Council of Europe and the EC. In their striving to be more 'European' than the others, national prejudices could re-emerge. One of the arguments by Eric Hobsbawm against the idea of Central Europe is that it involves a devaluation of 'less' European nations and states in the Balkan area.[49] According to Miklos Szabo, the pioneer role of Hungary in the system transformation and its European echo was instrumentalized by Hungarian nationalists against 'latecomer' countries, which according to this logic were less 'ripe' for European acceptance.[50] It is paradoxical that the European idea has become a type of measurement for national superiority in Eastern Europe.

The EC as the realm of modernity and democracy makes

it an inevitable 'reference group' for all political parties in East Central European countries. This means that despite all nationalist orientations, the nationalist parties are also parts of the 'Europeanist' political consensus which involves integration. The different levels of modernization and democratization between Eastern and Western Europe produce a schizophrenia between the nineteenth and twenty-first centuries, between past and future, in the Eastern European national consciousness.

While, in Ernest Gellner's terms, Western Europe is constructing 'the federal-cantonal common home', in the East the reminiscences of the past are still alive and there is a possibility that 'nationalism will be even stronger than it was the last time'.[51] Using Gellner's argument against his conclusion, the EC could be seen as a 'rival principle of association' to nation state and nationalism, affiliated with the modernization and democratization tendencies of Eastern societies, like a 'genuine craving for civil society, for pluralism, for the absence of political and ideological and economic monopoly'. Both external and internal factors push towards the unification of Europe, and we may hope that the possible future of integration will be stronger than the fascination of the national past.

The EC could, of course, be a 'rival principle of association' of 'national renaissance' in Eastern Europe, if there are plausible prospects for new democracies to reach the level of EC countries in modernization and democratization. The exclusion or inclusion of Eastern Europe in the EC, or the character and mode of its affiliation with it, is an object of sharpe debate among rival strategies among its members.[52] Miszlivetz has summed up the present state of the discussions in the East and in the West in the following way: 'Neither the Western integration nor the recently emancipated Eastern countries have a comprehensive framework for a new policy of common security. Political and social science analysis used to be dominated by the paradigm of the Cold War, and the prospects of security and economic policy were fitted into it.'[53] The strategy for the integration of the East is not ready yet, but 'the time is ripe for concrete and shared projects'. The outcome of the conflict between the 'civic' and 'ethnic' organization principles in Eastern Europe is highly dependent on the attitude of the EC. 'Central Europe cannot escape the challenge to establish new, unknown forms of effective and democratic cooperation in its countries. But Central European countries are not able to do this on the basis of their own resources and experiences. It is not to be expected that the European orientation itself will be able to establish a republican mind.'

The idea of homogeneous nation states with unlimited sovereignty will never function in this region, or at least never without pogroms, wars and conflicts. In their present condition, the Western peripheries of the former Soviet empire are not able to master the immense challenge which they are confronted with. The West's hesitation in providing its aid postpones the 'closing up' or 'comeback'.[54] Postponing the fulfilment of hopes in Eastern Europe could be dangerous for the community of established Western democracies as well. The victory of the 'ethnic' principle over the 'civic' one could result in immediate threats for Western Europe in terms of immigration and security problems. Let us hope with Ernest Gellner that in Eastern Europe communism will not be followed by a renaissance of 'ethnic irredentism' but by the 'federal-cantonal common home' beyond the nation state.

NOTES

1. On the concept of Eastern Europe, see Jenö Szücs, Three Historical Regions of Europe; in John Keane (ed.), *Civil Society and the State* (London: Verso, 1988), pp. 291–333. The analysis is actually limited to Poland, Hungary, Czechoslovakia and the former GDR, because in the Baltic states and in the Western parts of former Yugoslavia the problems of the dissolution of the present state and the nation building are still going on, while in the countries listed above the new political system has already become institutionalized.
2. Karl W. Deutsch, *Nationalism and its Alternatives* (New York: Alfred A. Knopf, 1969).
3. Eric J. Hobsbawm, *Nations and Nationalism since 1780* (Cambridge: Cambridge University Press, 1990), p. 177.
4. Ernest Gellner, Nationalism and Politics in Eastern Europe. *New Left Review*, no. 189/1991, pp. 127–37.
5. Friedrich Meinecke, *Weltbürgertum und Nationalstaat. Studien zur Genesis des deutschen Nationalstaates* (München und Berlin: R. Oldenbourg, 1928), pp. 1–23.
6. Deutsch, op. cit., pp. 37–67.

7. Jenö Szücs, Nation und Geschichte: Studien (Budapest: Akadémia, 1981).
8. Cited in Hobsbawm, op. cit., pp. 127–30.
9. Deutsch, op. cit., pp. 49–52.
10. Hugh Seton-Watson, *Eastern Europe between the Wars* (Boulder: Westview Press, 1982).
11. Hobsbawm, op. cit., p. 133.
12. Ibid., pp. 146–8.
13. See Francois Fejtö, *A History of People's Democracies* (London: Pelican Books, 1973).
14. See Bill Lomax, *Hungary 1956* (New York: St Martin's Press, 1976).
15. Deutsch, op. cit., p. 63.
16. See Miklos Szabo, Problems of Hungarian National Consciousness in the Second Half of the 20th Century. *Social Research*, vol. 55, no. 4/1988, pp. 679–714.
17. Deutsch, op. cit., pp. 52–9.
18. Charles Gati, *The Bloc that Failed* (Bloomington: Indiana University Press, 1991).
19. Charles Gati, *Hungary and the Soviet Bloc* (Durham: Duke University Press, 1986).
20. J. F. Brown, Conservatism and Nationalism in the Balkans: Albania, Bulgaria and Romania; in W. E. Griffith (ed.), *Central and Eastern Europe: The Opening Curtain* (Boulder: Westview Press, 1989), pp. 283–314.
21. Herbert Kitschelt, *The Formation of Party Systems and the Consolidation of Democracy in East Central Europe*. Manuscript, Duke University, 1991, p. 15.
22. George Schöpflin, Critical Currents in Hungary, 1968–1978; in R. L. Tökes (ed.), *Opposition in Eastern Europe* (London: Macmillan, 1979, pp. 142–87).
23. Maté Szabo, Die Rolle von sozialen Bewegungen im Systemwandel in Osteuropa. *Österreichische Zeitschrift für Politikwissenschaft*, no. 3/1991.
24. Zdenek Mlynar, Mitteleuropa in Ost-West Konflikt; in Sven Papcke und Werner Weidenfeld (eds), *Traumland Mitteleuropa?* (Darmstadt: Wissenschaftliche Buchgesellschaft, 1988), p. 49.
25. Adam Michnik, Zwei Visionen eines posttotalitären Europas; in R. Deppe, H. Dubiel und U. Rödel (eds), *Demokratischer Umbruch in Osteuropa* (Frankfurt am Main: Suhrkamp, 1991), p. 348.
26. Jacques Rupnik, Eisschrank oder Fegefeuer. Das Ende des Kommunismus und das Wiedererwachen der Nationalismen. *Transit*, no. 1/1991, pp. 132–42.
27 Jadwiga Staniszkis, Dilemmata der Demokratie in Osteuropa; in Deppe, Dubiel und Rödel, op. cit., pp. 339–45.
28. See Timothy Garton Ash, *Ein Jahrhundert wird abgewählt* (München: Hansen, 1990), pp. 188–227. See also F. Herterich und C. Semler (eds), *Dazwischen. Ostmitteleuropäische Reflexionen* (Frankfurt am Main: Suhrkamp, 1989), E. Busek und G. Wilfinger (eds), Aufbruch nach Mitteleuropa (Wien: Atelier, 1986) and H. P. Burmeister, F. Boldt

und G. Meszaros (eds), *Mitteleuropa – Traum oder Trauma?* (Bremen: Temmen, 1988).
29. György Dalos, *Ungarn. Vom roten Stern zur Stephanskrone* (Frankfurt am Main: Suhrkamp, 1991), pp. 111–28; Andreas Hegedüs, Karpaten-Becken und Mitteleuropa; in Papcke und Weidenfeld, op. cit., pp. 57–76.
30. Kathrin Sitzler, Regionale Kooperation und europäische Integration. *Südosteuropa*, no. 11-12/1990, pp. 686–708.
31. Rudolf L. Tökes, From Visegrad to Cracow. Cooperation, Competition and Coexistence in Central Europe. *Problems of Communism*, vol. XL, November-December 1991, pp. 100–15.
32. Ferenc Miszlivetz, Mitteleuropa – Der Weg nach Europa. *Die Neue Gesellschaft, Frankfurter Hefte*, no. 11/1991, p. 982.
33. Ibid., p. 983.
34. Cited in ibid., p. 972.
35. Kitschelt, op. cit., p. 7.
36. Seton-Watson, op. cit., p. 272.
37. A. Z. Kaminski and J. Kurczewska, Nation States and Civil Society in East Cenral Europe; in Herzog, Pradetto and Wagner (eds), op. cit., p. 57.
38. Seton-Watson, op. cit., p. 276.
39. Miklos Szabo, A nemzeti sérelmek szerepe a rendszervaltas folyamataban; in Sandor Kurtan, Peter Sandor and Laszlo Vass (eds), *Magyaroszag Politikai Evkönyve 1991* (Budapest, 1991), pp. 228–34.
40. Miklos Szabo, Restauration oder Aufarbeitung? Geschichte und politische Kultur in Ungarn. *Transit*, no. 2/1991, pp. 72–81.
41. George Schöpflin, Conservatism and Hungary's Transition. *Problems of Communism*, vol. XL, January–April 1991, p. 66.
42. Attila Agh, The Year of Incomplete Changes; in Kurtan, Sandor and Vass, op. cit., p. 20.
43. See special issue of *Szazadveg*, no. 2/1990, devoted to populist-urbanist discussions.
44. Andras Körösenyi, in *Political Quarterly*.
45. Andras Körösenyi, Politikai tagoltsag 1990; in Kurtan, Sandor and Vass, op. cit., pp. 75–81.
46. George Schöpflin, Post-Communism: Constructing New Democracies in Central Europe. *International Affairs*, vol. 67, no. 2/1991, pp. 245–51.
47. Schöpflin, Conservatism and Hungary's Transition, pp. 66–8.
48. Peter Hardi, Magyar külpolitika 1990; in Kurtan, Sandor and Vass, op. cit., pp. 409-12.
49. Miszlivetz, op. cit., p. 978.
50. Miklos Szabo, 1991, op. cit.
51. Gellner, op. cit., pp. 132–3.
52. August Pradetto, Europa nach der Revolution. Ost und West vor säkularen Herausforderungen. *Aus der Politik und Zeitgeschichte*, no. 6/1992, pp. 3–10.
53. Miszlivetz, op. cit., pp. 979, 982.
54. Ibid.

INDEX